Herman Friedrich Grimm, Sarah Holland Adams

Literature

Herman Friedrich Grimm, Sarah Holland Adams

Literature

ISBN/EAN: 9783337146085

Printed in Europe, USA, Canada, Australia, Japan

Cover: Foto ©Thomas Meinert / pixelio.de

More available books at **www.hansebooks.com**

LITERATURE

RALPH WALDO EMERSON.   FRANCE AND VOLTAIRE.

VOLTAIRE AND FREDERICK THE GREAT.

FREDERICK THE GREAT AND MACAULAY.   ALBERT DÜRER.

THE BROTHERS GRIMM.

BETTINA VON ARNIM.   DANTE ON THE RECENT ITALIAN STRUGGLE.

By HERMAN GRIMM.

„Wär' nicht das Auge sonnenhaft
Die Sonne könnt' es nie erbliden;
Lag nicht in uns des Gottes eigne Kraft,
Wie könnt' uns Göttliches entzüden."

GOETHE, *Epigrams.*

BOSTON:
CUPPLES, UPHAM, & CO., PUBLISHERS,
The Old Corner Bookstore,
283 WASHINGTON STREET.
1886.

TO

JAMES H. BEAL

THIS AMERICAN EDITION IS INSCRIBED BY THE TRANSLATOR AS

A Tribute

OF RESPECT, GRATITUDE, AND LOVE.

PREFACE.

An episode of peculiar import belongs to recent German history, revealing the character of a few literary men in a heroic light.

While offering to the public, in this little book, a brief notice of the "Brothers Grimm," perhaps a few words may be added to give an incident in the career of these men, already endeared to American readers by their unrivalled productions.

Emerson regretted that one must so often combine the adjectives "weak and literary"; intellect rises or sinks with character, "goodness itself being an eye." "Where there is depravity there is a slaughter-house style of thinking." It was Byron himself who insulted the glorious genius born within him, and well-nigh destroyed all claim to immortality, by lending expression to misanthropy and weaknesses of all kinds; putting what was personal and transitory in place of the eternal and universal. No greater contrast to this can be quoted in the whole history of literature than is presented by the Grimms; and it is the more pleasant to dwell on it, since in them also we find the truest representatives of Germany,— her highest culture, sweet sincerity, and simple soul-full life.

Jacob and William Grimm were Hessians, and born at Hanau. Their father was a lawyer, and they were educated for jurists. It was while studying Roman law under Savigny, in Paris, 1805, that the brothers (Jacob in his nineteenth year, William in his eighteenth) formed the resolution never to separate, and set before themselves the distinct aim of a revival of ancient German literature. In their school-days they had worked at one desk; later, they had two in one room; lastly, they wrote in adjacent rooms. In their united publications the Christian names are omitted. *Old German Poems, The Songs of the Edda,* the *Märchen* and *Sagen,* are by the "Brothers Grimm." In middle life each labored awhile in his separate province. William Grimm wrote *Heldensage,* a work of stupendous learning, embracing the whole range of German hero-lore, out of which the material had come for the innumerable tales, poems, and songs of the Middle Ages. He also, among other things, brought to light and edited a work by Freidank, written in the thirteenth century, on *Moderation, or Good Sense.* Jacob wrote the *German Grammar,* a *History of the German Language, German Mythology, Reinhard the Fox,* and the *German Rechtsalterthümer.*

But these men were not merely heroes with the pen. In 1833 William IV had given the Hanoverians a constitution which secured to the people many important rights. The brothers Grimm were at this time holding responsible positions in the Göttingen University, and were also in charge of the library there. Upon the death of William IV, Ernst Augustus, Duke of Cumberland, succeeded to the throne, and almost immediately thereupon abrogated this constitution. Against such a despotic act Dahlmann, Gervinus, and the brothers Grimm protested; they bravely demanded a repeal. It is the rarest thing for professors to rebel and protest: they submit, and oftener bar than open the gates to freedom. But these were live men, and seven of the Göttingen professors were instantly deprived of their professorships, and every other public trust that had been committed to them. This occurred in 1837. The excitement was terrific; the people were too timid to resist the decree of the king, and the Grimms were banished from the country. They retired to their old home in Cassel, grieved in spirit, but strong in the conviction of right. We read with the deepest reverence Jacob Grimm's simple statement that their proceeding was so natural as to seem much more insignificant to them at first.

> "Such men will help to save mankind,
>   Till public wrong be crumbled into dust,
> And drill the raw world for the march of mind,
>   Till crowds at length be sane, and crowns be just."

Jacob Grimm always hoped for, and in fact prophesied, the unity of Germany. On the accession of Frederick William IV the brothers were called to the Berlin University in the most flattering and honorable way, as members of the Prussian Academy of Science, of which Jacob had been for some years a foreign member.

It has not been my aim, in this brief preface, to give anything approaching a comprehensive idea of the labors of the Grimms. They were simply colossal, and require and deserve much greater space than I have allotted here. I only hoped to bring them personally a little nearer to my readers. In closing a centennial eulogy upon the "Brothers Grimm," last winter in Berlin, Scherer said:—

"Great learning not unfrequently leads to pride,

self-satisfaction, jealousy, and dogmatism. It is apt to interfere with intuitive perceptions and sound understanding. It plants subtile fancies and an artificial taste. Whole literary epochs have been poisoned by a pompous display of superiorities and vainglorious pretensions. It has often set up a false standard among men, and ranked a sum of esoteric knowledge, under the illusive name of education, higher than a human heart filled with its ancient mysterious power.

"The brothers Grimm — the noble pair! — from all the frivolity of false education and empty parade of wit were wholly free. In the zenith of their life and fame they remained simple, good men. They sympathized with children, as well as with the worldly-wise, with statesmen, and poets. Their unostentatious geniality radiates a soft splendor adown the coming years, for fate had dowered them with her choicest gift, — an immaculate beauty of soul."

Professor Herman Grimm, son of William Grimm, was born at Cassel, in 1828. In his thirteenth year he came to Berlin, from that time to be surrounded by the noblest men and women of Germany. Madame D'Arblay said of herself, "I never studied; at my father's fireside I drank in a world of intelligence."

But even at this time Berlin must also have afforded peculiar advantages for study of the exact sciences.

As in his father the artistic element predominated, while his uncle Jacob was rather the jurisprudent, our young professor's eyes instinctively sought the pictures of the old masters, and he early turned his studies chiefly in this direction. He published in 1860–63 the *Life and Times of Michael Angelo*, to use the German expression, an "epoch machenden" book. "Twenty-five years ago," said one of the professors to me, "no man dared lift his head in Germany who had not read it." Here was furnished the conception of a genuine biography, — the man in his surroundings, and as he looked to his own century. Some years later, and at Emerson's suggestion, Professor Grimm wrote, not precisely a *Life of Goethe* (although the work received this title in America), but a series of lectures on the great poet, throwing a vast deal of light on all the controverted points in Goethe's life and writings.

The essays on Emerson in this little volume which we now present to the public were written twenty-five years apart. Beside their intrinsic merits, they are interesting as proofs of a spiritual affinity great enough to enable these men to find each other in spite of the hindrance interposed by difference of language. Emerson is not appreciated in Germany even to-day, although his writings are slowly making their way; but Professor Grimm's admiration for him has been, and still is, considered one of the eccentricities of genius. Byron and Shelley were the first in England to speak with authority of Goethe as the great poet of the nineteenth century, although Byron knew little enough of the German language, and could not read the *Faust* without Shelley's aid.

In this age of dilutions and repetitions the refreshment afforded in turning to the pages of an independent, original thinker is indescribable. Professor Grimm's views on art are especially instructive and elevating; they are not taken from a one-sided artistic standpoint, but from a vastly higher and broader one, — the human standpoint, the value of art in the development of mankind. Hence we never meet in his writings with anything to remind us of Ruskin's par-. tial, dogmatic assertions, which, with a measure of truth in them, still do such violence to what is excluded from his range of vision. On the other hand, unless Professor Grimm's artistic manner of treating all subjects is understood, he must seem discursive. The unity is far deeper than appears, and is complete. He gives to every sketch its background; puts in the light and shade, and ends by bringing his figures directly into the foreground, where they remain indelibly stamped on our memories; therefore is he the very prince of essayists.

Van Helmont said: "It is my greatest desire that it may be granted unto atheists to have tasted, at least for one moment, what it is intellectually to understand. These men strain nerve and muscle to climb the highest mountains in order to gain broader views, and welcome telescopes which afford a still wider range of vision." Are not minds greater than our own intellectual telescopes, into which it must ever be our privilege and joy to obtain a glimpse, thereby winning for ourselves broader horizons? I must believe that in my native land there is a class of readers who will welcome these essays, which I have endeavored faithfully to translate.

SARAH H. ADAMS.

RALPH WALDO EMERSON.

FIRST ESSAY, PUBLISHED IN 1861.

A GOOD many years since, at the house of an American friend I happened to take up a volume of Emerson's Essays which was lying upon the table. I looked into it,— read a page, and was startled to find that I had understood nothing, though tolerably well acquainted with English. I inquired as to the author. In reply I was told that he was the first writer in America, an eminently gifted man, but somewhat crazed at times, and often unable to explain his own words. Notwithstanding, no one was held in such esteem for his character, and for his prose writings. In short, the opinion fell upon my ears as so strange that I reopened the book. Some sentences, upon a second reading, shot like a beam of light into my very soul, and I was moved to put the book in my pocket, that I might read it more attentively at home. I find it is a great deal to begin with if a book so far attracts us that we resolve, without urging, to look it through; since, as a measure of self-preservation, it is necessary to stand on the defensive now-a-days against books and people, if we would reserve time and inclination for our own thoughts.

I took Webster's Dictionary and began to read. The construction of the sentences struck me as very extraordinary. I soon discovered the secret: they were real thoughts, an individual language, a sincere man, that I had before me; naught superficial — second-hand. Enough! I bought the book! From that time I have never ceased to read Emerson's works, and whenever I take up a volume anew it seems to me as if I were reading it for the first time.

It is not easy to say what attracts us to a writer, and it is especially difficult to speak of a contemporary. We say in general, "I find him sympathetic." It is most natural for me to describe my feeling through a comparison with the physical laws of weight and gravity. I assume that there rests upon the soul of every man who has grown to manhood a certain burden, — the sum of his experiences, recollections, hopes, fears, and daily environments, — and that his happiness is in proportion to his success in escaping from this pressure and living in a sense of freedom. Hence we so often envy children, and even the good cattle.

The usual means for surmounting this burden of mortality is in regular occupation. Busied with this, we forget ourselves most easily and naturally. Let me say, incidentally, that for this reason I cannot agree with the views of many national economists, who regard the arduous labor of the poor man as a sacrifice he offers to the community, throwing a sort of halo about him, which should excite envy and secret shame in the minds of all people whose hands are not calloused by toil.

Another means of relief is sought in revelries and distracting pleasures. The highest relief, however, is found in the enjoyment of Nature and the Fine Arts.

To the latter study a man either wholly devotes himself, or allows it to fill the moments when, tried with business, the hunger of the soul must be appeased in another manner. We select from the wealth before us, each according to his idiosyncrasy;—one is absorbed with Goethe, another with Shakespeare and Raphael, Beethoven, Handel, and Plato. Others of less depth grasp the hand of some spirit on a lower plane, or eagerly welcome the latest sensation on the stage, in the book-stores, or in the concert-hall. A contrary fancy leads still others to pursue enthusiastically whatever is rare or unknown in books, engravings, and works of art, and to value these things in proportion to the difficulty of obtaining them. But none of these can satisfy a rightly constituted mind. The clear-headed man first contemplates, wholly unbiased, the phenomena around him; if anything clings to him and will not let him go, he stops! he enjoys! The question whether what has so captivated his senses is really beautiful is secondary; the first must always be, does it fascinate him, and for how long? With genuine modesty he then proceeds from enjoyment to knowledge, but full of caution, remembering the destructive spark which fell from Psyche's too rashly kindled lamp.

In truth, we rarely know what the specific property is in an intellectual work which has captivated us, or which the word that compels us to listen and to obey. One reads Plato through in translation like an agreeable story-book; another will hang on every word and particle, and find himself roused, sentence after sentence, to the most searching reflections; one says, "Goethe's *Elective Affinities* interested me very much;" a second, "It has struck me deeply;" a third, "The book contains fearful secrets." Each has a right to choose what pleases him, and to live in the spirit of it, provided only that it renders him the desired service, which is, — to lift him above the miseries of earth, to inspire a fresh, child-like hopefulness, which makes the ideal alone seem the real, and the wearisome cares of daily life a leaden dream which oppresses us. But those artists stand highest who, by their productions, accomplish the still greater miracle of taking up with steady hand this sorry every-day life, to unravel artistically the confused web, and bring out its intrinsic beauty. They transport us by no delusive dreams out of the world, but reveal to us the hidden glories surrounding every object in God's creation; they do not delude us out of our griefs, but cause them to disappear like the phantoms of an over-burdened imagination from which we had not power to free ourselves.

In Raphael and Goethe we have examples of this elevating influence in its fullest potency. What these artists portray does not overstep by one line the measure of the purely human. They nowhere entice us into marvellous, impossible regions; they simply open our eyes, and at once we see our ordinary existence for the first time in its true aspect, beautiful and bright. They stand in the closest affinity to nature; they hold up no magic mirror before us to magnify or belittle objects, and to present them either in a rose-colored light or wrapped in artificial gloom; they show us things as they are, — not as one in surly mood is apt to regard them on a sunless day, but as they would and must appear to candid observers, had not our eyes been injured and abused by a false education until they are no longer capable of discerning without help these primal glories.

They reconcile us to life. What depressed now fills me with joy, and I no longer wish to escape from it. I take it up, and it changes into beauty under my hands. Whatsoever these men touch is pure gold, is fair, as if the finger of God pointed to it, while a secret voice whispered, " Look only, and recognize it." I find within me the ability to perceive it so long as they show it me.

Emerson possesses this power in the highest degree. "Look at the stars," begins one of his essays, "if thou wilt be alone; the beams which flow from this heavenly world separate thee from thy surroundings. One might think the atmosphere was made transparent with this design,—to give man in the heavenly bodies the perpetual presence of the sublime. Seen in the streets of cities, how great they are! If the stars should appear one night in a thousand years, how would men believe and adore, and preserve for many generations the remembrance of the city of God which had been shown! But every night come out these preachers of beauty, and light the universe with their admonishing smile."

It is the opening of the essay called *Nature;* and as I went on reading sentence after sentence, I felt as if I had met with the simplest, sincerest man, and was listening to him as he talked to me.

I did not ask myself if he was brilliant and original, if he had any special purpose or hidden design in this essay? I simply read on, one page after another. It is possible that it was hard and confused, but it did not seem so to me. I followed the thought word for word; all was known and familiar, as if I had thought or dreamed it a thousand times myself, and yet perfectly new, as if I were learning it for the first time. If I laid the book aside awhile my independent spirit revolted against this all too potent spell. I suspected myself of being deluded and deceived. I reasoned within me, is he not a man like others, with their faults and questionable virtues, vain, moody, and susceptible to flattery? Then reading on again, the air of enchantment stole over me, freshening again the old, worn-out machinery of the world, and as if I had never tasted anything so pure. I was told lately by an American, who had heard Emerson lecture, that there was nothing more inspiring than to listen to this man. I believe it. For what is to be compared with the voice of one who is speaking out of his deepest soul what he believes to be true?

I know him only through his writings. But when through long years one receives from an author's works ever the same pure, soul-stirring impression, while so many others supposed to be genuine prove hollow and lifeless, and after experience has taught us that the consciousness in our own breasts can be the only safe standard, we rest satisfied that such faith in the power of a man is for us an indisputable possession. Again and again we see true genius misjudged, ostentation, pretension, and emptiness believed in, until we grow insensible to the floating opinion of the day.

But seeing, on the other hand, how the world is constantly longing for a man to whose true and sterling nature it may surrender for guidance, if we are so fortunate as to meet with a being who corresponds to this need, we must in the joy of our discovery impart this to others and publicly state as a truth what we can not but believe to be true.

I turned first to my most intimate friends, such as I knew understood English; it was only necessary for me to lay the book down and say, "Read." The first attempt was perfectly satisfactory, and confirmed me in my opinion. I now recommended Emerson's works at large, and began to have a pretty severe experience.

Emerson writes in English. Many Germans understand it so far as to be able to read the current literature, with which Tauchnitz is indefatigable in supplying the continent. Macaulay gives them no difficulty; even Carlyle is comprehended, as they make their way amid the disorder of his periods. But in Emerson's writings the broad turnpike is suddenly changed into a hazardous sandy foot-path. His thoughts and his style are American. He is not writing for Berlin, but for the people of Massachusetts. He uses every word in a sense that suits him at the moment, and whether the rest of mankind apprehend it or not is quite indifferent to him. It was Emerson's experience to be at first proscribed as heretical, insane, blasphemous; but he went on undisturbed, thinking and writing, and found himself later surrounded by admiring crowds wherever he appeared. How could he then be much affected by what was said of him anywhere, but especially in Europe, where he was understood with difficulty in English, or read cursorily through a German translation?

A second obstacle: Emerson is a cultivated man, and in speaking to his own people and the English has a cultivated audience in mind; that is, persons taking practical views of life, and having very clear conceptions as to the past and future of their native land. To all this the Germans present a wonderful contrast. We are extremely learned in our own department. We know life very minutely, but each under the narrowing aspect it wears in his particular career. Public spirit is only just awakening here and there, and gaining a slight victory over the special interests of different ranks and professions. Our historical works contain very accurate summaries of certain portions of history, but fail to afford a comprehensive idea of the general flow of the great stream of events. If, then, our greatest minds are so fettered within limitations, what is to be expected of the common herd? I believe there is nowhere on earth so much partial knowledge coupled with such general ignorance. Each knows what he must know, and knows it *as* he must know it. Men drive through the sciences as we rush through Europe in an express-train. The desired goal is reached, the journey is behind us, but we have had no active share in it, have heard nothing, seen nothing, only paid for our tickets, and passed the time in dreams. One may travel to-day from St. Petersburg to Madrid without doing more than opening and shutting the purse. There is no wish to see Germany or France, and the purpose of the trip is wholly fulfilled by reaching the Spanish capital. And thus it is with our learning! We have a wealth of knowledge in our heads; are a solvent people, ready at any instant to honor in sterling coin whatever demands may be made on our funds, no matter how great the run may be; but the union of scientific ideas with the spirit that harbors them is a cool marriage of convenience, without affinity or offspring. How scrupulously we avoid discussions in which knowledge is to be brought into practical relations with character! Man will draw no inferences. Everything which rises above the realm of the positive, and is demonstrated through books, is looked upon with suspicion. Only the obviously incontestible is asserted with boldness, and that opinion passed over in distrustful silence which has no other basis than the deep conviction of him who offers it. Only when it assumes imposing dimensions do we prick up our ears, and, if we can no longer refuse to think of it, commit it to memory.

Herein lies both the poverty and the wealth of our day. Emerson, who has shown so charmingly how Goethe was commissioned to take up into himself the infinite amount of rambling knowledge in his century, as so much manure to enrich and fertilize the soil of his mind, and thereby develop his personality,— Emerson, who had not become acquainted with Goethe through books others had fabricated about him, but from the great German's own writings,— speaks of him as being a man such as no other nation had produced,— the full bloom, as it were, of German nature, its highest qualities appearing symbolized in one individual. Hence he distinguishes him as "the writer" par excellence, as Shakespeare is "the poet" par excellence, giving to each his due, and pointing to their historic significance to the Germanic race, which they represent in two directions. What he says of both is deduced from the very essence of their characters, and is at once so terse and so profound that in many places almost every word seems to need a commentary.

A man must have had intercourse with the great world who is thus able to comprehend great characters. Emerson's friends are the first men in his country,— a country which has a magnificent political life, whilst until within a very few years we have had nothing of the sort. Goethe also associated with the leading spirits of his nation, as thoroughly harmonious natures do who rise to a height where a whole people recognize their superiority. For a light-house it requires not only a light to radiate its beams over the wide circle of waters, but a tower from whose summit the light must first be made visible.[1]

A nation has attained its zenith when all its powers, great and small, are stimulated into productive activity. Every man then has too much to do to trouble himself about his neighbors; entire frankness prevails; great faults and great virtues show themselves without disguise; no one is tempted to practise the unprofitable art of throwing a mystery over his own or other people's morals. Read Plato's *Banquet*, which, like a pleasing chapter in a modern novel, exhibits Socrates, Alcibiades, and their friends, in hours of social relaxation. Jupiter and all Olympus might have shared in it, so great and

---

[1] Mirabeau has somewhere said this.

godlike does it sound. What scintillations of genius! and withal what a firm, vigorous basis! Not the artificial *esprit* of the brilliant French epoch, nor the masked barbarism of the Augustan age (although both were heroic enough in comparison with many others), but pure taste, refinement, heroism, luxury, spontaneity, courage, manly ideals, with all their faults and weaknesses, unaffected, free, harmonious natures! A brilliancy imparted by the rarest and most perfect culture is over the whole. When Alcibiades, drunk, rises to eulogize Socrates, and further on into the night one after the other topples over, until, beside Socrates, only two or three remain to see the morning dawn on their revels, why are we not shocked? Yet to this day good men and true read and re-read these pages with care, and nobody thinks the worse of Plato for having written them. If a modern philosopher had fallen on such an expedient for putting immortal words into the mouth of drunken rakes, what a cry would be raised from Dan to Beer-sheba! And truly it would sound badly enough! Why is it that we scarcely dare to find fault with Aristophanes, whom Goethe indulgently calls "The Spoiled Darling of the Graces"? Because the culture of these Greeks, dead since two thousand years, surrounds their names and works as an imperishable bulwark, warding off the censure which might arise from other modes of thought, other customs, and other nationalities.

Emerson could have written for his country, but in

his sense such a romance as Plato wrote for Athens. In his description of how a gentleman enters a party we find the sturdy Germanic counterpart to the Platonic Alcibiades. I can conceive no more perfect ideal of manly character than Emerson has here given. It is a delight to read it, and to many perhaps a satisfaction that this pre-democratic American, who bows before nothing save his own will, and the glory of the Germanic race, still discloses to us the conditions under which an aristocracy is possible, necessary, beautiful; and that he regards the power to enter unembarrassed the most brilliant assemblies as the natural accompaniment of exalted rank. He is not speaking of what is *comme il faut*, or fashionable, but of the behavior of a cultivated man in the historic sense; not of the conventional classes, who set up imaginary barriers between themselves and those they consider their inferiors, but of such persons as by the natural course of events find their true and rightful place at the head of society. It may be that only birth, money, tact, or courage and buoyancy of soul have raised them, but there they stand, and no one denies that they are the aristocrats of the day, with a legitimate claim to their position.

He treats of the manners of these men, who whereever they appear constitute the aristocracy, and in the same sense handles all that comes within the realm of human experience, — love, friendship, politics, history, art, poetry, wisdom, spiritual laws, circles, the over-soul. Wherever he turns things fall into order before his eyes, and he speaks simply of what he has seen.

He views every phenomenon in its connection with the highest idea, and does not regard the poet, the prophet, the world reformer, alone as tools of providence, but finds the coal-heaver, the wood-cutter, the poorest day-laborer, just as valuable and essential in their different places. Greatness and heroism are not inherent to the material, but in the way it is handled, or according to how one fufils the task in life which out of its innumerable vocations he has chosen for his own. His teachings contain the very gospel of contentment, which seems well-nigh lost in our day, although it is extolled as the most precious dowry of all times. To-day, when everything seems in a state of disintegration, and the old accustomed forms in which the different careers of men were cast, in order to take fixed and pre-determined shapes, prove unsatisfactory, — when the young with timid curiosity, the old with sore misgivings, are seeking everywhere for a nucleus round which the fluent matter may collect, according to the law by which new crystals are formed, — Emerson quotes this law. He shows that the old barriers must fall away, because they impede our development, and that in this apparently uncurbed spontaneity and self-will is found the true element in which the character of the Germanic race is to unfold and gain its full power.

I thought every one must derive this from his book,

that his sentences must strike in like a ball from a pistol held close to the mark.

But I soon observed that insufficient knowledge of the language, and want of freedom in the soul, were not the only impediments; a third was added.

A person appears in a very strange light if he is all on fire with a subject which others regard without the slightest emotion. When a great singer transports the whole theatre, any man who claps and shouts is felt to be doing just the right thing, but if he is the only enraptured listener, while all the rest are cold and dumb, his enthusiasm may be ever so well founded, and perhaps shared by all four days later, yet it will make him at the time seem foolish and ridiculous enough. I spoke of Emerson as of a newly discovered planet. Men listened, but at the most were only rather curious to become acquainted with his books. It is marvelous how calmly the world looks toward the advent of what is really significant, and lets it draw near, as if conscious that it was not to be turned aside, and that it would be ineffaceable; not one step is taken to meet it; whilst we rush eagerly after ephemeral wares, to which the fleeting taste of the day alone gives any value, as if presentiment here also whispered, "Enjoy them while fresh; they will soon cease to please you." "One can foist anything upon the people," says Goethe, "only nothing to which they stand committed." My earnest way of recommending Emerson sufficed to excite misgivings. Many who later confessed to me that they had scarcely looked into his books coolly criticised him, while some refused out and out to have anything to do with his writings. They said I had allowed myself to be overawed by a mediocre man; and altogether, why did I talk of Emerson, who might be a clever author enough, but certainly the man was neither called for nor wanted in Germany.

I did not allow myself to be misled. I asked men to whom I ascribed a calm, unbiased receptivity of mind to turn their attention to Emerson's striking and forcible thoughts, and succeeded in persuading an acquaintance to read his *Essays* carefully. He wrote me the impression made on him. I had said that I was anxious to translate them. "So far as I personally am concerned," he replied, "I fear it will be to me forever a matter of indifference whether you translate Emerson or not. I feel him to be a poet and a poetical orator, but he has no element akin to my nature: he is an American. German he is not, nor will he ever be, however successful you may be in rendering his words in our language. I promise, at all events, to renew my effort to digest him, but hardly believe it will amount to much." What could I reply to such language? There was no antagonism in this case, not even the mildest shade of it. Every man has the right to turn aside from what does not please him. I did not feel called upon to convert the world by fire and sword to Emerson. The genuine finds its way; let a coppered gold-piece and a gilded copper have currency for a while and they will by degrees change their character without anybody's troubling himself to rub or scrub them. And so we thought with Emerson: because a man feels that an author has ministered to a want in his own nature, it does not follow that he must necessarily be so essential to others. Yet I will make one more attempt to say why I find so much comfort in his writings.

Comfort is the word which best expresses my feeling! For what do we need? what do we long for? It is *freedom!* Formerly this word had a suspicious import, before which princes and people alike stood in holy awe; to-day it is a harmless utterance, betokening the ideal of a well-regulated political constitution, toward the realization of which the princes and all the various parties consent to unite. But where is the happy mean betwixt law and self-will? No one knows! We are conscious that our best institutions are only provisional, and not in our country alone, but everywhere on this earthly ball. Parties organize; no party, however, being absolutely right, they are soon merged in one another; we attempt to say what we think, but feel that it is not the whole truth we either speak or hear from others, and know full well it will be impossible to present publicly this whole truth in its fulness and stand committed to it as its representative. This atmosphere weighs upon the land, and the highest mountains do not rise above it.

We aspire after a different condition. Every one longs to have a clearer path before him. We would enter into simpler relations with our fellow-men, and find in their silence more than the eloquence of speech. Uniforms, titles, insignia, have no longer any deep spiritual meaning. Catholicism and Protestantism, spite of the acumen with which they have been pitted against each other of late, are in reality no longer in such a state of antagonism that all men, the highest and the lowest, must alike be engrossed with it. Nobles and commoners meet peacefully, as optimates, where money and birth counterbalance; from the discordant elements of the day we do not anticipate that one party will arise victorious over the rest, but that all parties will blend and harmonize, until finally there shall remain only one Church and one State. But what next? The strife will then be to make this one sovereignty the Germanic, to which the Slavic, Mongolian, Romanic, and whatever the other races are called, shall submit.

This union of Church and State is nothing new to our race. It was represented in pope and emperor. It is in our blood, and not to be eradicated. We desire no restitution of the old order of things, — no more "Roman expeditions," for the world has broadened, and Italy is not now the hub of the universe. Neither is our work to-day merely the carrying out of elaborate theories. We must be satisfied, for the present, to see the goal clearly before us, and the path will widen as we proceed. Each man is now moving along by himself, but all hold to the one way. This is a peculiarity of our times: great masses, but isolated men; indefatigable piling up of knowledge and worldly possessions, and yet all this knowledge, all these possessions, are less valued than the straightforward glance of a man who looks candidly at things around him, and calls them by the names which he thinks right. A stone lies in the meadow to-day, lifted only to be thrown aside with vexation; to-morrow comes the man who, looking at it attentively, says, "It is a mine of wealth." Now everybody repeats this, and digs for the precious mineral. We do not value erudition at a penny's worth, but honor the learned man as a "scholar;" we do not care for poetic art, but distinguish one man as "a poet," another as "physician," or painter, or statesman; they may have studied where they would have gained their knowledge in whatever way they chose, — may first have been merchants, farmers, soldiers, or what not if now they only fill their places, and are able to make themselves a power in the land. We feel that we must look at life in this way: whoever is fit for anything is sure to find that which he is especially fitted to do. This is freedom. We are not quite educated up to this, but are working toward it. Emerson is the man who already stands upon this height.

We have a kind of shudder at the life in America. We see an immense edifice swayed to and fro by every gust of wind; the radical unrest does not seem consistent with any great natural development of character; the highest honors of the state are open to the lowest citizen: it has no past, with its established customs; its laws depend on the will of the moment; there is no permanently aristocratic class by whom good-breeding is fostered and made an essential qualification for entrance. There are only three acknowledged powers, — character, activity, money. It is surprising to see how these three act upon one another, and how justly each of the three is ranked. Character takes the highest place. Of this we have abundant proof; a number of energetic people, with the greatest amount of talent, stand everywhere at the head of affairs, and in positions they could never have obtained either by money or coarse strength. Below them comes a class of citizens whose less or greater efficiency determines the height on which they stand. The rest, without special intellectual ability, are estimated according to the money they possess. This organization in its simplicity forms an adamantine basis for American life.

Upon it stands Emerson. He contemplates the world as it lives and moves around him. What occurred, what was accomplished before his day, makes only one of the steps to the elevation on which he has placed himself. The living have the preference over the dead. The Greeks may have written, carved, philosophized, warred, triumphed, governed ever so nobly, — they are dead while we live! Had I never heard of them I should exist nevertheless, and the breath of spring delight me, and love and passion stir my soul. Shall I grow speechless listening to that which was said ere I was born? What matters it to me whether I am the epigone of a vanished age or the precursor of a coming one? keystone or foundation, last spark in the dead ashes or first faint glimmer in the rosy dawn of the future? Is this seed-corn the last product of a fast perishing plant or the germ of a new one just unfolding? Why burden my soul with knowledge I shall never use, or wear myself out over things whose utility I do not perceive? Learning is to many but a vain possession; like the Persian slaves on the sea-strand, they sit lashing the waves with their small rods. It is all useless labor; the sea rolls on unheeding. Stone upon stone, we burden ourselves from youth upward with an ever-increasing pile of knowledge, and when the moment comes for action must dislodge and free ourselves from some of it before we can take one step forward. Instead of acquiring a few things in the schools, and these few thoroughly, — because to know one thing well is the basis for future knowledge, — we have innumerable things driven into our heads by main force, in which to parade about for a while, until, God be thanked! in later years we have managed to forget them all.

It is an art to rise above what we have been taught.

Mechanical knowledge is simply the ladder by which to attain command of ideas which are not acquired, nor can they be imparted in the common mechanical fashion. All great men are seen to possess this freedom. They derive their standard from their own natures, and their observations on life are so natural and spontaneous that it would seem as if the most illiterate person with a scrap of common sense would have made the same. Instead of towering above us, they seem to place us above them, and unperceived to cloak our ignorance; we become wiser with them, and know not how the difficult appears easy and the involved plain; but in such a way that it would seem as if it had been always plain, and we had only been led into confusion by others.

Emerson possesses this noble manner of communicating himself. He inspires me with courage and confidence. He has read and seen, but conceals the labor. I meet in his works plenty of familiar facts, but he does not employ them to figure up anew the old worn-out problems: each stands on a new spot and serves for new combinations. From everything he sees the direct line issuing which connects it with the focus of life.

What I had scarcely ventured to think, because it struck me as all too bold, Emerson presents as serenely as if it were an every-day idea, and is so very natural that it would seem as if it could not be otherwise.

He is a perfect swimmer in the element of modern

life. He has no fear of the storms of the future, for he sees beyond, and the rest which will follow them: he hates nothing, contradicts nothing, contests nothing, for his understanding of men and their faults is too great, his love for them too mighty. I cannot follow his steps with other than the inmost reverence, and I observe with admiration how at his touch the chaotic elements of modern life are gently and dispassionately resolved into order and relegated to their different provinces. Had I found a single sentence in his writings which must be excepted from this judgment I should have begun to doubt the whole, and would not have ventured to utter a word; but long acquaintance has made me sure, and I feel in thinking of this man that in olden times there really may have been teachers with whom their scholars indissolubly linked their destiny, because without the inspiration of the chosen master everything seemed unreal and questionable. I will not say that I have surrendered myself with this blind devotion. Emerson is an American, and the nationality of his people has not yet had time to ripen and mellow like our own; what answers for them cannot so unconditionally be accepted as useful and applicable to us. As a character Emerson appears to me greater than when regarded as an author only.

It is certainly no misfortune that, as concerns intellectual things, while a false reputation is so cheaply won the real should remain difficult of attainment. Here neither gold nor persuasion will avail. Before we acknowledge the overwhelming power of an author we resist with might and main and seek every possible loop-hole of escape. We cannot make up our minds to it; with the dead, yes; with the living, not at any price. We do not willingly consider ourselves inferior to anybody. If a writer claims nothing more than the current recognition of the moment, this is granted without stint or hesitation,— that is to say, he is talked about, praised, admired, and those who are to give the final judgment, from which there will be no appeal, allow the thing to take its course, or even consent lightly thereto, keeping the back-door open all the while through which to retire, and with the feeling that we could probably do without this man, but that we must wait until the noise subsides to see what remains. Should any, however, try to cut off their retreat they are on their mettle instantly and rebel. One does not so easily give up his freedom. In the first case he was the Grand Seigneur, and such praise as he consented to give a gracious benefaction; in the second one he is a receiver of alms,— the man does not need our thanks, our praise is indifferent to him; we receive and enjoy, and are ashamed that we can give nothing in return.

Emerson, however, has not yet placed us in this dilemma. He is as good as unknown among us in Germany. The translation of his *Essays* is a labor which will not soon be accomplished; nothing ever cost me so much trouble as the attempt I made to translate some things in his works into German. He does not write, he seems to speak; at first one can detect no plan, no order, and we seek wonderingly for the hidden connection in these sentences, which seem to stand so detached and alien to one another, although in reality forming a closely linked chain. Soon, however, we discover the deep underlying law according to which these thoughts are evolved, and the strict sequence, notwithstanding that at the outset they digress right and left from the straight way until they seem lost to sight in the fields. It is not the law by which a tree is artificially reared on an espalier, when the gardener commands exactly where the branches shall grow and which shall be lopped off, but that of a healthy beech, throwing out its branches in all directions, and apparently in the wildest disorder, but uniting them to form a beautiful canopy over our heads, in which not the tiniest twig is unnecessary or out of place.

Some time ago I found Emerson's Essays in the hands of a lady whom I had formerly besought in vain to interest herself in them. She had always a thousand excuses for not reading the book, and tried to prove to me that we already possessed it all, and much more, in Goethe,—that we really did not need Emerson, even if he were indeed such as I represented him. Besides, she had read some of the things, and found them quite every-day matter,—thoughts she had long entertained herself, but never expressed.

As far as Goethe was concerned, she was not entirely in the wrong; this man's genius, which was mighty enough to turn thousands of mills and water-wheels, exists for most people only in the fountains and small cascades in which they occasionally rejoice.

In short, Emerson remained unread. But now suddenly she reopened the subject herself. "He was truly, after all," she said, "very remarkable. He sometimes made wonderfully simple observations which yet disentangled the most intricate trains of thought. I listened quietly, and acquiesced. Not long after she took me seriously to task, and imparted her admiration for the man in such a forcible manner, that I sat there as if I were the one to be converted. She grew quite impatient when I did not echo her words, and gave me to understand that in the end she comprehended him better, and felt him more deeply, than I did.

This experience has been repeated. With secret pleasure I have once or twice submitted to be instructed as to Emerson's value. With astonishment I see how he runs over, sooner or later, all his adversaries, and listen to the objections made to him. The old experience is here confirmed, — that but very few people are really capable of taking a sympathetic as well as analytic view of character. For the most part they fall upon separate trails here and there, or at the best succeed only in connecting two or three; the majority of readers pick out a few sentences like single fish from a great net where they had been floundering about, and first sort and arrange them in their own way in order to know what they possess. The result is flat contradictions, falsities, half truths, iridescences, affectations, attempts at wit, worn-out truisms, the superfluous magnified into the important, — everywhere blame and fault-finding in the richest measure. Through it all, however, they are impressed with the pure genius of the man; with the entire absence of vanity in his appearance; with the earnestness of his convictions, and, greatest of all, with his love for the human race, which renders his words fruitful and ennobling.

I doubt not that this feeling will spread further and sink more deeply, and that to a thorough appreciation of this character will succeed the comprehension and need of his works.

SECOND ESSAY,

WRITTEN AFTER THE DEATH OF EMERSON.

The Americans have the advantage of us in the use of their daily press. When upon Longfellow's death I read the New York and Boston papers, it struck me how intimate the relation was between those who have something to say and those who are willing to listen. The *Tribune*, like New York itself, was for some days absorbed with Longfellow. A series of articles poured forth about the man whose loss affected every home, and of whom so many had something to relate. A multitude of witnesses freely testified, and the assembled public constituted, as it were, a jury to listen to all that could be said concerning Longfellow. Justice was done to every kind of opinion, and from the varied contributions each chose the one most in harmony with his own. The like experience is now repeated with Emerson. Emerson had attended Longfellow's funeral. On the 27th of April the telegraph brought over the tidings of his death; fourteen days later the newspapers followed, and again on every page his name alone held the first place.

Between Longfellow and Emerson, however, a great distinction prevailed in all that was said. To Longfellow was awarded the high position he deserved, and the laurels were not stinted. The criticisms ring out perfectly clear and sure. Longfellow was a poet, and his place in the literary world had often been discussed. There could be no question as to what was his due. With Emerson the tone in which men spoke ranged at once higher and lower. It sounded as if something remained unexpressed. The effect of Emerson's writings and his personality struck deeper than Longfellow's, but was not so perceptible in its breadth. Emerson bore no official title to stamp him in the eyes of men. He began as a preacher, resigned the pulpit, and withdrew as a writer into a kind of solitude in which he remained. Now he is called by one an essayist, by another a philosopher, by a third a poet, and by many all these unitedly,— while others, still dissatisfied, say "Emerson was a prophet." In this, however, all agree, that Emerson was one of the greatest men America has produced. But this being accepted, it seems unnecessary to try to emphasize it, and it may be committed to future generations to prove in detail the ground for this conviction. One of the discourses on Emerson begins with these words: "Only Shakespeare can be named with Emerson." To whom would it ever occur to say so much of Longfellow? It would be natural to suppose that after such an opening the speaker would proceed to verify the statement, instead of which the discourse flows on in such measured tone that it would seem as if no proof were required, for every one had known it, and needed only to be reminded of it. In all that I have read of Emerson it is taken for granted that each American knows him, and knows what the country had in him and has lost in him.

Of the events of Emerson's life there is little to be said. His life was not romantic,— no extraordinary light rendered him conspicuous. Even a chronological setting of his works is unnecessary, for they are almost without exception of the same kind, and no one of them had instantaneous success. *Nature*, although the book (if we can so call the extended essay) produced a great sensation, required twelve years for the sale of five hundred copies. It is considered by many Emerson's greatest essay. It certainly shows his peculiar way of grasping his subject in full perfection, and is best calculated to introduce us to his views. Emerson starts with a leading idea which agitated America before it stirred us. But with us also to-day the question arises, How is it going to be possible for coming generations to deal with the enormous mass of intellectual production,—heir-loom of centuries, and which increases each day in more gigantic proportions, without injury to their legitimate work? Our best powers barely suffice to enable us to glance over what has been already accomplished. It would be hailed as a blessing if some one could convince us that the heritage of our ancestors is to be set aside, that untrammelled we may press on to the goal before us.

When intellectual resources of their own began to accumulate in America, this question caused more solicitude than with us, from the fact that their backs had not been trained to bend under the burden. Emerson's essay on *Nature* sprang from the feelings of a man who had entered deeply enough into European literature to be able to measure what might be lost in the acquisition of these riches. Emerson wished his people should preserve the advantage they had of exercising unfettered criticism on past events, and not allow themselves to be dwarfed under the weight of history and traditions sent over to them from the Old World. "Our age," *Nature* begins, "is retrospective. It builds the sepulchres of the fathers. It writes biographies, histories, and criticism. The foregoing generations beheld God and nature face to face; we, through their eyes. Why should not we also enjoy an original relation to the universe? Why should not we have a poetry and a philosophy of insight and not of tradition, and a religion by revelation to us, and not the history of theirs? Embosomed for a season in nature, whose floods of life stream around and through us, and invite us by the powers they supply to action proportioned to nature, why should we grope among the dry bones of the past, or put the living generation into masquerade out of its faded wardrobe? The sun shines to-day also. There is more wool and flax in the fields. There are new lands, new men, new thoughts. Let us demand our own works and laws and worship." And now Emerson develops what he calls his "theory of nature," or life, or creation, not in the sense of exact science, but bringing all the visible into a simple category, and placing the man of our age in the midst of it as the controlling power. How truly Emerson anticipated what is now the predominant idea in America, or how far his teachings have passed into the flesh and blood of the American, is shown by the nature of scientific activity there at present. We start with the single aim of pursuing science for its own sake, certainly the higher stand-point; in America it is studied chiefly with a view to what will be most serviceable to the learner, — in many cases the better way of attaining practical results. First, shall the living have justice done them?

I received to-day the last annual register of Cornell University, which was founded by the private citizen whose name it bears. On the title-page of the register Cornell's portrait is given, with the inscription around it, "I wish to found an institution in which every one can be instructed in every way." Under the general title, "Departments and special courses of study," I find in the book a section which offers a choice of prescribed plans of study adapted to prepare the scholars for their different positions in life. With the exception of theology and jurisprudence, everything requiring scientific training, from agriculture up to science and letters, is included. With profound understanding of the national character, a number of careers are marked out before the eyes of the student and the steps given by which he may advance. I take this example because it happens to offer itself; but whoever has had opportunity to become acquainted with American professors and students will have remarked their simple method of beginning directly with the essentials and the unconstrained freshness and courage with which they explore new paths, always finding the way to their aim. The American endeavors to comprehend everything, and without the loss of time to adapt all to his own use. Emerson's theory is that of the "sovereignty of the individual." To discover what a young man is good for, and to equip him for the path he is to strike out in life, regardless of any other consideration, is the great duty to which he calls attention. Emerson's essays are written with reference to this aim. He makes men self-reliant. He reveals to the eyes of the idealist the magnificent results of practical activity, and unfolds before the realist the grandeur of the ideal world of thought. No man is to allow himself, through prejudice, to make a mistake in choosing the task to which he will devote his life. Emerson's essays are, as it were, printed sermons,—all having this same text. The transition from preacher to independent lecturer was not in itself considered an unnatural one in America; they are behind us in the production of thought, but the interchange of ideas is much more eager and rapid. Emerson had a great predecessor, whom I name here because it will help us to understand what limited him in his ministry. Channing, the apostle of Unitarianism, had been at first only a preacher. But Channing knew how to control and awe a vast congregation, while Emerson loved best to speak or lecture to a few chosen disciples. His words did not sound above the discords of a crowd, but exacted reverential silence. There was nothing in his words any more than in his appearance that could kindle any definite thought. He only indicated the direction in which one must move.

To the charm of his presence many now testify. Carlyle said a supernal vision dawned on him when he first saw Ralph Waldo Emerson. Some one relates that when as a boy in the midst of his companions he once casually bowed to Emerson, who was about to pass them in the street, he returned the simple greeting in a way he could never forget. "Say to Emerson that I love and honor him," were Sumner's words on his death-bed. The earliest notice of Emerson that I find is in the letters of Frederika Bremer, who visited him in Concord somewhere about 1830. She grants that he remained to her a problem. At first she regarded his cool, incisive way of criticising everything as arrogant, but says at the same time that his nature made an utterly different impression on her from that of other arrogant natures she had met with. "There dwells in this man a loftier spirit," she concludes. This was before the times, we recall to-day, when Emerson's writings caused the young people sleepless nights. As Emerson himself said of Carlyle, his sentences indeed enchain us; they do not seem to be written, but graven on links of steel, as if Emerson had had a presentiment they were destined to last for centuries. It is not usual to speak of the immortality of men while they still live; but Whittier years ago expressed his belief in these words: "No verses written in the English language by any of the living poets bear so clearly imprinted upon them the stamp of immortality as Emerson's." The tribute to Emerson by the renowned physicist is echoed by hundreds this side of the water as well as in America, whose youthful souls were stimulated to their highest and best efforts by the peculiar inspiration of his words. Nobler homage cannot be offered from man to his fellow-man.

Therefore was it nowise astounding to read in the papers the simple statement, as if it were a fixed historical fact, that it was Emerson who had shaped the intellectual life of this century in America.

I became acquainted with Emerson's writings long years since, when I was young, and scarcely knew enough of English to force my way to an understanding of them. Never have I studied a language with such zeal as at that time. It often seemed to me impossible to fathom the meaning of his sentences. I do not know what impression these writings would make upon me now, thirty years later, if they were put in my hands for the first time. Time hardens us, and we are less hospitable to new ideas. But I had the feeling then that, as far as my knowledge went, no one had said such things, or said them in such a way, as Emerson. A sunny view of life radiated from him, — a simile I have often since heard repeated. He seemed to me to give utterance to the noblest contemplations on the past and the present. I attempted to study Emerson critically, but did not succeed. There dwelt within him a hidden power, which seemed his alone. A picture of Giotto in Assisi exhibits St. Francis restoring to life a woman who had died unconfessed, but only long enough for him to receive her confession. The woman lifts herself from the bier while he bends down to her. And in like manner Emerson animates whatever he touches, giving to Nature a voice that she may communicate her secrets, and we believe that he knows much more of them than he tells. Emerson has an incomprehensible way of inspiring the reader with the feeling of the matter without giving it a name or describing it, and without the art by which this is accomplished being anywhere perceptible. Allow me another comparison: As the night-wind passing through the woods and over the meadows comes to us laden with the sweet breath of trees and grasses and flowers which we have not seen, Emerson surrounds us with the atmosphere of things as if they were in reality near us. What was then my inmost conviction regarding Emerson's writings I have lived to hear expressed by many, and as if from the outset no one had held a different opinion. Goethe says, "It is impossible to show the day to the day." He means that the secret of the present is never laid bare to the present, namely, the continuity and relation of the ever-varying experiences, through whose mazes the human race like a vast herd is perpetually urged forward by a watchful Providence. We recognize this unseen force, and obey, timidly asking whither and whence? Everywhere is heard the cry: we recognize it, but no one believes in help from any of the voices. Emerson never asserted that he knew more than others, but his writings inspire the feeling that it must be so, and excite a hope that we may possibly draw from them answers to questions with which we had not consciously dealt. His words seem to me at different times to be capable of different interpretations. Many times have his thoughts presented themselves to my mind like single verses of an infinite poem whose design had still to be fully revealed, even to himself.

I had not glanced at Emerson's writings for many a year; when the telegram came with the tidings of his death, I took down the two-volumed edition of his works, given me by George Bancroft, opened them, and read. The wealth and harmony of his language overpowered and entranced me anew. But even now I cannot say wherein the secret of his influence lies. It is of a wholly individual nature. What he has written is like life itself, — the unbroken thread ever lengthened through the addition of the small events which make up each day's experience. His sentences often flow on monotonously and unaccented. They are series of thoughts. He begins as if continuing a discourse whose opening we had not heard, and ends as if only pausing to take breath before going on. Some one tells of calling on him the day before he was to lecture. He found him surrounded by papers, from which he was selecting and putting together whatever was appropriate to his subject. It does not detract from the value of his writings that their creation was a matter of chance. If we were to print them all together — the introductions excepted — we should see them forming a chain in which no links were missing. It would be like a panorama of ideas, for each minute with him seems to have borne its peculiar fruit. We feel that Emerson never wished to say more than just what at the moment presented itself to his soul. He never set up a system; never defended himself. He speaks as if he had never been assailed; as if all men were his friends, and held the same opinions as himself. He is never hasty, and always impartial. He labors after no effects in style. He speaks with perfect composure, as if translating from a language understood only by himself. He always addresses the same public,—the unknown multitude of those who buy and read his works and wish to listen to him,—and ever in the same tone of manly affability.

Nothing, however, is more comprehensible than that a man so conducting himself should be declared a pure idealist,—a *dilettante* who only floats above our earthly tabernacles because he is nowhere really at home. Reproaches of this nature Emerson has not escaped, for toward no one is the world, with justice, so sharp and merciless as to the man who requires of us implicit faith in his highest thoughts. But the superfluity of knowledge of every kind which Emerson utilizes is no longer regarded as the machinery with which a vain speaker seeks to surprise or attract the public. It is now perceived that when Emerson presents an antithesis, the antithesis exists in reality. Nature herself surprises us with dazzling lights and illumination.

Emerson's career is now ended. The attempt to classify him will repeatedly be made. At present the

American people feel only his loss. Emerson was one of the representatives of the national conscience. The various means of intercourse to-day bring the inhabitants of a great country into more sympathetic relations than formerly existed between those environed by the walls of a single city. There was more reserve in the old days, when men persecuted each other more for differences of opinion. Emerson was to many the highest moral tribunal, and his existence a comfort in the land. By his death America is not only impoverished by the loss of her greatest man, but at the same time regards Emerson as almost the last of a series of men who seem to have died out with him. He and Longfellow were the participators in a great intellectual movement which finds its historic close with them. But Emerson himself prepared the way for the transition to what now takes the place of the animus of those earlier days. He no longer addressed himself by preference to those who read or have read, but to those who only have ears to hear. Bret Harte describes in one of his stories the little house of an emigrant in the far West, where the sole intellectual store consisted of an edition of Shakespeare, and Emerson's portrait on the wall. We have already found Emerson placed beside Shakespeare, and he indeed resembles him in so far that he can be understood without preparation. In the same sense also it is said that, though he has written comparatively little verse, he was, properly speaking, a poet rather than a philosopher. If we admit the comparison with Shakespeare, we may refer to his spontaneity and wealth of thought, as well as his aptitude in the use of similes drawn directly, it would seem, from his own experience, and the absence of prejudice of any and every kind. He is to be compared with Goethe in his endeavor to possess himself of everything in the realm of science, and his inclination — in spite of his association with scholars — to hold himself aloof from them, although never tempted to put himself in opposition to them. In the æsthetic-political import of his writings he reminds us of Schiller, as well as by the democratic sentiment which shines forth from the works of both. Emerson, like Schiller, believed in the superiority of the guileless, ideal man over the man of statecraft and intrigue. Schiller inspires us to-day with the prospect of a great future, and with the certainty of the final appearance of a simple heroic people, each of whom, like Wallenstein's Max, will look down with contempt on our present artifice and cunning. The coming of this people Emerson also predicted to his compatriots. In another respect Emerson resembles Schiller. He stood ready to lift his voice whenever, wherever it was needed, and unhesitatingly came to the front in emergencies of all kinds, whilst Goethe only interfered in matters congenial to his nature, and postponed the rest.

Like St. Augustine, Emerson treats of the most subtile themes without lowering his voice, and in such a free, unconstrained way as to be attractive even to a child. With marvellous penetration he reduces the most involved questions to simple forms. This is especially conspicuous in *English Traits*, which was written after having twice visited England. The phenomena of English life are traced back to the character and constitution of the race, together with the natural qualities of the soil. I have never heard a country and a people more clearly described, and the value of the book is recognized on both sides of the ocean. The low estimate of foreigners among the English is proverbial, but they seem to have made an exception in favor of Emerson. Emerson's love of truth rings out clearly in every opinion he gives. "He was invested with the light of truth," begins a notice of him in *Harper's Weekly*, and English papers contain similar expressions. Emerson says the English is the first nation in the world, but ranks the German intellectually higher. The Englishman, he says, looks at everything singly, and does not know how to comprehend humanity as a whole, according to higher laws. He says, "The German thinks for Europe." But what distinguishes the English, Americans, and Germans,—the three people before whom, in common, stand the great problems of the world,— is often the subject of his demonstration. And here we must again mention Carlyle, whom Emerson has been supposed to imitate. Hero-worship was not an original idea either with Carlyle or Emerson. It is in the blood of English and Americans as one of their noblest capabilities. It is possible that, through Carlyle, Emerson was inspired to write his book on *Representative Men;* but it is a wholly different conception from Carlyle's *Heroes.* Carlyle's labored and, to our view, often intentionally peculiar style, can never for a moment be compared with Emerson's. And indeed the comparisons I have instituted between Emerson and others apply only to outward and accidental characteristics. He stands alone, and will have a special place in history. In the introduction to *Representative Men* Emerson says, in praise of great men, that each is useful to his people, in that his name enriches by a word the vocabulary of his native tongue. In the meaning of this "word," as he uses it, is contained an idea which could not be expressed by any other phraseology.

Emerson dwelt in Concord in a small one-story house, built, it would seem, chiefly of wood. One night it took fire and burned down. Emerson, seventy years of age, suddenly driven out into the cold night air, fell ill for the first time in his life. His friends suggested to him that he should go abroad to reinstate his health, the intention being during his absence to rebuild his house. Emerson went over California to India, returning home by Egypt and Europe. He reached Italy in the spring of 1873, and I saw him in Florence. A tall, slender figure, with the radiant smile which is peculiar to children and men of the highest order. His daughter Ellen was his companion, and devoted to him. The noblest culture raises men above national peculiarities and makes them perfectly unaffected. Emerson had an unpretentious dignity of demeanor, and I felt as if I had always known him. At that time he was still fresh and could work. Soon after an infirmity came upon him. He wholly lost his memory. One of my former hearers wrote me an account of his last visit to him. Emerson sat there, says the letter, like an old eagle in his eyrie. He greeted me in the most kind and friendly manner, but could no longer remember men or things. "It is natural to believe in great men," begins the introduction to Emerson's *Representative Men*. "Nature seems to exist for the excellent. The world is upheld by the veracity of good men; they make the earth wholesome. They who have lived with them found life glad and nutritious. Life is sweet and tolerable only in our belief in such society; and, actually or ideally, we manage to live with superiors. We call our children and our lands by their names. Their names are wrought into the verbs of language, their works and effigies are in our houses, and every circumstance of the day recalls an anecdote of them. The search after the great is the dream of youth, and the most serious occupation of manhood. We travel into foreign parts to find his works, if possible, to get a glimpse of him." The words to-day sound like his epitaph.

FRANCE AND VOLTAIRE.

When Alaric in his Italian campaign besieged Rome, the inhabitants, reduced through pestilence and famine to the last extremity, despatched messengers to the Gothic camp. Instead, however, of quietly awaiting, as they should, the verdict of their conquerors in whose hands their fate absolutely lay, they broke forth into the most arrogant threats, and returned to the city without having accomplished anything; even after Rome had actually fallen into the hands of the Goths, the comparatively lenient terms offered them by their victors were at first rejected with contempt.

Historians call it an inconceivable hallucination; for who could regard such stubbornness as patriotism, when the immeasurable wretchedness of the public condition was so clearly manifest? The Romans had seen with their own eyes the mortal terror of the populace at the approach of the enemy, the general fright, the helplessness, the want of leaders! Why then, in this utter absence of all power, such an ebullition of haughty pride?

I will neither compare the Germans of to-day with

the Goths under Alaric, although there could be no
detraction in the comparison with this noble people,
nor the French — especially the Parisians — with the
Italians and Romans at that time. But the extraordinary view the French took of the last war throws a
milder, or at all events an explanatory light on the conduct of the Romans, who in the midst of ruin rebelled
against the consciousness of being ruined, and also helps
us to understand the behavior of the French people.
We see that adversities of such enormous extent may so
unexpectedly overwhelm a people that the panic-struck
souls lose the capacity of taking in what is happening
before their very eyes. The Roman, without hope for
the future, unable to govern or to defend himself, worn
out with hunger and in the jaws of destruction, is yet
incapable, either of humbly negotiating or of conceiving
that Rome, which had stood unconquered more than a
thousand years, — Golden Imperial Rome! — could ever
be forced to admit the barbarian as conqueror within
her walls, and instead of surrendering he threatens.
The words of submission rebel against the lips which
would drive them forth. The Romans, deluded by a
glorious past like a Fata Morgana rising before him!
And even so in France to-day, though conquered and
prostrate, the prisoners from so many battles entertain
but one idea, raise but one cry, — "Betrayed!" The
Frenchman has a peculiar organization, rendering it
impossible for him to imagine himself beaten. Weary,
hopeless, and miserable he calls defeats victories, be-

lieves he can still grasp with convulsive hands Alsace and Lorraine, and threatens to demand the Rhine boundary.

To be sure nobody could foresee the extent of the terrible struggle into which the French nation was drawn; for no one dreamed that this organism, almost dissolved as it was by party passion, could yet give birth to such demonic power as Prussia had to acknowledge even while crushing it. Yet now that the phenomena stands complete there is nothing in it which the history of the country does not explain.

Three generations of Frenchmen have everywhere found rehearsed as articles of faith the invincibility of France, foremost among the nations, and the conquest of the Rhine boundary, as a sacred historical legacy. *Gloire* and *Victoire, France* and *Vaillance,* are rhymes for which the Almighty seems to have specially foreordained the French language. France conquered by Germany is in the eyes of the French people an illusion conjured up by the Evil One. They were spectral hosts that besieged Paris. Only a little patience, and with the returning sun the ancient arms of France will glitter as of yore and mirror themselves victoriously in the waves of the Rhine! Gustave Doré, as purely a national genius as ever lived, has glorified this expedition in a symbolic drawing, which illustrates the French idea of it better than anything which could be said or written. Every Frenchman who looks at it must exclaim, "Yes, so it shall be and so it will be!" That it will not be so is our hope.

What the Frenchman requires is *élan!* forward! without bag or baggage, no matter whither. All France hurrahed and rushed into the war with Prussia: it was a grand expedition. In the same spirit Brennus was hurried on to Rome, Bonaparte to Egypt, Napoleon to Russia. The Gaul needs about every twenty-five years a huge political exploring expedition, arms in hand, into this or that country which he is pleased for the nonce to declare the "terra incognita." They did not wish to fight with the noble German people; a promenade to Berlin was what they wanted, on account of Sadowa. They neither knew where Berlin lay, nor what had been contended for at Sadowa; an undefined thirst for battle pervaded the nation; it must find vent against the Prussians. The Emperor himself, certainly the greatest pessimist in all France, would have been glad enough to have avoided the war, but was obliged to yield to the pressure of the people.

Let us endeavor to gain a view of the phenomenon from a higher stand-point.

It is marvellous to observe how powerfully the love of renown has stirred in the heart of the French people from the hour they were first conscious of being a nation. Their conquests in arms and their great successes in art and literature have sprung from this source. They seize upon things intellectual with the same fire and boldness with which they attack foreign powers. They have unrivalled dexterity in grasping and expressing ideas. They are ready with their theory on the instant, but will cheerfully face death itself for it. It is well known what French specialists have done and are doing in all the various departments of science. They are greatest, however, when classifying whole masses of phenomena in conformity with new theories. They aim at an overwhelming general effect which shall silence all opposition. They expect their great men to shoot across the heavens like comets with fiery tails, straight through the constellations of fixed stars. And we must acknowledge, that for two hundred years the French have astonished themselves and all Europe with such men, soldiers, statesmen, savans, and artists. Happen what might, a brief interim, and France stood again at the head of nations; Paris, the brilliant centre of Europe, — hers the language in which everything could best be said; hers the soil, the air, in which great men sprang up and found the most rapid development; hers the honor and the glory and the hearth on whose burning coals the opinion of all Europe was formed!

How could this city, so long the heart and brain of Europe, even if actually in the grasp of the German army, be crushed or humiliated in the eyes of a Frenchman? This France not rise again with to-morrow's sun to revenge herself? Any moment they imagined might change the whole face of things! If the victory announced by Gambetta yesterday was won, may it not still come before to-day closes? It needs only the right general, at last, one no traitor like the rest, or that the gods who perchance have slumbered should awake to see what foul demons have brought upon France, to restore with one brave stroke the old order. Such thoughts were but too natural.

To us at this time Voltaire is of special significance, because he was the first and mightiest organizer of the dogma of the providentially intended preponderance of France among the nations, which from small beginnings gradually became an element of the French character. France had not always been the first nation. When Louis XIV began to consolidate his government Hapsburg was a giant in political affairs compared with France, while Italy exceeded her quite as much in culture; the precedence, therefore, was naturally yielded to both these nations, and art and literature openly recognized as an importation. This continued for decades, until the power of the Austrian and English monarchies declined, and France, by a series of victories, not only enlarged her boundaries formidably, but, remoulding all the heterogeneous elements thus gained, created a new French nationality with Paris for its centre. It now required only a few decades before the people living in perpetual contemplation of this prosperous state of things evolved the blessed gospel of the supremacy of France,— the prime article to-day in the creed of every individual Frenchman.

To establish this belief Voltaire contributed more than any one else. He first comprehended the whole wealth of his people, and exhibited it to France herself as well as to other countries, in its full splendor, as a living reality. To him this France, eclipsing the rest of the world in the unity of her land and people, was the product of the total development of humanity. The idea was natural, and nowhere met with opposition. Voltaire had simply formulated what all Europe had on the tongue. He was himself, however, the ripest fruit in this paradise of modern culture. All his experiences, even the worst, were typical of his nation. No writer ever arose in any part of the world to whom his people and country served as such an admirable foil as the French to Voltaire. A combination of many fortuitous circumstances is required before out of thousands who seemed called one is permitted to find the place where he develops perfectly and exhibits his full strength. Voltaire was singled out for such a rôle in France. His spirit represents the spirit of millions, and each individual Frenchman may be considered as an atom of his soul. He was greater, stronger, happier than them all, and the century in which he lived and worked bears his name.

Voltaire's long life embraces the most significant epoch in French history. As a youth he was educated in a lively consciousness of the undisputed supremacy which the powerful Louis XIV won for France; his death occurred while (although the French Revolution was hastening on) the rosy glimmer in the morning sky still promised a glorious day. Never have literary productions commanded so high a price as during the century in which Voltaire lived; never was a man more richly endowed for his career, nor one who used his talents less unsparingly. We have in our century had instances of books more popular with the masses; Sue's *Mysteries of Paris*, Renan's *Vie de Jésus*, or *Uncle Tom's Cabin* have netted authors and publishers much greater sums than did even Voltaire's works. As regards these books, however, there were certain strata among the people where we may say they as good as never existed, and even of those who read them with avidity, who has really found in them daily food, or lasting solace and enjoyment? But Voltaire's works were classics from the outset. Frederick the Great deemed it an understood fact that every man of taste must prefer the *Henriade* to the *Iliad*. Men studied Voltaire. His works and his life occupied the thoughts of the best classes of society in his day. Into religion, science, politics, the mind of this man gradually infused itself. Not indeed that he had a clique by whom his influence was made systematically effective.

Voltaire was too great for that! Men neither loved nor revered him. He was more hated and feared than any one, and through his whole life had only servants and coadjutors, but no friends. Yet no one, let the strength of his individuality be what it might, quite escaped Voltaire's influence, which, like the sirocco whirling desert sands through tent walls of treble thickness, is apparent, even over those who seem most energetically to have resisted it. Lessing, if we look at him dispassionately, has more Voltairean elements than would seem possible with such great personal contrast; and Diderot, together with many others whose natures were original and vigorous, rested largely upon him, although this may not have been perceived in his generation. One man only stood quite free of him, — Jean Jacques Rousseau; and he, too, was the only one Voltaire never manœuvred to win, but by ignoring him, and by other covert means (such as nowadays we could scarcely understand), held him at arm's-length.

For the rest, he was always open in his attacks, and brought into play the entire repertory of weapons in his arsenal, from the powerful big guns, whose every shot told, down to the meanest, most infamous weapons, which worked like poison in the blood. Voltaire simply acted out his instincts.

He was lion or rattlesnake, changing from one to the other without any effort of will. He was the latest edition of the old Homeric Proteus, whom he likewise resembled, in that, for the most part, he appeared to be placidly sleeping on the sea-shore in the sunshine, only when goaded rousing himself to the fight. But in truth he was always on the lookout, and it was only necessary that the poor mortal who met his gaze should strike him as worth the trouble for him to make his very existence seem a reproach and a shame. One thing he found absolutely insufferable, namely, to be obliged to acknowledge that he was not the sole literary power in the land.

Voltaire's history is the record of these dissonances and strifes. In the innermost depth of his nature he can hardly be said to have ever experienced development. All his phases are only external manifestations of something that was in itself complete from the beginning. He came upon the stage ripe and ready, springing from the brain of his native land, armed with shield and spear, and skilled in their use. With his first note he sent a challenge to right and left, fought battles all round, gave sharp thrusts, and never allowed the world any peace until he drew his last breath. In his whole life he never really learned anything new, although he steadily absorbed into himself the novelties of his day and generation; the germ of all was in his birth-right.

To the farthest points the web of his knowledge and personal relations was stretched; in those meshes friends and enemies, moths and elephants, alike were caught, while the great spider, with the monstrous understanding, sat in the midst, drawing the life-blood of his victims, ever lying in wait, with the same eyes, in the same form, and on the same spot.

A soil and atmosphere in which such an individual could display himself must indeed have been peculiar. The Paris which was Voltaire's school, in which he received his consecration and established his throne, was a unique product of historic evolution. At present there is a list of great cities beside Paris, — London, New York, Berlin, Vienna, and St. Petersburg, — which must be reckoned as about equal in value as vertebral points from which intellectual light radiates; but the Paris of the last century predominated over Rome, London, and Vienna (the only three cities which could be named in comparison) as decidedly as the French language did over the English and Italian.

The Parisians were at that time the favored representatives of the most cultivated nation. But the efforts they had been making for a whole century to attain this distinguished rank are not to be lightly estimated. We know not the laws that permit a wealth of great men suddenly to appear in the midst of a people; but in France we see during the seventeenth and eighteenth centuries such an extraordinary number of great men arising on all sides, that the combined lustre of their achievements has sufficient light-giving power to create a brilliant atmosphere over all France; something such as we observe at night over large cities, and in which even common things assume unwonted splendor.

Let us first look at their achievements in the literary field. At the time when Voltaire appeared the language had been elaborated and improved, until it had become an instrument of such fineness that the advent of a man who could exhibit its full power seemed a demand on the creative genuis of the nation. One might say that a man like Voltaire must come.

A hundred years before Voltaire, Corneille had appeared. He is the poet of the Fronde, Louis XIII, Anne of Austria, Richelieu and Mazarin, — of the nobility and the enfranchised citizens, armed against the king. Corneille found, as the happiest mirror for his day, the times of like import in Rome, when the families of Cæsar and Augustus rose to supremacy and imperial power over a number of other patrician families, equally powerful and equally entitled. During Corneille's most susceptible years France was in the hands of an almost independent body of nobles, with whom individually the king was forced to compromise. What rôle private family affairs played in all this, and what influence the beauty and intrigues of the women had, the history of that day informs us. Mazarin speaks of their extraordinary interference in state affairs as distinguishing France from Spain and Italy, where certainly *les grandes dames* also knew how to expedite or to hinder things. When Corneille makes Augustus say *Soyons amis, Cinna*, we might object to its wholly false effect, as an illustration of Roman history, since Augustus could only have said this to chaff a somewhat insignificant person. The public, however, before whom this was played saw in Augustus an incarnation of the united power of Richelieu and the king, and in Cinna, one of those dukes who, even as convicted traitors, were still powerful enough to count on having things settled in a friendly way.

Corneille's men are austere in speech, and his women, in whom politics and love seem chemically united, are powerful rather than feminine; even Chimène, the tenderest of all the poet's creations, never loses sight of her lofty political position. That the following generation, to which Racine belonged, cared no longer for such things is quite conceivable.

Racine is the court-poet of Louis XIV, whilst during the youth of the king the *vieille cœur* of Anne of Austria adheres to the great Corneille like a congregation to its old hymn-book. Racine glorifies the new France, which just as ardently clings to him. This new France of which we speak is composed of the nobility, restrained and educated by Louis, and Cinna the promiscuous French public, who make the first attempt to find recognition as an element proper. The old patriotic body of freemen, once able to close the gates of their city against the king, no longer held sway in Paris; now it was the great sea of the people, upon whom a blow was like a stroke upon water, which nothing separated, and which upheld all that rose to the surface, drop by drop, rising and broadening its flow, until, after a series of generations, the Revolution arose, and in its midst to-day the honor and glory of France seems to have sunk forever.

Racine needs despots, favorites, amorous young princes, who talk of nothing but their passions, and neither rebel against their country nor exert themselves to save it; ministers who have an opinion, but no will of their own, and if they speak of past or future refer only to their own predecessors or successors, and as spectators of the complications arising between such characters, — either a court where these things were matters of personal experience, or a nation deeming it the highest enjoyment to be near this court and gaze at it admiringly through the gilded lattices which shut it off from the rest of the world. He is the poet of the commoners, as yet unstable and powerless, truckling to the nobility, both the higher and the lower.

Molière is the greatest of the three poets. He created his world and ruled it. Corneille dared not say all he thought, and was, moreover, cramped by pupillage in the learned pedantry of the Academic clique on which he was dependent. Racine, one feels clearly, knew the court to be other than as he paints it; the single tragedy written out of his soul, *Berenice*, closes with a sigh; it might have ended quite differently, and he wrote nothing further of this kind. But Molière was perfectly untrammeled. His misanthropy breaks off with a dissonance, such as we meet with in life itself, which he knew through and through. His language is free, and the noblest manifestation of the genuine French spirit.

Corneille, Racine, and Molière put their own stamp on the language, and gave to their ideas the most plastic and artistic shapes. Clustered about them, and keeping step with their progress, were a number of writers who handled the language with ease and grace, and in admirable ways followed the bent of their idiosyncrasies. The language and literary form was wrought to such a pitch of perfection as to render it a difficult task to earn the right to use it for the public benefit or become a recognized author. Every writer was subjected to an uninterrupted series of the most irksome examinations, at which all Paris voted. Even a critic like Boileau despairs of expressing himself in correct French. The Parisian savants, together with the circle by whose final judgment the author was forced to abide, had become a secret power in which to share was matter of competition and supposed uncommon gifts. That a man dared to appear in Paris and claim public attention as a writer in itself, argued distinction of some sort. Writing and printing were not at that time what they are to-day. Far more was written and read to private audiences than appeared in print, or was exposed for sale in the bookstores.

Indeed, we may say that about the year 1700 all Paris wrote. Lords and valets composed gallant or satirical verses, epistles, memoirs, tragedies, and love-letters. They wrote and helped to circulate what was written, praised, censured, but insatiably asked for more. This excitement lasted up to the Revolution, when its character changed. From Corneille even to our time, a period of two hundred and fifty years, French literature swayed the taste of Europe. The different phases through which it passed were in conjunction with the revolutions in the general political condition.

As during these two hundred and fifty years the conduct of public affairs step by step passed out of the hands of the nobles into that of the democratic masses,—amongst whom to-day only wealth or talent gives weight and position,—the literature also in the gradual transit adapted itself as far as possible to the taste of those exercising the supreme control.

But this, too, is of the past! The mission of literature seems fulfilled in the sense of these centuries gone by. We start afresh! With us writing and printing is simply a vehicle of communication, the matter the essential thing. Naïve enjoyment in language as such is lost. To be sure he who revels in the artistic management of language will always win his audience and his fame; but if we regard literature as the servant of the forces governing mankind at the present day, we find the style of the roughest telegraphic despatch as effective over the masses as the most elegant and elaborately constructed sentences. This is most striking in France, England, and America. The nations do not seem to want books which can be slowly converted into friends, but special utterances of beloved or distinguished people, whose opinions can be at once accepted and put in practice. Reading is only a substitute for personal intercourse,—not for conversation, however, but for the business of life. Nobody is surprised to receive as answer to the question, "Have you read this or that book?" "No, but I know the author; he is a friend of mine."

The world-wide intercourse in which we all share makes reading and writing a labor; and only those cannot find enjoyment in it whose efforts are not demanded in any other sphere. At the time when Voltaire appeared, a hopeless stagnation prevailed throughout the political life of Europe. Men had no political ideals. Robinson Crusoe's rocky isle was the Utopia of national economy, beyond which the imagination of the people did not soar. Sure only of the present, they allowed themselves to relapse into mere enjoyment of it, and believed the deep ruts in which they were shuffling along the necessary requisites for a good road. That changes could be brought about by an impulse springing out of the heart of a united people was an idea which never had dawned even upon Montesquieu, when at the conclusion of his *Esprit des Lois* he constructed his model state. In general society the one thing to be done was to provide as good music as possible, that all might dance. For this the young were educated, and their elders found delight in it. Life seemed long, and its vicissitudes comparatively few. To fight against *ennui* was everybody's chief concern. Louis XIV (in his old age the regent of Louis XV) excelled in this species of warfare. Heaven and hell were set in commotion to defeat this enemy; of what immense value, then, must a man have been who wherever he appeared dissipated every shade of *ennui* as if by witchcraft; who (like the giant's daughter sweeping everything that came under her hand, changed to toys, into her apron) transformed all that his mind touched into the most entertaining playthings for the people, and this year after year, and on through many generations. To this end Voltaire could utilize the merest nothings, as well as the most prodigious questions of science, and the one, it would seem, as easily, as the other. Everything served him, and all gained equal weight in his hands.

Corneille would flatter the as yet torpid spirit of the people, which, unconscious of its power, seemed to have only a dim foreboding of the supremacy it finally assumed in Europe; Racine glorified the passions of the changing court, moving along proudly, treading upon laurels real and imaginary, to which a nation looked up as the Greeks and Romans to the eternally feasting Olympians. Voltaire aimed to astound, to thrill, to teach the great Parisian public, but all only to relieve it from *ennui*. "*Tous les genres sont bons hors l'ennui eux,*" was his motto. The people should be forced to laugh or to weep, no matter which, so they realized it was he who had the skill and cunning to do it. Voltaire was the most prodigious literary actor that ever found shelter on our planet,—herein perhaps wholly unique. An actor not in the common sense, but in the highest, such as Garrick was; for Voltaire identifies himself so completely with the rôle he plays as to transform himself into the character he represents, and the illusion is only destroyed for the spectator when he suddenly appears in a wholly different rôle. To laugh or to weep, to reflect seriously upon life and its duties, or to shrug one's shoulders over it in thoughtless frivolity, to find delight in the world, or to despise it, to plunge into the profoundest depths of scholarly research, or to thrust sceptically aside all learned contemplations,—to each in turn he summons us, and every time with equally convincing arguments; always, however, only for so and so long, not forever. His correspondence affords the best examples of this: there is not a single one of his very eloquent passages in which, sooner or later, the moment does not come when we say to ourselves, "This was written to produce some particular effect upon others, or at the best upon himself." At the same time we must not leave out of account the enormous expenditure of intellectual material involved in this play; nor indeed that it was in the gratification of this impulse that Voltaire saved the innocent from death when all France cried out against them. He was courageous and tough. He possessed immense power to make his thoughts those of the multitude, and if he often enough made use of it to avenge himself on his enemies, it proved no less potent when he espoused the cause of the oppressed.

Yet after having provided munificently for a distant granddaughter of Corneille's, when a rough, uncouth fellow presented himself proving nearer relationship and more intimate claims on the great poet, he speeded the poor creature on his way with only a friendly viaticum. Perhaps could Corneille himself have appeared in his old torn shoes, Voltaire would have given him a new pair, at the same time beseeching him to get out of his way. He did what he could, but still only what he would; people must not make themselves disagreeable, and if he was to be moved, the looks of the world must be upon him. Voltaire did not like situations in which the arrangements were not advantageous for him; nor did he often meddle with things that did not picture him in a fovorable light to the eyes of the curious world.

Voltaire is of moment to us to-day as poet, historian, and to the German nation especially as the friend of Frederick the Great.

For this reason it is valuable for every one to obtain a knowledge of his works and character. Voltaire sought to fairly exhaust the erudition of his time; but what he has himself contributed to religious philosophy, to the natural sciences, and to kindred branches of learning, is a matter of interest to those only who make these a specialty. His most legitimate renown attaches to his writings on historical subjects. These, unrivaled in form, and whose influence over the mind and destiny of France seem intimately connected with the final terrific ruin of his country, are to-day still fresh and readable.

Voltaire came into the world in 1694; his youth fell in the dull and stagnant years preceding the death of Louis XIV, when the people, enduring the misery of a despotic and firmly-interwoven Jesuit police system, awaited the departure of the superannuated monarch, without however attaching any prospective hopes to the hour when it should take place. St. Simon depicts this state of things admirably, bringing out the minutiæ with the sly, cool spitefulness peculiar to him. At that time, as well as later, public spirit was sustained by the vanity of the people in the triumphant position of France among the nations. Were they not the first, ably conducting their politics in silks and velvets,—what more could they wish? We all know how, upon the death of the king and the accession of the regent, this wearisome stagnation came to an end, and what mad doings followed. Nobles and citizens, hitherto residing separately in Versailles and Paris, now rushed together like two chemical elements whose union was complete as soon as they touched, and from that moment formed the "Parisian public governing the world." In the time of Corneille we read more than once in the memoirs of Madame de Motteville, "This year the court is absolutely deserted, for everybody has gone to the war." This certainly never happened in the days of Racine and Molière; for then Versailles, even in war-time, was not quite empty, only special blood must flow in the veins in order to be received there. But Voltaire needed not to bruise his spirit against any such limitations; he first learned to use his wings when, night after night, in the Palais Royal, play-actresses and duchesses, with their respective manly attachés, assembled as equals in rank, under the presiding regent. Still, the rest of Paris stood outside listening at the half-closed window-blinds in order to catch and circulate accounts of the scandal and uproar within. The days had come when lackeys and nobles, the two extremes in convivial intercourse, formed the warp and woof of society, whose only aim was to get money quickly in order to spend it again as quickly, and to create for themselves leisure only to waste it.

Notwithstanding all this, the external civic regulations, dating from past centuries, had been so firm and strong, that in the midst of confusion and bad management the state held out still a hundred years; and the intellectual culture of the seventeenth century having had an equally durable basis, there arose in the midst of all this frivolity and superficiality deep thinkers, and of genius, whose authority prevented the general level of public culture from sinking so low as it has to-day under an improved national economy and outward circumstances vastly more favorable. The solid beginnings operated yet. This was the rococo period of which the poets sing, and painters compose such charming pictures, where maidens with powdered heads peep out of the rose-embowered windows of village inns, just a walk from their fascinating country-houses, and who seem to have moved so airily in their heavy, rustling brocades as hardly to have touched the earth with the heel of their dainty slippers. When everybody paid in nothing less than shining Louis-d'or; when between marquis and marquises in pleasure palaces the incessant whisper of intrigue went on; when in open calash, with trim little postilions in the saddle, they whisked like the wind over the smooth roads of the glorious old kingdom of good old France, fifty per cent of whose population at that time lived doing nothing, from beggar and monk to duke and archbishop, and were nourished by the other fifty per cent who drudged and tilled the land, grovelling in the dust and living like cattle, — although precious little of this work in the mole-heap came to the knowledge of anybody, — all this seemed natural in France.

At seven years of age Voltaire had already written enchanting poetry. At twelve he was presented to the old Ninon de l'Enclos, who left him two thousand pounds in her will, that he might buy books. Voltaire was to be a jurist; but a relation, an abbé, who admired his intellect, took good care that the youth should be early enough taken into the best literary society of Paris to enable him to discover for what he really was intended.

He was not left dependent on such people as a poor author picks up in tavern and alehouse, but introduced at once into the society of rich financiers, abbés, and chevaliers, etc., whose connections were exclusively with the higher classes, and who dined and supped in palaces. At eighteen years of age Voltaire was thrown for the second time into the Bastile, because he had written verses satirizing the regent and his daughter; which, moreover, in the most humble letters and by all that was holy, he disowned and denied. Whilst in prison he wrote his first tragedy, the *Œdipus;* was released, had his work brought upon the stage, witnessed forty-five representations of it, received a gold medal and a pension from the regent, and, after its merits and defects had been made the subject of a bitter public discussion, contrived to have it printed with a preface by the most esteemed critic of the day, Monsieur de la Motte. He says that if the public, on seeing the tragedy acted, felt that a successor of Corneille and Racine had arisen in France, the reading of this work could but deepen and confirm the impression. All had happened before Voltaire was much more than twenty-five years of age. Matured by an experience which would have done honor to an older man, he had selected the most acceptable material and moulded it in the best form for a tragedy (making use of a model forgotten by everybody) and presented it to the public in brilliant and faultless alexandrines. A literary feat from the first to the last letter, without a spark of real feeling, poetry, or mystery; precision of expression, arrangement of scenes, and theatrical effect its sole aim.

It would, however, scarcely be right to discuss the peculiarities of Voltaire's dramas as illustrated in the *Œdipus*, which was his first and is to-day his least renowned work. *Mahomet, Zaire,* and *Tancred* are the tragedies of which we should speak. In these he incarnates the sum of his experiences and exhibits his full power. They are still quoted, read, perhaps admired; and that Goethe valued *Tancred* and *Mahomet* highly enough to translate them was indicative of their worth to the Germans.

Certainly it could never have escaped such a sharp-sighted critic as Voltaire, that one grand leading thought and character strongly marked were essential as the basis for tragedy; and further, how could one whose mind was at home in the literatures of all nations, and familiar with every literary expedient, fail to see before him a wealth of resources by which to lend to his dramas these two requisites. In truth, he went to work with such imposing clearness as to delude even Goethe. All that in cold blood can be made of a work of art Voltaire has accomplished in his tragedies. But let us compare one of his passages in *Mahomet* with Goethe's translation of it: —

> "Tremblant, saisi d'effroi, j'ai plangé dans son flanc
> Ce glaive con sacré qui dut verser son sang.
> J'ai voulu redoubler; ce vieillard vénèrable
> A jeté dans mes bras un cri si lamentable
> La nature a tracé dans ses regards mourants
> Un si grand caractère, et des traits si touchants!

De tendresse et d'effroi mon âme c'est semplie,
Et, plus mourant que lui, je déteste ma vie."
Le Fanatisme, Act IV. Scene 4.

How does Goethe render these rhetorical flights, so devoid of all graphic power?

"Mit Wuth ergriff ich ihn, der Schwache fiel.
Ich traf, ich zuckte schon zum zweiten Streich
Ein jämmerlicher Schrei zerriss mein ohr,
Von Staub herauf gebot die edelste
Gestalte mir Ehrfurcht seine Züge schienen
Verklärt, es schien ein Heil'ger zu verscheiden
Die Lampe warf ihr bleiches Licht auf ihn
Und düster floss das Blut aus senier Wunde."

Goethe has lent form and substance to the vague generalities in the Frenchman's production, and, feeling that even this was not enough, added the two last lines which give light and shade to the picture. Here we find what Voltaire lacked. His dramatic creations all shared that element of unreality which greatly impaired the effect of his first tragedy, and later, when inspired with the intention of making them the vehicle of great thoughts (these thoughts seemed so alien to the character of the piece that they might as well have been left out) they are dragged in head and shoulders, and their irrelevancy only disguised by the fact that in the public desire to meet a leading thought everywhere no discrimination was exercised as to its pertinence. As regards dramatic treatment, we see external accidents of the clap-trap kind made to bring about violent catastrophes. Not one original turn surprises us, and leads us to exclaim, "A poet wrote this!" "Only Voltaire could have conceived it!" Corneille and Racine are brimming over with lucky hits; Racine is so rich in other ways that his small talent for scenic arrangement is scarcely observed, but Voltaire, as dramatist, is not striking and original, never surprises us, and succeeds, at the most, only in worrying us.

Voltaire's inability to create characters, and to give the phenomena of life true color and form, is so very evident that it must be attributed to the idiosyncrasy of his whole nature. Among all his writings, both in prose and verse, I have never been so fortunate as to discover two sentences which afforded a picture. He does not succeed even in painting one where it would be the easiest thing in the world to do so, — as, for instance, when he wishes to describe, in a letter to a painter, the view from Ferney, on Lake Geneva, he takes pains to build up with words something like an actual landscape. Vain endeavor! Out of the complete disorder in which he brings the main features of the scene before us no one could tell what to look for above, below, in the middle, or to the right and left. This lack of power to excite the imagination by pictures is most curiously conspicuous in his great heroic poem the *Henriade*.

Among Voltaire's minor poems is one in which he assigns the position he holds among the epic poets.

Stanses sur les Poetes Epiques à Madame la Marquise du Châtelet.

Plein de beautés et de défauts
   Le vieil Homère a mon estime;
Il est, comme tous ses héros,
   Babillard, outré, mais sublime.

Virgill orne mieux la raison
   A plus d'art autant d'harmonie;
Mais il s'epuise avec Didon
   Et rate à la fin Lavinia.

De faux brillants, trop de magie,
   Mettent le classe un crane plus bas
   Mais que ne tolère l'on pas
Pour Armide et pour Herminee?

Milton, plus sublime qu'eux tous
   A des beautés — moins agréables;
Il semble chanter pour les fous,
   Pour les anges, et pour les diables.

Après Milton, après le Tasse,
   Parler de moi, serait trop fort;
   Et j'attendrai que je sois mort,
Pour apprendre quelle est ma place.

Vous, en qui tant d'ésprit abonde
   Tant de grâce et tant de douceur,
   Si ma place est dans votre cœur
Elle est la prémière du monde.

               VOLTAIRE, *Œuvres Complètes.*
           Paris: Didot, *Frères*, 1808, Vol. II. p. 575.

In the last verse Voltaire gives us to understand that for the present he will be satisfied with a firm place in the heart of the *Marquise du Châtelet;* but he certainly never doubted what the judgment of him by posterity would be. Had not Frederick the Great declared that Homer was nothing in comparison with him! (Which I may be allowed to quote twice, since the king so often repeated it.) If Voltaire in his old age calls La Harpe (the author of a now forgotten tragedy) Sophocles, who was crowning the aged Æschylus — that was himself — with flowers, he meant it quite seriously. "I have always believed, I do now believe, and shall continue to believe," he writes Horace Walpole (15th July, 1768), "that Paris in her tragedies and comedies surpasses Athens in every respect. I boldly assert that all the Greek tragedies seem like school-boy compositions compared with the glorious scenes in Corneille, and the consummate tragedies of Racine." Voltaire felt it to be so entirely beyond question that his time was the golden era in the ages, and he the poet of poets, that he talks of it coolly as of an established fact in regard to which modesty and immodesty did not come in play.

I have met with only one person out of the many I have asked, who professed to have read the *Henriade*. It is generally supposed to be a long-winded poem, that it is no loss not to be familiar with it, composed of many songs, dedicated to a rehearsal of the deeds of Henry IV. But the *Henriade* has little enough to do with its hero! It is (together with many other things which it is also) one of the ablest and sharpest attacks ever directed against the Church of Rome. If Pascal, in his letters *A Un Provincial* gave expression to the inimical feeling with which the enlightened community of the seventeenth century looked upon the Jesuit rule in France, Voltaire's *Henriade* incarnates the malignant opposition in the breasts of the philosophic portion of the Parisian public, to the absolute tyranny of the Romish Church. We must therefore speak of Voltaire's position toward the Church before coming to any opinion with regard to the *Henriade*.

The old tradition exists that Voltaire was an atheist, a scoffer at every thing holy, an enemy to religion. But he carefully avoided ever coming out directly against the Catholic religion. Voltaire soared much too high above his surroundings not to attain, in his loneliness, to the conception of a personal God, and far too well understood the wants of self-support in the masses not to look upon distinct formulas of belief as necessary to define their relation with God. He never, indeed, helped to shape these formulas for them, and he in the main disagreed with such as the Church offered. At his death he submitted formally to the authority of the Roman Catholicism; but before he had any thought of dying he once enacted a farce, in which, taking the part of the dying man, he accepted all the consolations of the Church, then, suddenly springing from the bed, mocked and jeered at the priests. He once went so far as in all seriousness to join the order of the Capuchins, and mounted the pulpit to deliver a thrilling penitential discourse. Yet he said the most abusive things about the popes, and to a pope dedicated his tragedy of *Mahomet*, in which, under the guise of Mahometanism, an attack upon the fanaticism of the Church was intended. The same performance is repeated in the *Henriade*. He has ventured in this poem to expose things against Rome which, had they been couched in less crafty language, would have cost him his life. But withal, he humbly proposed to an old Jesuit, "revered as a father," to expurgate every word in it militating against the Catholic religion, — to whose honor and glory, in fact, the poem was written. Lastly, Cardinal Quirint translated the *Henriade* into Italian.

France, like all the other Catholic countries at that time, was filled with a clergy representing every grade of culture and every rank in life, and having at their disposition an enormous amount of property in money and lands. Moreau de Janvers reckoned the income of the entire French nobility, for the year 1700, at five hundred and twenty millions, the king (including everything) at nine hundred and fifty-four millions, the clergy at five hundred and twelve millions; and this fourth of the whole revenue was in the hands of only about three hundred and ten thousand individuals.

This power, however, would have been less dangerous if, as in the times preceding Voltaire, it had been forced to maintain itself in the face of an inimical worldly element warring against it. But, as we saw at the beginning of the eighteenth century, nobles and commonors moving on together, we now find the clergy also included in the general union. Fierce antagonisms, dating from the time of Louis, when questions of church discipline were handled as matters of life and death, all at once shrank into nothingness, because Paris had lost the power to be interested in anything, whatever it might be, more than three days. For in these very words Voltaire himself branded the indifferentism of his age. More and more frivolous became the tone of the great crowd, more and more formidable the power of the priesthood; and so it came about that, at the same time when one strata of society dared openly proclaim its denial of all religion, for the smallest breach of form (if the interests of the clergy demanded) they could pounce upon whom they would, and were usually sure of their victim. The public looked on without sympathy, and allowed them free swing. It was this tyranny (which, owing to the support of Rome and other Catholic powers, was of boundless extent) that Voltaire sought to undermine. To hope to make any progress here, however, the first necessity was to créate an excitement. Religious ideas, which had long ceased to stir anybody, must again be made to rouse the passions of the educated. I do not think that the systematic conflict Voltaire later waged against the clergy arose in the beginning from the convictions which were the strength and fire of his old age. When he wrote the *Henriade* he was a young man. There lived and worked in his soul a revolutionary power, fitted to stir the masses, but which the general laxity of the nation denied him opportunity to bring into action. Three powers in France formed the basis on which all else rested, — royalty, nobility, and the church.

To fight against the first two was not to be thought of; therefore, "On without loss of time against the Church!" We have in the *Henriade,* as it were, the correspondence between irritated diplomates which precedes a war, whose final aim is determined in part by the course of events. Hence in the poem the strenuous effort to say the most cutting things without seeming to have said them, and the striving in the face of deadly insult to assume a most flattering tone of submission. Voltaire, like a hornet, is playing round the fruits and flowers (apparently a most innocent creature), until he suddenly swoops upon his victim and seems to have hesitated so long only to find the best place to inflict the wound and insert his poison. Here he is a perfect devil, and the terror his attacks inspired was as great a safeguard as the subtlety with which he afterwards defended himself.

Voltaire's relations to the Catholic Church later became so complicated as to demand the exercise of all his talents. Endowed by nature with marvellous gifts for intellectual conflicts, he found incessant practice for them. He was never in his whole life without these strifes. No passion so completely developed all his mental power as *hate*. As a hater he is unrivalled except perhaps by Aretin, who is certainly the only one to contest the palm with him. Voltaire was untiring where he hated. He hunted people to death; he lied, he slandered, he hit upon the most original devices for bringing his rival into disgrace. It was as if to add the last sublime touch to his infamy that on his death-bed he uttered the lie that he should leave the world without any feeling of hatred toward his enemies. If Voltaire had met Maupertius (who alienated Frederic II from him) in Charon's boat, he would then and there have seized him by the throat and tried to fling him into the Styx. A thirst for revenge, — an enemy, — was a living need to his soul; he had a positive talent for provoking insults, as if longing to have an adversary that he might persecute him.

Regarded from this point of view, Voltaire's character must awaken a contempt not wholly counterbalanced by his noble defence and self-sacrifice in the cause of the innocent ones who were basely accused and deserted by the rest of the world. In the war against the prejudices of the Church and the Law Voltaire won victories in favor of some poor souls who must have been ruthlessly murdered but for him, which have lent to his name imperishable splendor. Nevertheless, whosoever reads the passages in his writings, where out of sheer revenge he casts suspicion on the private life of Frederick the Great, must feel an inextinguishable aversion to a man who could descend to such low insults. The only salvation for Voltaire here is in taking into account his nationality, and therefore only are we able to believe that his life-long war against Rome for freedom of thought, in the beginning grew out of casual, purely accidental, circumstances.

It was mainly owing to the *Henriade* that Voltaire in 1746 was created historiographer of France. This title best expresses wherein his forte lay. He was a born historian. A native instinct impelled him, like Machiavelli, to write out with mechanical impartiality all he could gather concerning the events which came under his notice. His prose style is simple and without affectation. The masterpieces he produced as historian must and always will be regarded as masterpieces. The most excellent among these works is the *Siècle de Louis XIV*. For, considering the value of the *Henriade*, the tragedies, epistles, poems, romances, and whatever else fills so many pages in his writings, as active, essential portions of universal literature, it seems as if we could dispense with them all ; but the history of the *Siècle de Louis XIV* steadily increases in value; and whoever reads it must decide that it is one of the books which it is necessary for every one to have read.

There are three means of instructing mankind as to what has happened, or is happening,—plastic art, poetry, and historiography. Plastic art is the purest and simplest. A Greek statue literally tells us nothing save how far an epoch was able to sustain the highest conception of human beauty. Of the earliest Egyptian times, all knowledge is wanting of deeds and personalities; we have only names and works of art, but the latter so eloquent, so convincing, that we do not need written documents to persuade us men thought and felt as we to-day. When we see the living stream so distinctly, why tell us it was a stream with its windings through rocks and shoals which at times impeded and at times accelerated its course? Poetry is the transition from art to history, and deals also only with the universal, the ever-living, the unchangeable in the midst of changing conditions. To discover and explain these conditions is the task of the historian. It is for him to spread out before us the transitory external circumstances and their influence over the formation of human character, and the aspect of human actions.

If the incidents before Troy which Homer's *Iliad* pictures had ever actually taken place, how very differently the historian must have narrated them! The relative power of Agamemnon and Achilles would have been discussed; the partisans of the two princes, their secret, selfish motives either for inciting or appeasing the quarrel, would have been exposed, and statistics given respecting the general outward condition of both Trojans and Greeks. We should have been told what the Greek trade amounted to at that time on the shores of Asia Minor! what interest Egypt had in this war! and as regards the description, statements made by Trojan prisoners would have thrown flashes of light on the tone of the city, while from gossiping slaves the debates between the Greek chieftains, and the negotiations of Menelaus with his brother, would have been brought to light. The inconsistency of private counsel with public speech, and the influence of personal interests in bringing about great effects, must have been exposed. These things skilfully interwoven, and each alternately appearing in its proper order, — what interest! what an abundance of so-called material!

But supposing all this had been at Homer's service, of what use would it have been to him; without a glance he must have turned aside from all these precise and interesting details consciously to invent just what the *Iliad* contains. He could only present symbolic deeds, only out of his own imagination create situations in which was contained what blank reality never brought to sight. The *Iliad* is the product of marvelous poetic calculations. What Voltaire in his *Henriade* vainly sought to attain, by rehearsing the deeds of Henry IV, Homer achieved. The poetic power in this man is beyond all comprehension. An old man with the fire of youth, a young man with the experience of age! The situations in which Achilles' character is developed represent him ever in new lights, and ever greater, until at last out of Titanic savagery a child-like reverence and gentleness is attained. Achilles' behavior to the suppliant Priam is the most touching thing ever put into human language. By degrees Achilles rises above his surroundings, until at last he stands out in solitary grandeur, sole hero of the poem. More than once Homer withdraws him from our sight, but only to make his reappearance the more imposing. What modern poet surpasses Homer in the art of ever fascinating us afresh by change of scenery. Scenes by day alternate with scenes by night, meetings with gods and men, surging billows with woods and mountains! Very natural is the tradition that Homer was a blind, wandering, lonely beggar, for only a human life through long years turned in upon itself could give the power to compose such a poem; only tried experience teach such careful weighing of antithesis, such unerring skill in dropping and resuming the threads, or such inexorable criticism, which does not allow one superfluous thought in so many thousand verses, but steadily moves on to the end.

Homer succeeded in doing just what Dante did many centuries later: he gave to his people a picture of their own character, and made his poem an ideal bond uniting the different tribes. Could any historian have achieved this? Neither Herodotus nor Thucydides, neither Livy nor Tacitus nor Machiavelli, were able, like Dante and Homer, to fill the souls of their people with a consciousness of their world-historical position.

But not every age gives birth to such poets! Virgil, although he has held the admiration of the world for two thousand years, has never been able to do more than entertain his readers; and as regards Voltaire's *Henriade*, although in his own century it was read with avidity, it never more than excited a certain sense of piquant enjoyment. There are unpoetic epochs, suited only to historic representation. Voltaire tried in vain to make himself appear a kind of Prometheus forming men in his own image. The clay took shape under his fingers, but all his blowing could not lend to it one breath of life. As historian, on the other hand, he does what no one could have done better. By his manner of representing events he proves how much originality is required in a historian, even if his mission be somewhat less exalted than the poet's. It does not suffice to hunt up the sources, to separate the false from the true, to arrange and classify a mass of material. Genuine scientific investigation is prompted by an instinct whose origin defies our penetration. A mysterious connection between the man and his subject appears essential here from the beginning. The true historian suggests the picture of the successful gambler, behind whom stands a demon who directs his eyes and hand to the numbers he must hit.

Voltaire as historian was a creative genius. With a sagacity nothing escapes he reviews the actions of those long dead who once gloriously directed the destinies of their country, conjuring up at the same time these shadowy forms to speak for themselves, with a life-like power, motion, and individuality. The capacity was his to apprehend the past constellations of those who once held the sovereignty in their hands; to put in as background the turmoil of the people in their every-day life, and to illuminate the whole by letting the great ideas of the time shine forth, beneath whose fertilizing beams important movements were carried through and their aims made clear. It was Voltaire's intention to write a history which should represent his people as the last and greatest among the nations that had played a conspicuous part in the history of the world. To us, indeed, to-day the trivial nature of the French supremacy in the seventeenth century comes out more and more clearly, and we hardly feel it worth while to devote much study to this epoch. We know its main features, and long ago ceased to cherish any extraordinary respect for Richelieu, Mazarin, and the French dukes and marshals. Yet we should like to see the person who, after reading Voltaire's *Siècle de Louis XIV*, could maintain this indifference. Voltaire succeeded in giving a universal impression of this age which will be imperishable. His finger followed the course of men and events, and perhaps only the lines which he has traced will ever impel coming generations to trouble themselves to obtain a closer view of what occurred in France between 1650 and 1700.

The idea *Siècle de Louis XIV* did not originate with Voltaire, — rather with the court poets, court savans, etc., who already in the lifetime of the king had taken advantage of the flattering term. Voltaire in his book never once degenerates into this tone. He nowhere even makes an attempt to pass over from the rôle of reporter to that of panegyrist. The king is not exhibited in any special splendor, nor even in an attractive light. He is merely the axle of the huge mill-wheel by the help of which for fifty years European events were pressed and turned to the glory of France. Everything was carried as grist to this mill, and at last, when foreign corn began to fail, the mill-stones slowly ground themselves to powder. With stern, uncompromising truthfulness Voltaire sets this before us.

Frederick II said of Voltaire, that he was not a savan, but a whole academy; and one might add, not an actor, but the whole theatre, not an individual Frenchman, but the whole nation. He was epic, lyric, and dramatic poet, philosopher, mathematician, scientist; in each department so rich and so absolutely skilful that it would seem as if it must have been his only one. As historian, he reaped the advantage of this monstrous versatility. He knew precisely what he wanted to do. He writes to D'Argenson (1740, after he had begun the work): "I will say something which may seem odd to you, namely, that only those who are capable of writing tragedies can lend an interest to our dry and barbarous history. It requires, like the drama, exposition, plot, dénoûment. And, further, why only and forever a history of the kings that of the nation must be written; one would suppose there had been nothing in Gaul worth the trouble of committing to history for fourteen hundred years but kings, ministers, and generals; are, then, our customs, our laws, and the genius of our people, to be esteemed as nothing?" Here we have Voltaire's programme. He is to write the history of the golden era in France. At home, everywhere, he understands men and things, with marvellous insight finding his way to the heart of all. As regards style, the unsparing amount of self-criticism to which he has subjected his writings for long years now served him in good stead; for if the works of strangers rarely impressed him, his own satisfied him least of all. He pruned his productions unmercifully, and was untiring in his efforts to improve them. To all this must be added his great political experience. In France, England, Germany, and Italy he stood in personal relations with the most eminent men, and knew exactly how his words would strike and influence each and all. Voltaire's *Henriade* was the work of a young man who, groping, had found the only way in which to move onward; his *Siècle de Louis XIV* is the same work repeated by an experienced man, who knows the meaning of every step he takes, and is familiar and satisfied with the path he has struck.

As regards the simplicity of Voltaire's manner of presenting his subject, so that for the most part he seems to speak only *mezza voce*, we must take into consideration that it was not necessary for him to persuade his public, Frenchmen and others, that France was the first nation on earth and Louis XIV the greatest king. He is so certain of this, that at the outset he thinks it rather important to reduce this feeling to the proper measure. According to his deepest convictions there would still remain more glory over than one could use. His intention was to expose the failings of his country, and under such circumstances he surely might venture to do it. When Cicero, Sallust, and Tacitus exposed the depravity of their fellow-citizens, and spoke of the evils which finally led to the decline of Rome, they had no other thought than that Rome herself was to lead Rome back into the paths of virtue. In the same spirit Voltaire speaks of the injury done to France. What would he have said had anybody dared to suggest that at some future day Germany might take the lead, politically and intellectually, in setting things to rights. Voltaire hoped for a new blossoming-time in France, and from her own fresh shoots. His *Siècle de Louis XIV* was to be simply a mirror held up before the eyes of his nation. Voltaire truly considered the material condition of France in his own time as vastly more satisfactory than during the heroic epoch of the former century. "*Voici l'âge d'or qui succède à l'âge de fer. Cela donne trop envie de vivre!*" he writes to M. Dupont. Only in matters of religion were things in a bad way, and needing correction. But he no longer makes direct assaults upon the Church, as in the *Henriade*, — rather, taking higher view, seeks objectively and without an accent of passion to enlighten his readers in regard to the historic development of ecclesiastical relations.

In the *Henriade* Voltaire rejects Calvinism roughly and curtly. He pictures it as falling away from Henry at the moment of his conversion, like some bodily disease, which until then had obstinately clung to him. In France and the Catholic countries generally, after the Council of Trent, Protestantism had been treated systematically like a kind of pestilential disease, which must sometimes be endured, but never shown; the consciousness of its existence as a religion was well-nigh lost. Protestantism was negation, and Henry's conversion is not as with an idolater, a Mohametan, or a Jew, — a transition from one form of worship to another, — but a step from nothing to something. The truth which changes Henry's convictions is not proved to him by controversy, but by external phenomenon, somewhat as in a romance where a good and beautiful maiden, of noble family, simply by her appearance rescues a dissipated young man from his low life and raises him to herself.

How differently Voltaire regards the matter later on! The second chapter treats of the state of Germany. All the free cities had accepted the Evangelical religion "*secte, qui a semble plus convenable que la religion Catholique à des peuples jaloux de leur liberté,*" and in his essay *Sur les Mœurs et l'Esprit des Nations* he speaks of the rise of Protestantism and its necessity as serenely as any Protestant.

Voltaire's great idea was *tolerance*. Frederick II, in his eulogy on Voltaire after his death, points to the service which he rendered mankind in this direction as being his greatest and most lasting one. The idea developed gradually in his mind with all its consequences, until it became a centralized force, giving unity of meaning to all his varied efforts. He made this the watchword of his school and party. Tolerance, although a positive idea, was conceived by Voltaire as intensely active; he waged open war against intolerance, and rightly found in this the germ of the Revolution. He says that about 1740 the new ideas came to France and began to be adopted by the people. Beyond this beginning, however, Voltaire himself never went. He never contemplated an overthrow of all existing things, but went on calmly planning reforms, since they seemed somewhat necessary. This may account for his hatred of Rousseau, and his dislike of Montesquieu. Montesquieu went to work like a statesman. Beginning with the Frankish times, he pictures French constitutional life from a juristical point of view, shows the way to proceed, and builds up a state composed of honest people. Rousseau, on the other hand, wished to create a new earth, new people, new ideas, — in short, anything that had never been. Voltaire did not care to trouble himself about the future. He knew the limit of his powers, and let a matter alone for which he was not equipped. His aim was to stand in the front, to make his books a power and a joy, to be the herald of a great idea, and for the rest to follow his own bent and say just what he chose. His special delight was in speaking things out as free and boldly as he saw them. He never used flattery except for some distinctly personal end; if there was no actual need of it, he perfectly revelled in setting forth the naked truth. His *Siècle de Louis XIV* is written with such impartiality that we are sometimes tempted to suspect that he is jeering at his hero. After attributing the rise of Louis and the height to which he rose to a series of lucky accidents, in which many times the king personally had little share enough, he pictures the gradual decline of the monarch, the monarchy, and the French genius with so much truth and so convincingly, that we need only continue in the given direction to arrive at the point *après nous le deluge.* Voltaire foresaw it all clearly, but to build a Noah's ark in preparation never entered his mind; where all must swim, he would take his chance with the rest. In this sense he was a genuine Revolutionist, and Goethe was right when (Nov., 1799) he said, "Voltaire had dissolved all the good old human bonds."

But it would be unjust to make him responsible for the Revolution, although it may have seemed so at that time to Goethe. We know to-day that the *old* must have gone down and the *new* arisen if Voltaire had never lived. This "new" of the French Revolution was the irresistible uprising of the *Tiers État.* But we could more easily to-day imagine the conquest of

Europe by a horde of gorillas than Voltaire, or even Rousseau, who certainly wanted to revolutionize things, could conceive of the coming into action of that power which made the Revolution, and whose final mastery in France has been signed and sealed by recent events.

This element was not to be discerned by any one in Voltaire's age. The French Revolution of the last hundred years is the rising up of the Celtic mother soil through the Romanic superstratum, which till then had represented the genuis, power, and wealth of the country. France, that for two thousand years had manured the soil of the Celts with Germanic and Romanic blood, has to-day again become old Gaul.

Drained to the last drop, worked out, exhausted, in the best meaning of the word, the French race has once more made place for the old Celtic mob, which, rising like the emancipated leaven of the people, covered with its foam the remnant of Romanic existence, and dragged it down to itself. We see this done, time after time, as the aggressive power grows stronger and the defence ever weaker, feeling that the moment must come when this resistance will draw its last breath, and the primal Gaul, commanded by the Druids, celebrate his decisive victory. If we would understand these people thoroughly we must consult Cæsar or the most recent French histories.

Gaul, converted to a Roman province, had in the course of five or six hundred years become decidedly Roman in its every aspect, with a people speaking the

Roman language, and having a Roman organization. Cultivated forests grew luxuriantly where formerly stood only pines and firs. But this existence drew its vital strength from Rome and languished with the decay of imperialism there. Too powerful, however, was this overgrowth to permit the Celts again to assume the rôle they had lost five hundred years earlier. The Franks came over from Germany, and, uniting with the Romans, in the course of three hundred years formed a new element from which the city and country nobles of the following century sprang. Again it needed half a thousand years in order to consume this. We have lived to see it accomplished, and to-day, when there are no more Franks to be found capable of holding them in lasting subjection, the leaderless Celts attempt once more to be a nation by themselves. The fancy of the crowd offers to this man or that the supreme power, only after weeks or months to give it to another, with whom the pleasure of ruling for a few short days stands higher than any considerations of the danger to his country, of which all alike seem unconscious.

Voltaire would have thought this a frightful dream. He wrought himself into such a fury against the Romish Church, that this conflict at last became the sole interest of his life. Yet a Romanist and a Frenchman, in the Romanic sense, he always remained. Protestantism, rational and impassionate,— therefore, as he acknowledged, suited to Germany,— would alone in his eyes have been sufficient reason for excluding the Germanic nation forever from occupying the position which France, as successor to Spain, enjoyed as her legitimate world-historic right. In these contradictions is to be found the solution of Voltaire's often puzzling and apparently double-faced attitude toward the Romish Church.

He who had attacked and insulted Rome and her priests yet believed just as firmly as Machiavelli had done earlier in the indispensableness of this authority to the management of cosmopolitical affairs. Both argued from the existing state of things. Machiavelli, who saw in the Roman hierarchy the source of all evils, was yet, set him down which way he would, linked in bonds of friendship and interest with representatives of this fraternity; and it was the same with Voltaire. His attitude toward Rome was like that of a good monarchist to his court, which he abhors, without on that account becoming a republican. The Roman church and the French monarchy, good or bad, were stubborn facts. Apart from the development of this Romanic-French element, for which he thought and wrote, Voltaire's very existence would be inconceivable. To be sure, Celtic features break out even in him, but only as subordinate qualities. He would have shuddered at a vision of the monstrous storm-tide of 1790, which brought such immense tracts of the old Gallic soil once more in contact with the sunlight.

VOLTAIRE AND FREDERICK THE GREAT.

VOLTAIRE'S *Siècle de Louis XIV* brings us to Frederick the Great. And not because the king appreciated it more than any one else in Europe, but because Voltaire was chiefly occupied with this work during his second stay in Berlin and Potsdam. When in 1740 the letter was written in which he explains his ideas to D'Argenson, he had already confided the book in manuscript two years before to Frederick. It was not, however, completed until after the Berlin times. In this work, as in all Voltaire's historical and political compositions, we trace the permanent influence England had over him. A letter to my Lord Hervey, Keeper of the Great Seal of England, in which he discusses how far Louis XIV was worthy to be made the subject of an historical work, is usually given as preface to the book, but it owed its final stamp to the influence of Frederick the Great. Voltaire had to learn from personal experience what it is to have a great sovereign directly over one, to live with him in the same house, to eat at his table, to be the sharer of his best but also of his worst hours.

Voltaire stood in need of a strong position outside his native land. As a young man he had fled to England, won friends for himself, and for his writings a constant public. Whoever has been once accepted in England finds the English loyal. His books were printed in the Netherlands, the great central book-market for the period which ushered in the Revolution, as Venice in the sixteenth century for the period of the Reformation. What Voltaire thought, wrote, and printed, like the works of Montesquieu and others, entered France only as contraband. But even in the Netherlands books did not come out so smoothly as among us nowadays. Very rarely was a book planned, written, printed and offered to the public, all within a settled time. From various causes important books often came out without the foreknowledge of their authors, and with modifications. Being for the most part circulated at first in manuscript they were exposed to mutilations of the text and indiscreet communications to the bookseller. Not infrequently they were obliged to be printed anonymously; hence many were attributed to authors quite innocent of them. Voltaire's correspondence is full of matters of this sort. We hear of manuscripts being eloped with out of the hands of booksellers who had come by them unfairly, the whole account sounding not a whit less romantic than the release of fair damsels from the hands of robbers. Voltaire writes to Frederick that he has succeeded in abducting one of his manuscripts from the bookseller under the pretext of wishing to correct some errors in it. The man, after much diplomacy, brings it forth, but does not let Voltaire out of his sight, who now sets to work with ink and eraser, not to correct, but to convert the whole into nonsense.

The reason Voltaire required foreign support was the necessity he felt of holding up before the Parisians the Gorgon-head of his unimpeachable reputation, based on the decision of all the rest of Europe; neither the people nor the court of Versailles must ever dream that it made any difference to him whether he was regarded with friendly or hostile eyes, or even if they chose to ignore him altogether. Yet it was his weakness that he could not live without the gossip of the Parisians. Like the breath of life to him was the feeling that France was dying of curiosity to know what would be the next surprise out of his lips; and we see him forever exerting himself to keep up this excitement. He alone could play tragedy and comedy at the same time, and the world should look on and manifest applause. All his power was directed to securing this. But we must acknowledge that no one was ever sent into the world with such capacity for managing his public. Only considered from this point of view can Voltaire's relations to Frederick II be rightly judged. Frederick and Voltaire were the two great actors upon the stage of public life in their epoch. They were necessary to one another. In the beginning, however, Voltaire was the more dependent of the two, and it was not until much later that the parties stood on equal ground. Frederick was, to a certain extent, wholly sufficient to himself, and often bade the rest of mankind "adieu;" in this solitary realm he was only the king and the general. Voltaire lacked this power of sustaining himself alone. Here Frederick had the advantage. But Voltaire was untiring, inexhaustible, more knowing than any, more capable of expressing himself; and Frederick, when he descended from his height, — since it was not possible always to live in solitude, — again and again found only Voltaire. Herein lay Voltaire's ascendency over Frederick. The history of their friendship is the alternate struggle of each to maintain his superiority.

The record of Voltaire's and Frederick's intercourse has been handed down to posterity in three volumes of their printed correspondence. The first is from their earliest acquaintance to Frederick's accession to the throne, or from 1736 – 1740. The second volume, from 1740 to their rupture in 1753. The third volume contains the intercourse resumed by letter from 1754 until the death of Voltaire in 1778. The youth, manhood, and age of the king correspond to these three segments. In no correspondence does Frederick speak out so openly, and Voltaire summon all his resources to exert influence over another. Their relation is in itself a drama. — In the first act, the hope of meeting face to face and living together; in the second, the realization of this hope; in the third, a revulsion, growing out of the natural impossibility that two beings, each of whom needed such a wide sphere of personal freedom, should stand so near together; in the fourth and last, a reconcilement, owing to the fact that they could not live without one another. Their correspondence consists of what stirred the world within the years 1736 – 78. These three volumes belong to those books we are glad to take up in a leisure hour.

The correspondence opens with Frederick's sending a letter to Voltaire from Berlin, 1736; a young man of twenty-four years, feeling like a caged eagle, and with a yearning for the intellectual excitement of France, to a man almost double his age, — a renowned leader in the intellectual realm, and revelling in the fulness of all which he craves. We must not for one instant suppose that Voltaire's recent personal trials had in the least dimmed the lustre of his fame. He lived in retirement in the country, with his friend, the Marquise du Châtelet. His *Letters on England* had been publicly burned by the hangman's hand in Paris, and he himself only escaped imprisonment by flight. His enemies, taking advantage of his absence, had circulated libellous papers and reports against him; his admission into the Academy, for which he had been proposed, seemed doubtful. All this might trouble him but little; very welcome, however, at such a moment, was to him the voluntary homage of a king's son. Frederick's letter, breathing the utmost devotion, gave Voltaire to understand what high value the prince attached to a friendly intercourse with the greatest poet of his age. Voltaire's seductive flatteries denote no less plainly the intention to profit by this godsend. A decided purpose shining forth on both sides rivets the bond from the beginning. Frederick and Voltaire, each in his way, knew men and the world thoroughly. Neither concealed from the other how advantageous the new alliance seemed to him; but one, like the other, soon shows just how far he intends to go.

Even before Frederick had expressed more than in a general way the wish to see Voltaire *in propria persona*, we suddenly find (at the end of 1736) in many newspapers the report that Voltaire is visiting the crown-prince, who has also sent him his picture. To both these rumors Frederick was far from indifferent. To invite Voltaire to visit him at Rheinsberg, at a time when, to raise only twelve thousand thalers behind the back of his father, he had to carry on a long and tedious correspondence with Suhm, was not possible; and just as little dared he, in the face of his father, send his picture to a man already reputed an atheist. The manner in which he discusses these two points with Voltaire shows that, with all his enthusiasm, he knew exactly how he stood with him and how he had to treat him. His portrait he roundly refuses to give him, and, with respect to the visit, remarks somewhat sharply, that it would seem as if some mischievous imp had whispered these stories into the ears of the Dutch journalists, since they coincided so literally. Meantime the thing appeared to him the more improbable, just because everybody knew of it. He said to himself that Voltaire would not have made use of the newspapers to announce his intended visit to the prince, but would have chosen a more direct and friendly way. Voltaire could not fail to perceive that Frederick understood him and was on his guard, and he soon found out who gave Frederick the key to his character and proceedings: one Theiriot was Frederick's correspondent in Paris. To dislodge this inconvenient spy is henceforth Voltaire's chief endeavor. Soon letters from the Marquise du Châtelet, who had likewise entered into friendly relations with the crown-prince, contain bitter complaints that he allows Theiriot to send him all the stray papers and brochures issued against Voltaire in Paris. Upon this, Frederick declares distinctly that he shall continue to profit by Theiriot. Notwithstanding, we see their mutual relation gradually become what it was intended to be from the outset. Voltaire corrects the crown-prince's literary efforts, and in polished phrases says flattering things to him, in exchange for which he has glorious prospects of what his pupil will do for him when he becomes king. Voltaire's letters, in this honeymoon of their acquaintance, have the single aim of accustoming Frederick to the gentle murmur of charming, appreciative epistles from the literary potentate of Europe, and to render himself indispensable to him.

Had fate not imposed upon Frederick the task of being a great king, he would have become a better writer than was consistent with the duties attendant on his high vocation. His writings, considered apart from their author, are those of a *dilettante*. But writings sometimes are *not* to be considered apart from their author, whilst their mere outward form and style may be disregarded. Frederick's works will always stand as his very own, and the value they receive from this fact outweighs their deficiencies. As a writer, Frederick lacked the primary essentials for an author,— a language. Alfieri relates in his memoirs how he was forced one day to acknowledge to himself that the two mother tongues which he inherited — the bad French and equally bad Italian — spoken in Turin, were neither of them adequate to the expression of ideas. He went to Florence, and there acquired a richer language Frederick was not so well off. His German was uncultured and uncertain. He had, indeed, a rough-and-ready speech at his command for every-day matters, but when he wished to use select expressions, as in some letters to his younger brothers, he did so with awkwardness, and like a foreigner. While his French, on the other hand, was the colorless Parisian jargon of the better classes, circulated throughout Europe by wandering nobles, soldiers, actors, dancing-masters, and wig-makers, — an idiom which, by study of the grammar and the classics, could be distilled to a point of chemical purity. Berlin, through its French colony, still in its first generation, offered better opportunities for the acquirement of good French than any other place in Germany. Yet facility in speaking does not compensate for what is an indispensable requisite in writing; namely, a language either wrought out by the writer himself from its provincial peculiarities to general clearness and strength, as by Goethe, Lessing, and Schiller; or one which, through constant interchange in the intellectual centre of a nation, has gained such wealth and flexibility as to well dispense with its local characteristics. Frederick was not born in France, therefore the first was out of the question; the other, as he could not live in Paris, he must obtain artificially. With genuine royal instinct he appealed to the highest source, and herein lies the secret of Voltaire's indispensableness to Frederick and the guaranty for their lifelong intercourse. Frederick writes to D'Argens, at a moment when he was justified in hating Voltaire, "He deserves to be branded as a galley-slave, but his French, not himself, is of consequence to me." And this same French, one day, led Frederick again to overlook and forget all these "galley-slave" deserts.

In considering Frederick's writings, however, the French form may be left out of sight. When we reflect how constantly and actively his personal supervision was demanded in both civic and military affairs, we discover him to have been an eminently gifted genius, not only as a man, but as an author. His writings interested him so deeply that he felt everything else to be an interruption. He declared literary fame to be the only fame that deserved the name. In critical situations, when his mind craved relief from the unutterably depressing feelings of the moment, his literary occupations alone afforded it.

It was in September, 1759. The Russians and Austrians threatened Berlin, and the deadly struggle which Frederick was carrying on for Prussia and Germany seemed about to concentrate at the capital. Despairing as to his future, with little to hope for from his army, the king saw himself in the wretched plight of one limited to the defensive who must await his enemies' movements. Long months already had this state of things continued. In August he writes to D'Argens: "Believe me, mere firmness and resolution are not sufficient to sustain one in a situation like mine. But I tell you plainly, that if fortune now deserts me I shall not outlive my fall and the despair of my country." Instead of any decisive change, however, day succeeded day with wearisome monotony. It was in this mood that Frederick wrote his *Thoughts Concerning the Military Talent of Charles XII*. He finds himself on almost the same spot of earth, opposed to the same enemies, and in the same situation. He weighs what that prince, in thinking over his campaign, may have had to reproach himself with, and what had been his own mistakes. He reviews and criticises Charles's career in its main features. "My intention was," he begins, "to obtain for my own instruction an exact idea of the military character of Charles XII, King of

Sweden. I judge him neither from the exaggerated representations of his admirers, nor from the distorted traits his detractors have lent to his picture. I rely on eye-witnesses, and on those facts in which all his biographers agree. We regard with distrust the detailed accounts of historians, enveloped as they are in a mass of lying insipidities and anecdotes; only the core of great events is authentic and credible." In this spirit Frederick goes on. He grapples to his work, however, not merely because of this similarity in his fate to that of Charles, but because he finds in this literary labor the only means of sustaining himself in his unhappy situation. When in later days Frederick records the history of his times and his wars which thrilled all Europe, he speaks of events which he had conjured up and participated in. His writings are like the hieroglyphics which an advancing glacier, while forcing its way onward, scratches on the mountain walls. Where works of such import are in question, the style or construction of sentences are very secondary considerations.

By no such path did fate ever entice Voltaire to write. His experiences were in a wholly different realm from those of his royal friend. And this difference was yet another guaranty for the indissolubleness of their friendship. Voltaire knew the entire world of his epoch, but with such a nature as Frederick's he had never met; and Frederick could say the same of him.

Voltaire appeared in Berlin (1743) after Frederick had become king. How brilliantly these first years sped away at the court of the young monarch has often been described. As yet there was no Sans-Souci; and the festivities were held at Charlottesburg, where a number of youthful brothers and sisters surrounded the king, breathing freely at last after the long heaviness and constraint. A certain exuberance of life, wit, and caprice reigned, and a crowd of great and little lights moved to and fro while Frederick and Voltaire were the grand central chandeliers outshining them all.

We need only to remind ourselves in what circles Voltaire had hitherto moved to feel that if he now bewitched the king and his court, he did it consciously, in the way of his trade, and not because he was for the first time *à son aise* in Berlin, and the intellectual lava-stream burst forth involuntarily. Voltaire was almost fifty years of age, and he had entered upon life very early. It must certainly have pleased and flattered him to find that he united in his person the whole scale of attractions, and all the machinery necessary for the exercise of his magic power; but never did he for a moment lose the feeling that he was a foreign star upon this stage in the land of the barbarian, nor ever make the slightest attempt to disabuse himself or his friends of this idea.

What mattered this, however, either to himself or Frederick? Both were actors in a glorious drama and in the eyes of all Europe; they divided honestly the cost as well as the success of the undertaking. Voltaire knew perfectly well of what value Frederick was to him. The invitation sent him by the young monarch, to whom he had himself drawn the attention of the world as to an infallible Solomon or Alexander, having made to a great extent his Europeon renown; his reception in Berlin, where, as philosopher, poet, greatest of the great men of his age, he formed the centre of all the court courtesies, gave him a chance to revenge himself, in the way most consonant to his nature, on Versailles and Paris. Now they saw clearly what they had lost, or might lose, in him, and took steps to recover possession. On the other hand, Frederick, through Voltaire, attracted all eyes to his capital. He gave to the scarcely recognized Prussian monarchy — to the *royaume des grandes frontières* — an intellectual focus whose beams radiated over all Germany. The century in which Voltaire and Frederick lived was not to be baited alone with diplomatic and martial fame. The princes had too much accustomed their subjects to wars and alliances, planned, without their co-operation, in the chambers and ante-chambers of unapproachable castles, whose results often affected them alone. It was not France which made war at that time, but the Pompadour. The nations did not bear any ill-will to one another. The intellectual portion of the people knew only of artistic and literary interests, and Frederick, if he aspired to any real success, must appeal to these sympathies. He makes Voltaire, as it were, his prime minister in the realm of intellect and culture, that Prussia may be properly represented in the great republic of the educated; and Voltaire understands his position. His first work is to finish *The Anti-Machiavelli*, and on the printing of this book to do what none beside him could have done, namely, to enhance the sensation it naturally produced in Europe to such a degree as to make it a grand success. Voltaire was able to lay before the king letters containing testimony to his royal literary fame from all countries, but especially from France, where Cardinal Fleury himself wrote to him. The twenty thousand livres, together with the equipage, etc., which Voltaire later received yearly in Berlin, was not money squandered to entice a distinguished author into the service of a prince, who, in his leisure hours, amuses himself writing books. Frederick was much too sharp an economist to make any unnecessary outlay, and understood human nature far too well to seek in this way to reward a truly attached friend, or try to bind him closer to himself. In this, as in all else, Frederick kept the main thing in view. Therefore Voltaire's "dirty money matters," as he calls them, — his intrigues, his calumnies, — were not the cause of his rupture with the king. Frederick had lived through too much to regard these as anything more than inconveniences, and disagreeable. He knew Voltaire's groundless fancies well enough, and knew him to be under the tyrannical control of every thought which passion suggested; while as for the money, Voltaire was obliged to earn a fortune. His talents were not of the kind to admit of his living like St. Francis, happily married, on a modest income. Frederick, who realized the power money gives, saw through this more clearly than anybody else, and the ways in which Voltaire sought to increase his pile were not the worst, considering the times. In the end the income of one hundred and sixty thousand francs, on which Voltaire lived like a lord at Ferney, gave to his power a solid, indispensable basis, and none of the charges against him of cheating, speculating, and unfair dealings were ever substantiated, though there were always plenty of spies ever upon his track.

Voltaire and Frederick separated because two men, each of whom was born to rule supreme, must one day feel that they were not intended for personal intercourse. Frederick, a young king just come into power, of daring, imperative nature, issuing day by day irrevocable commands to be straightway fulfilled, — standing before the mass of Europe to contemplate the overthrow of kingdoms, which he knew must sooner or later succumb to the power of the Prussians and Germans; a man who, as a promising author had been treated for many years by Voltaire himself as a demigod, could not be sure that, on entering into the intimate communion of mind with mind, he should always be able to subordinate himself to Voltaire with that delicacy of feeling which the poet in these moments might expect. It is neglects of this sort of which Voltaire afterward complains in the bitterest tone. From the very first day he must have perceived that, even in the open province of philosophy, his *confrere* wanted, as king, to speak the decisive word. In many such cases Frederick undoubtedly displayed his royal authority. This was probably observed at the outset; else why, after his successful *début*, did Voltaire's friends so urgently dissuade him from entering permanently into the service of Prussia? Voltaire asserted later that the blue eyes of the king had captivated him. We will not think too slightingly of this confession: there must have been a fire in the king's glance which kindled and charmed irresistibly; and charm and incentive were all Voltaire asked for in this world. Frederick, when he called him into his service, had just ended the Silesian war victoriously. It was as if to fulfil Voltaire's prophecy he had in a few years vanquished the oldest power in Europe, against which France had vainly contended for a century. Voltaire felt he had had an active share in the deeds he had predicted. What hitherto had been flattery on his part was now a legitimate tribute of admiration. Frederick was his pride. With what labor and toil indeed had he equipped this young philosopher as his scholar for such triumphs! And Frederick's letters and offers corresponded so wholly to his expectations! To be sure, they knew each other, and had passed through some experiences already, but recent events seemed to have matured and elevated their friendship. Formerly it had been Alcibiades who treated Socrates at his side with a mixture of love and petulance, — forgiven in him all the exuberance of youthful vigor and genius; but now Alexander seemed to have called Aristotle. Voltaire accepted the call. But he as well as Frederick followed more recklessly than ever the bent of his own nature, and the catastrophe which ensued was inevitable.

One is inclined to-day to judge Frederick, on the whole, somewhat severely. But we have only to cast our glance round upon contemporary European sovereigns to feel that Voltaire's names, "Hero, Solomon of the North, Alexander," and others, even if flattery, were not misplaced. Voltaire never maligned nor flattered without some real foundation. Frederick was a prince of heroic courage, of great ideas, and without pettiness, — a national product of which old mother Germany may be eternally proud, whatever the future may bring forth. That "something more" than mere "firmness and resolution," as Frederick writes to D'Argens, is necessary, in order to hold his head erect, was recognized by Voltaire in those early days, and the world will feel it so long as his name lives in history. And this power of volition, so prodigious when brought to bear on public affairs, manifested itself in his private conduct as well. No one can rise wholly above his birth and education. His father's odd whim, in retaining Gundlach as learned man and court fool in one, we see reappears in Frederick, and not merely toward Pollnitz. Frederick could carry out a hard joke to the point of cruelty against his nearest and dearest friends. We feel the smart in our own souls, when, in the course of the correspondence with D'Argens, who was so dear to the king, the letter finally comes in which the marquis, then living in the south of France, bitterly complains of one of Frederick's literary jokes, made at his expense, not considering how deeply it must wound D'Argens, who, as an old man, had naturally longed to see his birthplace once more. In this same way he wounded many. His early training implanted this germ of hardness in him. He was suspicious; he was pitiless; and the experiences of his later life too often only strengthened the impressions of his boyish days. Yet, in the real depth of his nature there was kindness and a guileless disposition to do good and make others happy when he was perfectly sure that he should not be imposed upon. We have unquestionable proofs of this. What repels in Frederick is the perishable alloy of his century. His unbounded sense of duty toward his people has been a permanent benefit to every single individual.

Voltaire was similiarly organized. He, too, possessed this "something more," which carried him safely through all the vicissitudes of life. He also was hard, inconsiderate of those about him, and disinclined to put any restraint on himself. To be forced to obey was a new experience; but Frederick commanded, and for a while Voltaire suffered the unheard-of martyrdom of conforming to the will and humors of a master, who often enough, in his eyes, was nothing, after all, but a poor scribbler. And others forced their way in between them, spirits of the second rank, who in Berlin were allowed to make themselves conspicuous, whilst in Paris they would have been snubbed. Against these people, at least, Voltaire thought he might set his face. But in vain! The king would not allow it. These people fought for their very existence. When superior people are alienated from one another, it is always largely owing to the intrigues of low, ordinary natures who stand between them. They make the breach and keep it open. A rabble rout, who disappear like flies when we would strike them from our foreheads. Thus we see the ideal companionship of these two great men suddenly ruptured, and invisible hands busy in rendering any approach in the future impossible. Frederick, irritated and stung to the quick, did not hesitate to abuse his royal power by setting the police on to harass Voltaire, which insulting treatment, as the king very well knew, could not make Voltaire any the less a sovereign in a higher realm. Voltaire, on the other hand, lowers himself so far as from Frankfort to address to the Roman emperor a rousing letter, full of indictments against Frederick, and privately to compose that description of the life at Sans-Souci, which, if it is the truth, tells equally against him who participated in it at the time. To be sure, Voltaire never published this, and may possibly have forgotten that he ever wrote the thing;

but he should not have allowed it to have been found among his papers.

This prelude, however, was necessary to convince Frederick and Voltaire that fate had determined them for one another. What they had lost each could soon count on his fingers. For almost twenty years their friendship had been the envy and astonishment of the princes on one side and of the literati on the other. Now all saw what had come of it! Voltaire before the eyes of the world ignominiously kicked out by his royal friend (the vulgar phrase assumes an almost tragic significance); Frederick, after having deluded the world with the glamour of his philosophy and culture, unveils himself as only a somewhat more carefully whitewashed despot of the ordinary stamp. Fallen from their high position, both now appear in their respective places, no better nor worse than the rest of mankind.

They knew well enough that they had injured themselves! But for the present it was impossible to do more than keep each other in view. Voltaire, after discovering that France was no longer the right place for him, established himself permanently in Switzerland, there *in villegiatura* soon to find all eyes in Europe again riveted upon him. Frederick began the war in which, for seven long years, he fought for his crown. Where was now the man who, during the first war, had been the great interpreter of his actions? Popular, in the present sense of the word, Frederick never was. His personality and his successes so impressed the masses as to surround his figure with heroic splendor. Frederick and his grenadiers became military ideals; the "Zietheuscher Husaren" were the "Uhlans" of the last century, and Frederick's *bon-mots* began to be a staple article in miscellaneous literature. To all this was added, by common consent, the German language, and a simple geniality peculiar to the German people, but of which Frederick had little enough. The king's real self is not mirrored in Germany's admiration of him. Frederick was lonely. He did not enter, even with his generals, into right hearty natural relations. He always carried his library and literary work about with him. Every leisure moment was devoted to them. Not as Napoleon, sailing to Egypt, read *Werther*, and whose whole expedition was directed either by historic or modern scientific ideas. Frederick, in general, read and wrote only of what bore the least possible reference to his surroundings. When he could give himself up to refreshing thoughts it was to correspond with people to whom the war in its most important phases had little interest. What did the Catholic Marquis d'Argens care whether the good cause of Germany and Protestantism triumphed or not? And even Frederick's historical works had no public. Of his *Charles XII* not more than a dozen copies were struck off for distribution among his friends. He lost his old companions without finding any to take their place. His mother died. His sister, the Margravine of Baireuth, who was nearest of all to his heart, died also. The decline of France and her literature he comprehended, but not the rise of Germany. He missed Voltaire! And it is to Voltaire that he turns at last, and from whose fresh missives he derives consolation and diversion. There is something touching in this testimony to the poverty of human life. These two men, who thought they were separated forever, now approach one another for the second time, but very quietly and with a certain reticence, as if feeling they must not again imperil the precious mutual possession.

Unfortunately the correspondence is not here wholly preserved. Voltaire had just made some advances, but was shipwrecked because Frederick could not help seeing that he was to be enticed into saying something which should reinstate Voltaire in the eyes of the world, and also which might possibly compromise his old patron. This was in 1754, a year after the rupture. Three years later it was the king who took the first steps. Letters were written at that time of which we have no knowledge except from Voltaire's allusions, but it is pretty certain that Frederick first took up the broken threads. Perhaps his nature prompted him to wait until the moment when it had become indifferent to Voltaire whether his relation to the king had a sequence or not. Whenever prominent men have quarreled, a perfect *tabula rasa* is essential to a reconciliation. Frederick, to use Goethe's expression, had been "threshed by Fate" until he felt able to do without all and everything except the one man who, out of millions of half-petrified spectators, saw exactly what the matter was. Voltaire, on the other hand, had tasted so many of life's condiments, that in the end it was all the same to him in whose kitchen they were cooked up,— whether of high or low,— so they tickled his palate, and the "sauce à la Frédéric" continued after all to be the most piquant; yet even this he had learned to do without. Nothing remained, therefore, but for Frederick to give Voltaire a hint that he needed him.

We now see the two men for the first time in the genuine relation of like to like. On the 4th of April, 1757, Voltaire informs the Duke de Richelieu (one of those gilded hangers-on in the world's history, who, present everywhere, have nowhere done anything) that "the King of Prussia has written to me." Beuchot, Voltaire's latest editor, adds to this: "The letter was dated January 19, from Dresden." Nevertheless, with the exception of one insignificant sentence, it has remained unknown to the German publishers. This letter is the important one. In the beginning the correspondence is rather meagre. It betrays an endeavor on both sides to yield nothing, to appear independent, if possible indifferent; not until 1759 does it flow on in the old way. From this time nothing disturbs the mutual understanding. Lines of demarcation, to be sure, are precisely indicated and firmly sustained: Frederick and Voltaire were too old not to channel their course very distinctly. The reader must not, therefore, be led astray if occasionally, when Voltaire tries to play the mediator in diplomatic affairs, he is unmercifully snubbed by the king; it is on the simply human ground that Voltaire and Frederick now meet without misunderstanding.

The letters in which the king, in the critical moments of the war, gives vent to his despair, contain the deepest and truest revelation of himself that he ever put into words; and those wherein Voltaire seeks to sustain him will always be quoted so long as his writings have any claim to immortality. If at other times he parades his satisfaction at the king's return to him, and boasts that he has saved Frederick from suicide, this is characteristic of Voltaire, whose letters to Frederick lose nothing in depth and weight thereby. Nor is Voltaire lowered by his persistent attempts to regain his old honors and be triumphantly recalled to Berlin. In these things Frederick remains firm; Voltaire inserts his wedge in vain. In the end this makes him independent and outspoken to the last degree.

"Blessed be the day of my death," writes Voltaire, April 21st, 1760, "when my sufferings, which you have chiefly conjured up for me, shall have an end. I shall not leave the world without the wish that all the happiness may be vouchsafed you which perhaps, as king, you really are not capable of attaining. Would that philosophy might one day enable you to develop the glorious inner core of your being, which is distorted by passion, by unrestrained imagination, by ill-temper (if only occasionally), and by your peculiar experiences, which irritate with their sting, and infuse poison into your soul, and, finally, by the unfortunate pleasure (quite indispensable to you) which you take in humiliating the human creatures around you, and saying to them sharp, insulting things, both by writing and word of mouth, that seems the more unworthy of your majesty, because intellect and rank have raised you so high above them. You must feel that these are truths I am uttering."

Frederick was very little moved by this letter. Voltaire had begun by putting the king on his mettle as "philosopher." "I will not," was the reply, after first writing of indifferent matters, lay the past upon the rack to extort confessions. Your behavior no philosopher would have endured calmly. All shall be forgiven and forgotten. But remember this! If you had not had to do with some one who was possessed with a kind of insane passion for your genius, you would not have come off as well as you did. Once for all, let me say to you, never bother me again with your ill-treated niece [Madame Denys, who, in Frankfort, was arrested with Voltaire]; she tires me, and has not the merit of her uncle, to compensate through many excellences for her many defects. Molière's servant-maid will be remembered by thousands; Voltaire's niece, by no living soul. My verses are of no special interest to me. I have more important affairs in my head, and the muses are pensioned off."

Frederick then passes on to other things. "In June," he writes, "begins the new campaign. There will be little to laugh, but perhaps much to weep, over," etc. We feel that these things absorb him so completely, that he treats the old personal quarrel with Voltaire as a secondary matter, of which he disposes curtly and distinctly, in order to come to the main point. After all, Voltaire was the only man with whom he could discuss the present and the future. For the rest, he might say, or leave unsaid, what he chose. In 1761 D'Argens writes to the king that Voltaire had purchased the freedom of returning to Paris by his dedication of *Tancred*, wherein he apostrophizes the Pompadour as tutelary genius of the noblest intellectual interests of France, and Frederick replies that this is to him an affair of the utmost indifference. It will not be long ere Voltaire again will venture some species of impertinence to the court of Versailles, and be forced anew to make off with himself. "There is no calculating on this man. The only thing in which he is consistent, is the scraping together of money by the most ignoble means; and he never can get enough."

Voltaire's public abasement before the Pompadour was all the more pitiful that he ranked as the most eminent literary man in Europe, and arrogated to himself the censorship of vice and virtue. Yet, shortly afterwards, in the face of court, justice, clergy, and public opinion, he heroically appears in defence of the family Calas, for whom he alone upon God's wide earth is pleading, and whose innocence he proves as clear as daylight. Voltaire neither flinched nor flagged until their honor had been restored to these people. "Truly," as Frederick said, "there was no reckoning on this man." He had openly scoffed at the king's literary efforts; still, Frederick continues to send him what he writes, begging for his opinion. He alone could furnish an ode which gave true expression to Frederick's pain and grief at the death of his sister. Frederick, as survivor of the two, honored Voltaire's memory in Berlin by an oration upon his death which will always redound to the credit of both. Voltaire, on his side, sharply took Frederick's part as an author against the French Academy, and, without the king's knowledge, earnestly pleaded for his admittance. The Abbé d'Olivet, in a new edition of his work upon prosody, had criticised Frederick's writings with much severity. Voltaire refuted this attack in a letter which had the authority of a manifesto in Paris, and in which he exhibited the king as worthy of an honorable literary position. On the same day, January 5, 1767, he writes to Frederick, but makes no mention of this defence.

The years now draw on when the king and Voltaire come to stand side by side, as old people who have a happy past behind them, for which the present does not offer, nor the future promise, any compensation. They contemplate themselves with calm objectivity. "Am I not a man with faults like others?" writes Voltaire, in the year 1776; and the king replies, "Had you thus spoken twenty years ago you would be with me now." This was only half his thoughts, but the other half, "And I should not be sitting here so bereft and lonely," rises to every mind. Frederick felt the world was becoming strange to him; all around had grown old or died; Voltaire alone remained young as ever. They now try to be of comfort to one another, and the correspondence at last goes on peacefully, as it had begun.

Eminent men require their historical background in proportion to their importance. For Frederick, a part of Goethe's shadow suffices to relieve the outlines of his figure. Herder and Lessing demand the eighteenth century; Goethe's background embraces all the grand moments in German development; for Blucher, only the "Freiheitskriege" is necessary; for Stein, the social revolutions in two centuries; for Frederick the Great, like Goethe, the entire history of Germany; for France — for Chateaubriand — the years of the French Revolution are enough; for Diderot and Rousseau, their own century; but in order to estimate Voltaire properly, we must bring before us the whole history of Romanic life, from its beginning to its very close. Conceived only as the product of his century, Voltaire would be a kind of *genre* figure, alternating betwixt jest and earnest. As fruit of the whole Romanic development he assumes graver and grander proportions. The accidental is effaced, and the essential comes out in strong traits which disclose the secret of his existence and his influence.

There is going on to-day before our eyes a worldwide revolution unlike any that has preceded it, so far back as our eyes can reach. The different nations of Europe suddenly desire to exist each for itself. The mutual influence of races upon one another (in theory utterly denied) is in practice to be limited to a minimum. And this new view is not the fruit of a theory broached by the learned, but a spontaneous impulse, thrilling the people to their very depths. It does not appear in individuals, but stirs in the masses.

It would be false to attribute the origin of this struggle for separation and isolation to recent political events. They have been only the awakening sun shining straight into the face of a feeling which had long slumbered, waiting for the light. For example, the aversion of the Germans to everything French after the Napoleonic wars, and the present hatred of the Romanic nations to everything German, are not to be ascribed to the victories on either side, nor to conscious party effort. The enmity also between the Slavs and Germans is quite independent of any such causes. That a man like Garibaldi, in whose life and conduct every heart-throb of the Romanic race was to be noted, could take the field with France against Germany is to be attributed to something deeper than mere infatuation for the name of a republic. Unnoticed a fruit had ripened, and recent events were the storm which shook it from the tree. There is a universal law by whose commanding force great masses of people attract or repel one another, and, by moving in concert, or by their separate exertions, help on the general intellectual progress. Nations demand alliances or refuse them. They subordinate themselves voluntarily, though knowing they are strong enough to resist or rebel like madmen, in spite of the consciousness of a weakness which prophesies destruction. At the time of the so-called inroad of the barbarians, all the Germanic people, sooner or later, adopted Romanic forms. To-day, the most wretched Celt would rather go naked than see himself decked out in German garments.

What we understand by history is the knowledge of the mutual relations of the different races which have occupied, for the last three or four thousand years, the peninsula called Europe, — to the geologist such an insignificant space of time that it scarcely serves as a cipher in his calculations. During this epoch we see distinct nations (which we assume emigrated from the heart of Asia) settled in the same spots, showing the same characteristics, speaking the same languages. As regards the same places, they have only changed as large vessels when at anchor are driven to and fro, though tethered to one spot by wind and tide. As regards characteristics, they have been developed and modified by the culture of different centuries, but remain essentially the same. In the languages, the change has apparently been very striking; but it is a question if the period which comes under our observation is long enough to admit of positive conclusions. These nations, Greek, Romanic, Celtic, Germanic, and Slavic, have remained the same, not only in themselves, but in their relation toward each other. They form one vast organism. The Romans contended with the Greeks for the possession of the coast of the Mediterranean; the Germans with the Celts for the Rhine, with the Italians for the Alps, with the Slavs for the lands lying on the Vistula. The boundaries of each vary from time to time, but never overleaped certain limits. The only real change that has taken place in this great body during the three or four thousand years which come within our knowledge, is that the power has been transferred from one race to another, while even this change seems to correspond in its direction with the general movement of the peoples from the southeast to the northwest. It is our hypothesis that the Germans reached their present habitation as part of one of the very earliest immigrations from the east, and it now looks as if they would move still farther west, even to America, there to lay the foundation of new nationalities. Yet it must never be forgotten that this assumption of an Asiatic origin is merely the result of scientific speculation; for the European races all look upon themselves in accordance with their traditions, as aborigines. And a patriotic affection for one's native soil is firmly interwoven with this belief, whilst as regards America, there is no proof, as yet, that what originates there will continue through the centuries to preserve its Germanic nature.

The transfer of power within the circle of the European nations comes clearly under our observation. All the development of strength seems to have this aim. Twice within four thousand years has this change of leadership shown itself. From the Greek race, whose origin is so remote as to be legendary, who made the connecting link with central Asia, we see the leadership pass over to the Romanic, and later to the Germanic, race.

There was a time when the Greek element pervaded all Europe, and there was a time when Europe, part of Asia, and America were inundated by Romanic streams; to-day the whole earth seems becoming Germanized. But within each of these three great epochs we notice fluctuations of rulership among the various nations composing the race in power. The various epochs of the Romanic supremacy are well-defined and familiar to us. The first object was to overmaster and absorb the Greek spirit. When this was accomplished, the Germanic, Celtic, and Hibernian nations in their turn were also vanquished and incorporated. From Rome the leadership was next transferred to Spain, and from Spain to France. The papacy was the central and one important creation of the Romanic race, its last and greatest achievement establishing the undisputed supremacy of France, to oppose the growing tendency toward a Germanic empire. Voltaire's *Siècle de Louis XIV* is not only a description of the period in which a great king raised his nation to the height of prosperity, but it is the genius of the Romanic race taking literary form and flaring up mightily before its final extinction. Like Voltaire, all these great men of the *Siècle de Louis XIV* lacked the lightness and buoyancy of youth. They seem to have come into the world old in thought, as if the approaching destruction of the Romanic world weighed upon them. They rush violently forward and crush their enemies; but for what? There is no future before them. They astound all Europe with the fulness of their culture, their wit, their art, their poetry; but this culture is, after all, only a piquantly flavored rehash of the old Romanic spirit. The wit is forced and cold, the art a distortion and regilding of the classic ornaments which the inhabitants of Italy once ravished from the Greeks, their language the last, blossomless, colorless shoots, springing from the mutilated Romanic roots.

These are the powers from which and for which Voltaire was begotten. His nature is an expression of the entire Romanic existence, whose brilliant decline was through him to be immortalized. In this sense it was Goethe who, with nice historic perceptions, best understood him and knew how to picture him in the place to which he belongs.

We read in the appendix to *Rameau's Nephew:* "When a family has sustained itself through generations, we see that nature finally produces an individual who includes in himself the qualities of all his ancestors, and who unites and brings to complete development all these varied gifts, of which hitherto we have had only faint indications or isolated examples. Even so it is with natives whose aggregate accomplishments may, if fortune favors, be brought to expression in one individual. Thus was incarnated in Louis XIV the highest ideal of a French king, and in Voltaire the literary genius of the nation."

Goethe next proceeds to enumerate the qualifications it would be well for a literary man to possess, — depth, genius, intuition, elevation, individuality, merit, nobility, spontaneity, etc., — ending with style, harmony, purity, correctness, elegance, and perfection. "Of all these varied forms of intellectual expression," he continues, " only Voltaire's right to the first and the last — depth of conception and perfection in execution — can be disputed. Whatever else of capacity and skill rouses the enthusiasm of the wide world Voltaire possessed, and thereby won his fame."

But Goethe, in conceiving Voltaire as the personification of France, denies to the nation itself depth and perfection ; and it is curious to observe that France here reminds us of the Greek world, which, in its last phases, no longer possessed these two qualities which so preëminently distinguished it in its palmy days.

Any attempt at a discussion to-day of the final aims of the Germanic race would lead to mere vain imaginings. Nothing remains for us in the immediate future but to live and struggle, and, as the early Romans drew their spiritual life from the culture bequeathed to them by the Greeks, so to lay the foundation of our own in that of both Greeks and Romans. The safest guide to the development of our own spirit can be no other than a knowledge of the past as far back as our sight can reach. Luther's new Germanic creation grew out of a thorough comprehension of Romanic theology, Goethe's poems from an entire absorption of Romanic culture, Frederick the Second's truly Germanic politics from his clearly seeing through the mass of Romanic intrigues which Machiavelli (if only as an objective observer) had put together in his book on "The Prince." Frederick's Anti-Machiavelli formed the starting-point for his later career. Frederick, who was a pupil of Voltaire, who only spoke and wrote French, who misjudged German literature, and often did not understand German nature, was yet in an eminent sense the first German prince. His declaration that he was only the head-servant in his kingdom contains the radical idea on which modern Germany is based, for everything would go to ruin among us if the feeling were once lost which now leads each man, the highest as well as the lowest, to regard himself as in duty bound to the service of his country. In Voltaire's school, however, Frederick gained strength and light, and therefore we have to thank him, so far as his influence here came in.

This sense of duty is the strength and power of the German nation at the present day. The astonishing absence of it in the Romanic race is the conspicuous symptom which betrays its retirement as a governing one. In this light, the recent efforts of the Romish Church appear like the desperate attempt, by means of a formula in which dwells unlimited compulsory power, to lend to the individual that support which is wanting in his own nature. In any case, these means can only avail among the Romanic nations.

Voltaire, when he took the field against the Romish clergy, dreamed of nothing of this kind. Perhaps should such a man appear to-day and be deeply moved by the danger to his race, he might be found on the side of the Church. It was gratuitous spite in the Catholic clergy, during the Restoration, to order Voltaire's bones taken out of his grave in the Pantheon, and scattered to the winds, that no trace of the great Frenchman's body should be found to serve as a relic. The Orleans were said to have succeeded in hunting up the bones again, and had them reinterred in the old place. It is questioned however, if they really were the right ones.

The memory of a great genius, who once moved the world, has nothing to do with the frail, earthly material in which it was once confined. Personal vices, and even virtues, become matter of indifference. We see the earth inhabited since time began by innumerable, ever renewed masses of people. These we find inclosed in an organization whose connection has been uninterrupted so far back as our knowledge goes. The aim of this organization is to furnish to each individual, in an ever-increasing measure, and for his own progress toward perfection, a judgment regarding his fellow-men and the earth which we inhabit. In the striving after this aim there is no cessation, only at times a hesitating movement which is generally succeeded by very rapid hurrying forward. When this stagnation occurs we see the masses left to their own guidance, helpless, not knowing how to go on; but, on the other hand, when the movement is rapid, we see this brought about by the influence of single men, who, through their own power and the confidence reposed in them by the people, gain the leadership. The memory of such men may remain living through thousands of years, and then we call them "immortal." But if their power abides beyond a certain space of time, it appears so immense that it is no longer believed in as an emanation from a single person, and the individual, as time goes on, is gradually resolved into the race from which he sprang. Thus Homer's poems are no longer regarded as the work of one man; they are the poetry of all Greece; and the time may come when Goethe's writings will be attributed to no individual phenomenon, but looked upon as the precipitate of the entire inspiration of the Germanic race at a certain period, and Shakespeare's poems appear as the collective expression of an earlier epoch. And thus Voltaire, also, will perhaps one day be used merely as a word by which to designate the last dying tones in the literature of Romanic genius.

FREDERICK THE GREAT AND MACAULAY.

A PHOTOGRAPH represents, as it were, the expression of the moment, stiffened, as the thing looked at the very instant it was fixed by the light of the sun on the metal-plate, as it never had looked before, and never will look again. For a change in the subject is proved to be constantly going on. The sun moves farther, and the sharpness of its light depends on the ever-varying conditions of the atmosphere. During the few seconds required to photograph a building, it changes in appearance; and the face of a man, be the sitting ever so short, reflects quite another thought at its close than that which decided the look when the signal was given to uncover the apparatus. Our eyes are not practised enough to discern this in the picture. But no force works independently, or by itself alone. The incessant changes in matter, the never-resting thoughts, intersect each other in all directions. Our senses are not sufficiently acute to follow out these radiations; the coarsest only reveal themselves, and we say (because we cannot do otherwise) things look just as they always have, until the change is so marked we are able to observe it.

The thoughts of the individual, and those of mankind in general, meet and act upon one another according to laws as yet unknown; these involutions are among the great mysteries. One thought suddenly interrupts another and forces itself into its place. We strive to break the train by substituting a fresh idea. Impossible! We give it up. Uncalled for it returns; and it may do the same to-morrow or after long years. A certain thought impels us to an act. Of this we are not conscious at the moment we yield to it, — nay, often believe ourselves influenced by a very different thought beneath which the first lies hidden. The will of another attracts ours as by magnetic force, and at the moment the change of action occurs we imagine ourselves the guiding power. In a few seconds we often decide for and against a thing, conclude to do it, and after all give it up again; and it may be a stone we stumble over, or a bird soaring above our heads, or something which mechanically catches our attention, that turns the scale, and, in spite of the vacillation, one thing or the other is done. Like a grain of sand falling into a clock and stopping the wheels at the hour of twelve, it might have happened one, twenty, or sixty minutes later. The grain of sand had nothing to do with the point of time; it was accidental.

We know little indeed of the ways our own thoughts take; still less of those of our best friends. What, then, can we know of the thoughts of men whom we never saw, who lived centuries before us? What of the intellectual current which prevailed when they lived? For each age has its peculiar atmosphere, through which it must be viewed if we are to understand it clearly. After the Thirty Years' War Germany was exhausted. Men knew little of the natural sciences compared with the knowledge of to-day, and were living under the influence of customs and habits which now are obsolete. Who would think of judging what was written, thought, or done at that time as if it were the product of our age? This change in the current of thought occurred not only in the course of centuries, but sometimes in days and months, as with us. The Anglo-Indian war, for instance, affected the entire atmosphere of Europe. We have regarded differently since this war the relations of the Germanic peoples to the Asiatic. In fact it has reawakened our interest in those distant nations and brought them nearer to us. We have also seen that cruelties are possible in our day such as were hardly conceived by the wildest imagination.

In a like way the Prussian war has changed our mental horizon. So, too, the gigantic extension of steam-power and telegraphs.

Who would think of judging Cæsar's military operations in Germany as if there had been telegraphic despatches in his day; it would be ridiculous! But soon, when these inventions have become part and parcel of ourselves, it will be indeed very hard to imagine any life without them.

Shakespeare describes Cæsar as fighting with cannon; of course we all know better. But how his battles were carried on no one can say; for, were his own accounts of them twice as clear and exact as they are, there would still be so much omitted that was familiar to his contemporaries that we should need the Roman public of his day to interpret Cæsar's words precisely in the sense in which he uses them, to enable us to obtain a distinct picture of his manner of action.

I by no means wish to suggest that we can know nothing because all is not laid open to our observation. I would only express the opinion that he who thinks to enter into the nature of things by anatomizing them, to understand thoughts by disentangling them, and pursuing each singly, to comprehend the fate of men and nations by dividing them into small parts, and these again into smaller and still smaller, proposes to himself an endless piece of work, and one for which his imperfect human faculties are wholly inadequate. Let any one appear with scent fine as that of a dog, eyes sharp as those of a lynx, hearing keener than the Indians in Cooper's romances, who with the tips of his fingers can recognize colors, with money and health enough to roam incessantly about the wide earth, still the brevity of his life, the prejudices of his age — arising from ignorance of what is still undiscovered — will debar him from that comprehension of the whole to which he hopes to attain by study of the infinite details. All our knowledge is fragmentary. What we admire in great scholars is, not their monstrous store of facts, but the mysterious instinct through which they were led to collect and group them so as to deduce therefrom intellectual perceptions. This is the miracle wrought, when through the contemplation of outward things the human mind becomes one of the creative powers of the universe. A precience of the whole reveals to the true scientist order and connection in the heterogeneous mass of detail into which our entire life seems to split when we contemplate it in its meanest aspects. It enables him to grasp this world firmly, which is always threatening to resolve itself into atoms, and to hold it so firmly that not one particle of its infinity is lost. Our curiosity to know the before and after is no mere child's play, without aim or object. If the sentiment of things is in us, we learn to know them accordingly. Everything takes form and becomes real. The whole world, illuminated by the brightest sun that ever shone, would be as good as non-existence without the eye of man; the whole heaven full of melody, voiceless without the ear of man; libraries replete with the most interesting facts, dead letters without the mind that gives them meaning. Life becomes real only when mirrored in the soul of man. Of things and phenomena we know little indeed in ourselves, and see them only as some particular man has taught us to see them, and name them as he has named them. He came forth and observed things. He was endowed with a mysterious perception of their nature, — we may say with creative love for them, — and according as he was writer or artist found words to represent, or power to shape as he saw them, the forms about him. Whilst endeavoring to penetrate to the core of all phenomena, in order to confirm his intuitions, he brought into life something new, — a book, a treatise, or a picture, by whose help we are enabled to see what he alone had seen, and to approach things closely as he alone at first had done. No one sees the most common fact without the spectacles which he who observed it first has placed upon our eyes. It is surprising what curious discoveries we make when applying this maxim to art and science! We find that one great artist's conception of the human figure had through long years deprived all his successors of the power to see or paint it otherwise, while these in their turn had drawn the public after them. Postures of the body, which for more than a century were thought beautiful and natural, or at any rate possible, are to-day called ugly, unnatural, and impossible; yet men and their anatomical structure have not changed, and artists studied the nude at that time as they do to-day. So little can a man dispose of his own eyes! The trees were mountains of moving foliage for thousands of years, until Claude Lorraine and his followers painted them. Now we see what is picturesque everywhere in the landscape. Our German language was a clumsy instrument, which none knew how to play upon; Goethe drew from it divinest melodies, and henceforth the art was inherited as so much given capital. Our minds receive a conscious and an unconscious education, but for all, even the most trivial, of our acquirements we are indebted to men whose names perhaps are never heard. What has not been pointed out to us, or we have not discovered by our own power, does not exist for us. An infinity of knowledge in all departments will yet be revealed, and when it is we shall wonder how we could have been so blind. From the whole wide field I select history, which alone is of importance to us here.

It is conceivable that the human mind released from flesh and sense might float above the earth, reflecting like a mirror what is happening below. I do not suggest this as an article of faith; it is a mere fancy. But let us assume that the immortality of some men take this form; that, untrammelled by what had formerly blinded them, they hover over the earth, and see clearly revealed all the vicissitudes of the world and of men, from the very birth of the planet. The past would be to them a web of harmonious beauty. Every single thought, every deed, which we call good or condemn, would constitute an integral part of it. The falling of a leaf and the yawning of the earth to swallow up whole cities would take equal rank among events, because the same Power had ordained and directed all.

But now, suppose that, dreaming on, we should see this spirit, which had so freely surveyed all things, suddenly forced to unite itself again to a mortal body.

If the highest talents of every kind were bestowed upon him, would even the faintest recollection of his former state be possible to him? He would be born in a certain epoch; he would have father and mother, a country, a profession, a heart that loved and hated, vanities, sorrows, joys, vexations, despair, and rapture. When, even for a moment, could he enjoy that absolute clarity of mind which formerly was his element? He would begin to doubt whether he actually ever had this freedom, and soon the very memory of it would retreat like a dying echo into the hidden depths of his soul. The prejudices of others would be his, however little they might influence him. His family would give him class prejudices, either of wealth or poverty, of nobility or people; his fatherland would make him partial, his beloved would claim and receive his best feelings. What would remain for the enjoyment of that boundless, colorless knowledge into which he was formerly resolved? A longing after it would be the abnegation of all human feelings. But if, notwithstanding, he makes the history of the past his chosen study, must not his work suffer from the hindrances which cloud his soul and prevent a free comprehension? He writes for the men who surround him, and hopes for their applause, however few it may be whose judgment is to him of any value. He must espouse a party; his country and his family compel him to do so. Whilst in earlier days he had had the hearts of men before his eyes like a bee-hive, where he saw the thoughts fly in and out and do their work, he must now guess at them as secrets. Scraps of letters, false confessions, partial one-sided accounts of contemporaries, marred, unfinished, or untrue copies of works by their hand, fragmentary memorials of every kind, outward matter, all from which to build up a new man and exhibit him to the world, as if he had looked thus in life. The spirit he infuses into this form cannot be deeper than his own. Qualities the original once possessed, but of which he who recreates the character has no knowledge, or no correct understanding, he cannot bestow on this new figure; and if he were fortunate enough by any means to learn the innermost thoughts of the original he would lack the capacity to interpret them rightly, and therefore they would not benefit his productions.

Every historical work is the one-sided view of a limited man. He may be the wisest of his age; nevertheless, a time will come when his standpoint also will be out of date and his limitations only too apparent, because others have succeeded him who taught mankind a higher wisdom and informed them with deeper and broader knowledge. The historian tells the little suggested to him by the memorials of past days (which often enough he does not fully comprehend) as genuinely as his country and personal surroundings permit, and in the way he thinks most intelligible to those who will read his writings. He conceals many things intentionally, often the most important. An historical work which aimed to be something like a photographic reproduction of the events of which it treats would be a contradiction. One cannot copy what he has not bodily before him. Who delineates the past to-day can only represent what takes form in his mind, while exposing it to be worked upon by the memorials that remain. The question is, not whether the picture thus gained is mathematically correct, but whether it has life and soul in it, and will be of any service to mankind. We acclimitize plants and animals from other lands and zones. It is not our object to develop them precisely as they were in their own home. Soil, light, and temperature may cause them to grow into something quite different. The only question is, can they exist with us and are they of any use? The history of Rome which is being written to-day has little to do with old Rome. Every land, every age, indeed, every individual scholar, will conceive it differently. Its author reads and studies the vestiges still to be found of the Roman people, and, in conjunction with the ideal which education and country have implanted in his soul, arises a conception which he puts into words; but how is it possible that this should be a true, colorless picture of the condition of things thousands of years ago? Like poetry, sculpture, and painting, historiography requires an artist. Raphael did not represent what he had before him. Let any one compare his studies and the draperies with the figures themselves for which they served. He only completes with their help a picture which did not at once stand clearly enough before his soul; he uses, as it were, an alloy, as one adds copper to gold in order to be able to stamp the coin. The historian knows the facts, and in the course of his life has formed certain theories which, in his opinion, would benefit the people. These last are the main thing, and the history which he writes only the illustration. Who writes history in any other way heaps up a confused mass of apparently correct facts for whose veracity there is no guaranty. For facts in which a definite idea is not laid down hardly admit of representation; they are virtually outside of intellectual knowledge.

Man himself is the standard for human actions. To many, history consists simply in the enumeration of their ancestors, whether they were good or bad being matter of indifference. The Egyptians are satisfied with lists of their kings, and with knowing the length of time each reigned; the Jews, with the simplest genealogy. Every nation writes its own history until it comes into contact with another nation which is its intellectual superior, and whose prejudices rest on a nobler basis than its own. To-day the Germans take foremost rank among the European nations. That a German should write a history of France, Italy, Russia, or Turkey would seem nowise unsuitable or contradictory; but imagine an Italian, Frenchman, or Turk undertaking to write a history of Germany! If the book, by any chance, imposed on some innocent mind, because written in a foreign language, it would be only necessary to translate it. A Russian has written a life of Mozart, and, elated by the success of his work, one also of Beethoven. Music certainly would not seem to be confined to one nationality; but is this Mozart? is this Beethoven? They are two musicians to whom certain works are ascribed; but as living individuals they have no sort of connection with these books or with the opinions expressed in them. Is it Goethe of whom Lewes has written two volumes? I think that we Germans know him better. The Goethe of Mr. Lewes is a brave English gentleman, accidentally born in Frankfort-on-the-Main in 1749, whom he invests with Goethe's life experiences (knowledge of which he obtained at second, third, or even fifth hand), and who, moreover, is said to have written Goethe's works. The book evinces great industry, but there is little of the German Goethe in it. The English are Germanic like ourselves, but they are not Germans; and what Goethe was to us we alone realize. Macaulay writes an essay on Frederick the Great. Is this the king to whom Germany owes her greatness? One would almost believe it, so graphically is he portrayed; but look at him more closely! It is a pinched-up, crabbed lord's face, with snuff on his nose, — a man in the very worst society, without concentration or morality, who, for the most trivial reasons, begins a rapacious war against Austria, pursues it aimlessly, and wins at last by sheer accident, what he had in no wise earned. In this light our hero is shown up to us. Our enthusiasm for him is a national error; not virtues, but the faults of a tyrant, have been made by the Germans the object of idolatry. He was no mighty sovereign who by noble, legitimate effort restored the decaying honor of his country, and thereby of all Germany; but simply, as Lord Byron said of Blucher, in reference to Napoleon, "a stone over which Austria stumbled and broke her leg."

Macaulay's essay is the criticism of a book which appeared in London in 1842, — *Frederick the Great, and his Times. Edited, with an Introduction, by Thomas Campbell, Esq. 2 vols. 8vo.* "This work," he begins, "which has the high honor of being introduced to the world by the author of *Lochiel* and *Hohenlinden*, is not wholly unworthy of so distinguished a chaperon. It professes, indeed, to be no more than a compilation, but it is an exceedingly amusing compilation, and we shall be glad to have more of it. The narrative comes down at present only to the commencement of the Seven Years' War, and therefore does not comprise the most interesting portion of Frederick's reign."

Macaulay first gives a brief historical sketch of the kingdom of Prussia. Frederick's grandfather makes himself king, and ridiculous at the same time, in the eyes of all Europe. His son and successor is a brutal tyrant. Frederick II, constantly repressed and kept in subjection during his youth, as soon as he mounts the throne manifests all the evil qualities of his father, and becomes even a worse tyrant. He is stingy and vicious. His court, which is a caricature, is peopled with French nonentities or scoundrels. Out of the whole there were but two persons near him fit to be called human, — Lord Marishal and his brother, two Englishmen. Frederick is a wretched fabricator of verses written in the worst possible taste. Without a shadow of justice he begins a war with Austria, recruits his army by the most despicable means, depreciates the currency, pays no one but his soldiers, and conquers at last, simply because, owing to a variety of accidents, the political conjunction in Europe demanded peace. These are the contents of the essay. To be sure, withal, Frederick is styled the greatest of the kings ever born to a throne; his practical talent, his perspicacity, and other superior qualities are recognized and duly admired; yet we close the book with the impression that this renowned monarch was, after all, a detestable creature. Nowhere, at the first glance, does Macaulay seem to have misstated the facts, or handled them unfairly; and yet we might call the whole false and untrue.

One cannot demand of an Englishman, advertising an English book in an English journal to the English public, that he should flatter Prussian patriotism, or pay any regard to it. Even if he were the most impartial of men, we could not expect him to make the Prussian point of view his own. The English consider other nations as a species of barbarians. They esteem and hate those who withstand them, whilst such as yield to them are despised rather than loved. At the time when Macaulay wrote his essay England was a little less estranged from Austria than it is at present, but Prussia was an object of jealously and dislike; of this we find ample proof. England, owing to her position, would not be inclined to regard with pleasure the increasing prosperity of the North German States. In the last war the English signalized the German ships to the Danish cruisers. Their policy toward Schleswig-Holstein is well known, and their efforts to prevent the creation of a Prussian navy.

This enmity, if we may so call it, results from the character of the people and their circumstances. It is no intentional malice, but a natural feeling, which, owing to change of circumstances, is by degrees passing away. The antipathy steadily lessens. North Germany and England are dependant on each other in so many ways that, in spite of jealousies, the English and the Germans will draw nearer together, just as America and England, notwithstanding occasional rudenesses and hostilities, must grow more and more friendly. It seems decreed that England, America, and Germany shall rule the earth. If in former times the Romanic belief in kingship permeated all Europe, today it is the Germanic conception of freedom which is remoulding the nations. We have at last come to a consciousness of this, and opposition has ceased. But Macaulay wrote his essay before 1848, at the time when Louis Philippe was king, and the world in general old and worn out. To-day it is young and energetic. Romanic law, religion, and literature no longer permeate the soil from which spring the seeds of life and action. The German nation had never willingly yielded to this influence. The Reformation, however, was the first decided step against it; the Thirty Years' War brought things back into the old ruts. Frederick the Great's victories were the second step, and this, too, the triumphs of Napoleon seemed to render of no avail. Then came the "Freiheiteskriege." The scales oscillated, until finally things shaped themselves as if impelled by an inward necessity. The gigantic efforts of Louis Napoleon and the Italian church, opposed as they were to the quiet progress of the Germanic races and their faith, appeared to many another reaction. But it was not so in reality. Let Austria, Russia, and Italy be once completely intersected with railways, and the spirit of Germanic independence will find an abiding-place in these countries.

Frederick the Great was French by education, wrote in French, philosophized in French, and discussed the Romish church in the tone of the Voltairean school. He never banished nor persecuted the Catholics, nevertheless his victories over France and Austria must be conceived to-day as triumphs of the North German Protestant spirit over the Romanic south. These two sections of our country are still opposed to each other as Catholic and Protestant. But no one thinks the South German church identical with the Italian. Seen from Rome, all Germany is Protestant. Were the language of Rome German instead of Italian, we should all long ago have understood that the distinction is rather one of nationality than faith. The Romans demand a formula and a tyrant. They do not ask why you are a heretic, but whether you are one or not. If you are not a heretic, it makes no difference what you do; if you are a heretic, do what you will there is no help for you. But even the mere question with regard to these things, or the slightest coercion attempted over the inward spiritual life of a man, is thoroughly hateful to a German, whether born and educated north or south of the Main. The external tyrannical influence of the Italian church over faith and unbelief had, since the tenth century (when the Spaniards reformed the papacy), developed into an all-pervading police system. Against this Frederick's hate was directed. He abhorred fanaticism. This is one of the reasons why his wars were never unpopular. North Germany should be extended that she might assert herself more effectually against Romanic South Germany; therefore he took Silesia, — where more than half the population was Protestant, — and therefore he kept it. Macaulay styles his invasion "base treachery," and adds, that as it was an assault on the whole community of civilized nations (the strife not being a mere Austria-Prussian one), deserved to be branded with a condemnation much more severe. If a contract like the Pragmatic Sanction, which had been set up and guaranteed in the face of all Europe, had proved insufficient to protect Maria Theresa, what sacred right or title, as Macaulay asks, could protect any nation from arbitrary attacks? Frederick's own words are: "Ambition, interest, the desire of making people talk about me, carried the day, and I decided for war." All Prussia's claims to Silesia were artfully contrived pretensions. And now he goes on to describe the beautiful young empress, pale from her last accouchement, the prince upon her arm, in tears begging protection of her people, whose enthusiasm breaks forth in the cry: "Rex nostra Maria Theresa!"

We demand of Macaulay neither Protestant nor Prussian sympathies, but the manner in which he contrasts the lovely, innocent, forlorn woman with the atheistic, vain, unattractive man, shows that he has not only strong sympathies with Austria, but also with Maria Theresa personally; and here we all agree with him, — she was a superior woman, the pride of Germany! But Macaulay goes further yet. Frederick's personality is repulsive to him, and this once recognized, his narrative loses the sacredness which his unbiased convictions would have retained had he simply followed his enthusiasm. The prejudice betrayed deprives his work at once of more than half its value. So accustomed are we to reading the

Prussian estimate of Frederick the Great, that it certainly would be useful if an opinion of him in the broader European sense could find its way to the public mind. But if a book appears which makes this pretension, or if we ascribe such to it and the book disappoints us in this respect, we must refuse to accept it, and may not conceal the reasons why.

Supposing Frederick's claims to Silesia had been far more apparent than they were, and supposing he had been provoked to the invasion so that it was not unexpected, still had he done the same thing to-day he would have been blamed, and justly. Count Gotter, whom he sent to Vienna with war or peace in his pocket, arrived there two days after the Prussians had entered Silesia. Frederick relates this himself. To the Austrian envoy at Berlin, who apprised his court of the preparations going on, and expressed a suspicion of the king's designs, Maria Theresa replied, "We will not, we cannot believe it." Frederick's move was really, therefore, an unwarranted assault.

If Sardinia to-day, in the faith that she had claims on Lombardy, without first demanding in Vienna to have them peacefully conceded, should invade the empire, this would be an outrage, and, as Macaulay says, not only "gross perfidy toward Austria, but toward the whole community of civilized nations." But the Silesian war was carried on a century ago. Only sixty years earlier Louis XIV had taken possession of Strasburg in the same way. This was gross treachery toward Germany, but did not disturb the peace of Europe, for the French succeeded in the stroke, and the ignominy falls upon Germany of having allowed it. Louis was at that time the more powerful, and he knew that his *coup* would not break the treaty of peace just ratified.

Even so Frederick's invasion in his time was no outrage, — it was a challenge! He attacked the mightiest power, and wanted the war. The King of Prussia was then, in the eyes of the overbearing French nobility, only the Marquis of Brandenburg, — a poor parvenue, beneath consideration. Frederick's father before him had sought occasion for war in order to give weight to the Prussian name. The hobby he made of his troops was the most useful one he could have ridden. Frederick now had an army at his disposition. He was young. No great ruler has ever been reproached for his ambition, neither Alexander, nor Cæsar, nor Napoleon. He was the weaker. He contended against terrible odds, and had to take every advantage. Austria must not have a day for preparation. Therefore he entered the country at once and filled it with his troops. His manner of prosecuting war had still a smack of the Middle Ages in it, for so had the King of France and the Emperor mutually invaded each other's territories centuries earlier, looking out only for their own advantage, and finding pleasure in war. The conception of truth and honesty which obtained in private intercourse was never carried into political relations. Nor is it even to-day. The nations still fall upon one another like wild animals, and the weaker is swallowed up. So it has been from time immemorial. Frederick felt that neither he nor his country enjoyed the consideration to which they were entitled by their intrinsic strength. He took the bull by the horns, and compelled the nations to realize what he was. To-day this might be considered a foolhardy proceeding, — but perfidious, if he could carry it through, never. He was stirred by the power within him, and demanded a sphere of action. He did not, like a wolf, attack an innocent fold, but openly challenged a war with the most powerful antagonist in Europe. Frederick was son of the man George II had styled the "père coporal," the "roi des grands chemins," "archisablier de l'Empire Romain," and who was treated with the utmost contempt by all the old courts, which contempt extended to his officers and subjects. Now he, upon assuming the reins of government, demands satisfaction. He is resolved to occupy a position that is something more than merely conceded to him with lofty condescension. This is the reason why he begins the war, as he plainly tells us in his *Histoire de mon Temps*, and Macaulay might at least have cited it without mitigating the severity of his sentence. Never was "ambition, interest, and the desire to be talked about" more justifiable than in this instance, and Frederick was the man to fight it through.

Of all this, however, Macaulay makes no mention. He gives a picture of European politics, and yet of the rank of the different nations intellectually says nothing, what is merely casual or accidental forming the whole. If we may not agree with those who see in every battle lost or won an indication of the will of Heaven, the view is forlorn indeed which regards universal history as a mere web of accidents, and assumes the highest aim of a nation to be to make its life as tolerable as possible. There is an ideal growth of nations, and Frederick the Great has infinitely promoted ours.

Macaulay's personal dislike of the king is even more plainly betrayed by the way in which he speaks of his youthful days up to his ascension to the throne. Life at Rheinsberg consists in dining and supping well and holding romantic literary tournaments. When the crown-prince becomes king he dismisses his associates, as Henry the Fourth Falstaff and company. Macaulay might have told even worse things than these: how Frederick laid before his father calculations in political economy purporting to be his own, but really drawn up by others; how he secretly borrowed from the Austrian ambassador a sum of money which he needed, and was almost in despair when the king, who had been mortally ill, showed signs of recovery; but neither these things nor those quoted by Macaulay touch the main springs of action, from which alone any correct judgment of the crown-prince is to be formed. Although he allows that he was badly treated by his father, he gives it a comical-genre aspect. Yet here lay the real cause of all the inward miseries Frederick experienced. He was born with an inflexible nature, which through mistaken treatment was driven to desperation. If Rheinsberg was to be mentioned at all his marriage should have been discussed, against which he struggled in vain and was forced into at last; that from the outset he was surrounded with spies who pretended friendship for him, . and then reported everything to the old king in Berlin; how shamefully they took advantage of the bad relations existing between father and son, and would have been glad to make the breach irreparable. This was the mental experience of those years; it might and really ought to have been emphasized. No one who looks carefully into this Rheinsberg life will ever derive the impression that eating and drinking was the main thing.

It was at Rheinsberg that the crown-prince wrote his essay *Considérations sur l'État présent du Corps Diplomatique de l'Europe* and the *Ante-Machiavelli,* — two very important works in which the principles of his later policy are clearly set forth. In the first he pictures the relations of the European powers to one another at that time; its pregnancy is in the proof that all Austria's efforts had been directed to making the German Imperial dignity — which was dependent on the pre-choice of the princes — a hereditary prerogative of the house of Hapsburg. The *Anti-Machiavelli*, which created a great sensation, contains no learned criticism or refutation of the principles of the Florentine diplomat, who never intended to furnish a political standard for all time, but simply to represent his own experience. Frederick's book is rather to be considered as the first opposition made by a German prince to the system of government which prevailed generally at that time. According to Machiavelli, the sovereign, with his glory, his interests, and his wealth, is the centre around which revolves the fate of his subjects. Frederick says that the welfare of the people must form this central point. Here is the Germanic doctrine of the relation of prince to people born anew in Prussia, and in Prussia for the first time put into practice. The thousand villanous wiles and intrigues between sovereign and people which Machiavelli enumerates as known and in frequent use in his day (none of which are his invention, — he has simply catalogued them), and which had been in common practice in princely palaces since the sixteenth century, roused the burning indignation of Frederick's soul at their immorality. He attacked Machiavelli for the sake of having a tangible antagonist, but in his heart meant the Romanic system of government all around him, and in this sense the book was interpreted. To-day we notice only the points in which he misunderstood Machiavelli, who was neither a great man nor a great politician, and more admired by later generations for his penetration than esteemed by his contemporaries. Macaulay's renowned essay on Machiavelli contains erroneous views, arising plainly from the author's want of acquaintance with the sources of Florentine history.

Macaulay hurries over the account of Frederick's Rheinsberg friends. Perhaps we could not expect him to do otherwise in an essay necessarily limited to essentials, and yet if he could find room for a sentence of ten lines in which to speak of the disappointment of a few, who thought after Frederick's coronation they had reached the promised land, and were disagreeably startled out of their dreams by the harsh words, "Now there is an end to these tomfooleries!" there might also have been room enough to mention some who had a different experience. Macaulay's few, however, belonged too appropriately to the dinners and suppers of Rheinsberg to admit of his spoiling the unity of his picture by naming these men later as sharing Frederick's victories and his renown. Frederick, whom he describes as the meanest of the mean, at any rate never let these men famish. Kurd von Schlözer has given us a picture of this Rheinsberg circle in his *Chasot*. That those who thought best of the crown-prince expected a Telemachus after Fénélon's pattern is a curious assertion of the English author.

Frederick assumed the government at twenty-eight years of age. He had already announced his political principles. His character was matured, and his friends knew him too well to expect anything of the kind. "Others," continues Macaulay, "predicted the approach of a Medicean age, — an age propitious to learning and art, and not unpropitious to pleasure." If any imagined this they were by no means disappointed at first; for the assertion is false, that as soon as Frederick touched the crown he became a changed man, imbued with the spirit of an unbounded miserliness, which broke out over night like some inherited disease. He is accused of having proved faithless to everything he had said or loved as crown-prince. In truth, his personal experience, especially his wars, did make it somewhat difficult for him to follow in the footsteps of the Medici; but so long as he lived he was devoted to the arts and sciences, and spent a great deal of money in their service. His tastes did not rise to the purely classic, and to dabble in *dilettanti* fashion in poetry and science, especially in the department of medicine (although it escaped the sharp scrutiny of our critic), was a weakness, but a weakness of his time. In his printed correspondence we find proof that he was always in earnest about these matters, and eager to know the ablest men in each province. Indeed, in comparison with his zeal for what was positively useful, or for the promotion of art and science, his own verse-making was a mere innocent pastime, — the more so, that he never filched a moment from the state affairs for his poetical effusions, nor demanded the flattery of the public by having them printed.[1] To-day, when all these papers have been dragged to light and published, we are apt to forget this. What the king did send into the world in his lifetime were things of weight and importance. If really ambitious, as Macaulay says, of being handed down to posterity as a great author, he at any rate took pains to deserve it. His writings are elaborate works in the composition of which he had his nation in view that he hoped to benefit; and if, secondarily, posterity shared his thought, he did not flatter himself with illusions. Those who have no prejudice against his productions, from the style and the French, cannot fail to admire the clear arrangement of material, the simplicity of narration, and the unreserved way in which he speaks of his own faults.

"No one," says Macaulay (I come back to the expectations cherished of the king on his ascension to the throne), "had the least suspicion that a tyrant of extraordinary military and political talent, of industry more extraordinary still, without fear, without faith, and without mercy, had ascended the throne."

This contains the pith of his criticism. That a man like Macaulay is always fascinating, that his account of the Seven Years' War, and of the Silesian campaigns, attest descriptive power of the very highest kind, I need not tell those who have read the essay. The author's forte lies in just such rapid retrospects of

---

[1] He only allowed some of his early poems to be printed for a small circle of his intimate friends.

eventful times. Nothing could be more brilliant than his manner, for instance, of depicting the conquest of India by Lord Clive. Our steps are close beside the hero's, and we experience his victories with him. So, too, with Frederick. We see the wave which raises him, and the succeeding one beneath which he sinks; and how again with renewed strength and unclouded eye he raises and sustains himself above the stormy waters. Macaulay's manner of writing gives the impression that he is wholly infallible. All the more is contradiction demanded when this extraordinary talent is used to exhibit false and damaging views, as if they were results of clear, conscientious observations.

Let us grant for a moment that the king was without fear and without mercy. To demand of a military leader that he should be swayed by sympathy and pity, when a kingdom and his honor were at stake, is to demand too much. But never has Frederick been called cruel or inhuman. He had no Croates or Pandours in his army. He was harsh toward his people, his own family, and most of all toward his brothers. The manner in which he treats Prince Henry, an eminent diplomat and general, even into old age, is often perfectly insulting. But even here he is always consistent and intelligible, never acting from cruel, arbitrary impulse, like a brute tyrant; never a hint gives the impression that to punish gives him pleasure, or that he takes satisfaction in cutting men to the heart.

We, on the contrary, often see clearly that he is unconscious how hard he is. From his earliest years, trained in a hard school, severity and suspicion became infused into his blood. He was always solitary; from youth up he never met with a soul he dared to trust,— not even his sister whom he loved so dearly. Perhaps he never uttered the inmost feelings of his heart; and he to whom this is denied must be unhappy. The time has not yet come to form a perfectly unbiased judgment of Frederick. He is too near our own day; many of his written utterances are still unprinted! But whatever may be said in the future about him, he will never be reputed a tyrant without loyalty, shame, or mercy, as Macaulay has styled him. Neither in public nor private relations was he this! Never did he bind the fate of a people to his own, and then coldly sacrifice it to circumstances. Never did he appeal to the love of plunder in his troops to stimulate their bravery, never persecuted the conquered to gratify personal revenge. Necessity forced him to drain Saxony; but his own country fared no better. It possessed less and yielded less. He destroyed Bruhl's palace in Dresden; but this was richly deserved punishment for the count's intriguing policy. Ludwig Sforza and Cæsar Borgia were men without shame, truth, or mercy; but even Wallenstein is not so severely condemned, although he prosecuted war in a most inhuman fashion, and ended as a so-called traitor; or Louis Quatorze, who let loose a herd of tigers in the

Palatinate, when "political necessity" led him to devastate this innocent land. We judge them with more leniency, because in other directions their characters appear too grand to allow us to pass such a sweeping sentence on them as a whole. Faithless and merciless we call princes whose deeds show that their life-giving impulses are devoid of all truth and mercy. Whether it be justifiable to wage war when it can be avoided, or to open a war not positively called for in self-defence, may admit of discussion in the abstract; but this much is certain, that nations have always been proud of their victorious kings, and the question has never been raised on what ground they made war.

When Frederick took possession of Silesia, Prussia had between two and three millions of inhabitants, and her revenues amounted to seven and a half millions. The army consisted of somewhat over eighty-three thousand men. The country had no debt, and in the treasury was about nine millions of thalers. The territories belonging to the crown were, however, for the most part widely scattered, and even the compact centre had no safe boundaries. Of the troops, twenty-six thousand were foreign hirelings. Prussia possessed neither Saxony, Silesia, Pomerania, Poland, nor the Rhine lands. But Austria, when Frederick attacked her, possessed Silesia, the provinces of the Netherlands, and an altogether different influence in the empire from what it has to-day. The electorate of Cologne, Mayence, Treves, and Bavaria, all adding their considerable quotas, stood at Austria's service. At that time the princes trafficked with their regiments as oxen-dealers with their herds.[1]

Had Frederick been overwhelmed by this superior force which he had challenged, we might indeed have accused him of wanton rashness. But he won his cause. "Prussia was" — these are his words — "a kind of hermaphrodite, and more electorate than kingdom. It was a glorious task to decide finally which of the two it should be, and the recognition of this necessity it was which nerved the king's arm for the terrible task he set before him." Like Cæsar, Frederick always speaks of himself in the third person.

He would no longer suffer the tokens of contempt which his father had quietly borne. They had taught him that he must win for himself, and more especially for his nation, the respect due to both; that moderation is a virtue statesmen must not carry too far, inasmuch as the corruption everywhere does not allow of it; and lastly, since a change of government had come in, that it was more advisable to manifest his power than meekly to submit. At the close of her wars Prussia was no longer a contemptible interloper among the royal powers, but a dreaded peer, whose will must be consulted before a single shot could be fired in Europe.

How was it possible to leave this view of things so

---

[1] "L'electeur de Cologne entretenait huit à douze milles hommes, dont il trafignait comme un bouvier avec ses bestraux." — *Histoire de mon Temps,* I. 28.

wholly out of sight if any correct judgment of Frederick's wars was to be gained? And yet Macaulay ignores it completely. He lays great emphasis on single traits in the king's character, but nowhere shows the focus in which all unite, or the genesis which explains their *raison d'être*. He says the peculiarities of his father broke out again in him! Possibly he may be borne out in this statement; but what does it signify, when speaking of such a grand, unique individuality, to fall back on the one-sided theory of fatalistic natural inheritance, when the circumstances which really formed and must form it are so clearly discernible? Macaulay has eyes only for what was genre-like and whimsical in the man. His one dirty, shabby old coat, his snuff-box, his crutch-cane, — in a word, what rendered him a conspicuous figure in the street and a favorite subject in wax-cabinet exhibitions, is graphically portrayed; about the man himself our author is silent. I believe, however, this is not owing to malice prepense, as it might appear; for with Macaulay the clothes of men always form an important part of their soul. He is a brilliant advocate for or against a person, and his words have the accent of a special pleader who would move the jury on the instant to say "yes" or "no." His essay on Frederick is directed against the great king. No falser method than that of not doing full justice to him upon whom the judge is to pronounce sentence, and thus making it appear as if something more than a fair judgment was demanded.

I think if Macaulay had started with the intention of being perfectly just and impartial he would not have reiterated as he does the expression, "to do justice to the king." After hearing him through we are in the frame of mind to let justice have its course, and declare the accused guilty. Among the most contemptible means for compelling such a verdict is the artifice of mentioning at the outset one of the most damaging imputations against the moral life of the king, — thus interpreting all his actions *a priori* as those of a reprobate crowned by blind fate with success. It cannot be my purpose here to defend Frederick. I am only trying to throw a little light on the tactics of his accuser.

He handles his subject skilfully indeed, and has the advantage on his side of being a renowned historian. Perhaps among us this gives him even more weight than in his own country. In truth, this is the reason why the essay assumes such importance in our eyes.

The question whether it is allowable to make use of history for political aims would be answered differently in England than with us. We contemplate the past from a certain philosophic remoteness; we become partisans, but belong to no special party as represented at the present day. The main point is to set forth the truth, not to make proselytes. We leave people free to make their own choice. But in England it has always been the custom to utilize the storehouses of history for political purposes, and Macaulay may have done it this time without a thought of harm, even if fully conscious of his intention.

In this way we explain the frivolity with which he handles the facts. The whole tone of his essay, however, is less strange when we call to mind a wondrous peculiarity of our epoch. All that is mythical in times gone by our age rejects. No one believes any longer in heroes whose characters were unaffected by the little prosaic needs of human life, whose thoughts were a perpetual inspiration, and whose feelings were guided by immortal passions. Such figures are banished from the realm of history, and scarcely tolerated in that of poetry. With the same composure with which we observe the various eras in the formation of our planet we dig out the roots of the oldest nations from the legendary soil in which they flourished, shake off the mould from their fine fibres, and compare the plants with those which are to-day blooming and bearing fruit. Mommsen comes and blows aside the old gray mists resting over the swamps on the Tiber banks, and we see the city of Romulus arise as naturally as among us the foundations are laid and the walls raised for soldiers' barracks. The same labor and the same material was expended to build a wall thousands of years ago as now, and the ancient elephant hungered, fed, and digested according to the same laws as the elephant of to-day. This point of view is so consonant to modern thought that it has become the ruling one in all the sciences.

To politics and history it was first most boldly applied in England. A parliament sits in London, where the doings of kings and emperors are discussed as formerly in the Roman senate. A member of Parliament deems himself one of the arbitrators of peace and war for the whole world, and the other gentlemen in Europe had better take their resolutions accordingly. Hence, also, the method of putting themselves on a very familiar footing with historical personages. Macaulay handles Frederick the Great exactly as if he were his equal, and his school imitates his example. Cæsar and Pompey, whose faults and virtues have been hitherto covered with a veil which threw over them a vague poetic light, are now people like ourselves; they are dragged forth into the full light of day, the dust knocked out of their togas, the rusty old weapons cleaned and furbished up again, while they are told without ceremony to their faces, "Here you were clever, and there you made fools of yourselves." Frederick gets as sound a drubbing as if the things had happened yesterday, and a newspaper correspondent had reported them to a London paper.

And who will forbid this? Were they not all mortal men like ourselves, who ate, drank, thought, acted, and repented as we do? Calmly we ask, and appear to forget entirely the monstrous distinction that we live while they are dead. The years between their time and ours are a sea which no ship traverses. The life of a dead man may not be subjected to the same measure by which we estimate the deeds of the living. The myth is no artificial rust that is to render the appearance of things more interesting, but the genuine platina which we cannot destroy without destroying the monument itself, whose accessory only it seems to be. Every dead man, even if but just buried, has become already a mythical person; and every year in its flight adds to the mysterious halo that surrounds him. What the sculptor does at the moment when he chisels the bust of a living man Time slowly and gradually does for the dead. The passage of years renders more and more general the features it transmits, and the less individual. They grow more and more beautiful of superior men, whilst those of the insignificant masses soon fade into nothingness. We may say, in truth, that a great man absorbs and unites in himself the best features of a generation that, in itself, is fast vanishing and passing into oblivion. We discover through a telescope that a star is a small glittering point, and that the rays we perceive with our naked eye are only illusory; but there is no such instrument for the men whom death removes beyond our vision. "De mortuis nil nisi bene," is no mere good-natured adage inspired by vague, universal sympathy. Every man, as soon as he is dead, is seen through a tenderer light, and his discordant being assumes harmonious shape.

What we never forgive the living we forgive the dead. Their faults do not cease to be faults, but the hatred is silenced that once followed them. They have entered a higher sphere, which it would be inhuman not to respect.

Yet how natural in struggling with a political party to call the past to our aid, and, identifying it with the present, deal out to our historical antagonist the blows intended for the living! It is a political right arrogated by the present in regard to the past, but one which will never be acknowledged in Germany. With us science can never be used as means to further party aims. We are the only people who can and do judge events from an ideal standpoint; we have been made to suffer for this, but can never give it up, for it is in harmony with our nature, and our one stay and support. We should be as weak and powerless without this inward light, as we have often enough been tempted to represent ourselves. In Germany, historiography will never be permitted to take a one-sided political standpoint, but must so conceive and describe the deeds of nations as they most clearly reveal the god-like power of humanity.

In many cases even Macaulay cannot do otherwise. In his essay on Byron he enumerates a great number of single traits, exhibits him in every conceivable position, and remains throughout so cool and unbiased that his calm observation is nowhere resolved into partiality; but he winds up by saying, "To us he is now only the poet, young, noble, unhappy." Thus he writes directly after Byron's death, claiming for him, even then, the purifying, absolving power of history, which he seems to have wholly forgotten in the case of our great king. We have not forgotten it.

We will not upbraid him, however, for what he has chosen to say about Frederick; had he been a German he would have written very differently. I believe his opinion stands alone, even in England, and there, too, encounters just contradiction. If he had been a German, he must have been accused of perfidy, ignorance, and want of patriotism. Macaulay, in this essay, has given expression to a rashly-formed opinion of a foreign prince, but we should deserve severe censure if we took from such a source our knowledge of the man who has contributed so powerfully to the greatness of Germany.

ALBERT DÜRER.

WHEN speaking of distinguished poets or artists, of Shakespeare, Goethe, Schiller, Raphael, or Rubens, their principal works — the works from which they derive their fame — rise involuntarily before our view. We say Goethe, and think of *Iphigenia, Werther, Faust;* or Raphael, and mean the *Stanzas* of the Vatican and the *Sistine Madonna.* And so, likewise, of great generals and renowned scholars, their names are synonyms for glorious battles, or books which in themselves were eras.

The artist of whom we are now to speak does not seem to have reared any such lofty pedestal to his fame. Albert Dürer! he is universally known as an eminent painter, as foremost in rank; but where are his masterpieces? Where is the one great work with which he came forward to kindle the enthusiasm of the world, as Goethe with *Werther,* Corneille with the *Cid,* Michael Angelo with the *Pietà?* What was the crowning point of his activity, of his life?

He lived in Nuremberg. His house there has been carefully restored, and is now visited as a pilgrim shrine. Dürer himself stands before us a magnificent man, tall, with clear eyes, and dark blonde curls falling over his shoulders; but this is almost all we know of him. We indeed remember here and there having had occasionally some bit pointed out to us as being Dürer's work; but no one ever stood lost in rapture before a picture of Dürer's, as so many have done before Raphael's Madonnas. Dürer's productions float before us a maze of small things, — engravings, woodcuts, drawings, pretty paintings in miniature on parchment, carvings in wood and ivory; more like treasures and relics than pictures, which by their power or beauty assert a right to a distinguished position. And yet no one questions Dürer's having been a great artist. Are his works, then, lost or destroyed, or have they been carried away into distant lands? On what does his reputation rest? Where are the proofs of his greatness?

And here, at once, this may be said, — Dürer's fame, exalting him so high, and comprehending the whole man, is of recent date; Dürer's name was always honored, but the tone in which it is uttered to-day is struck for the first time. In treating of him personally, therefore, we must include some discussion of the characteristics of our age, which has first brought him forward in this radiant light.

Our age is one of scientific research. Every man who has been able in any respect to lift himself out of the callous state of brute ignorance strives to share in the labors of the great fraternity devoted to the scientific investigation of all that exists. A potent charm emanates from such labors, and not from their material value, enormous as this has been, but from the fact that they have tended to establish the laws governing the universe. Whoever pursues scientific studies at the present day, with a view to mercantile advantage, and is successful in obtaining results, is respected; but the absolutely noble are the laborers in the cause of truth itself. No more genuine aristocracy exists to-day than the aristocracy of learning.

Two facts have grown out of this bias of the present generation toward science, of radical effect,— the gigantic increase in numbers of men dedicating their lives to scientific research and following upon new views a speedy deduction of the extremest consequences. A freedom devoid of limitations or prejudice has appeared which we regard with some perplexity. The elder among us (using this word in its mildest sense) were brought up in the faith that the original progenitors of mankind had enjoyed immediate intercourse with the Deity; but now, when the transmitted records of Scripture are no longer the sole authority, when everything that can give answer is questioned (and every tiniest stone and drop of water gives answer to-day), we are led to think that our connection is with the monkeys. A vast multitude of people, — and more perhaps than we imagine, — calmly acquiesce, with all seriousness, in the notion that we derive our origin from these animals, and this, too, merely because science has to a certain extent plausibly demonstrated the connection between man and monkey. In place of ancestors, mighty, heroic ideals, their descendants must strive after in vain, we have now the wretched savage dwellers in the lake cities whose veritable bones we anatomize. No one ventures to doubt these palpable records of the oldest history or to resist the conclusions derived from them. Nor is it better in the province of religion. What could exceed in purity the primal aspect of Christianity and its evidences? But this beginning is treated of to-day as if it were a question concerning something which lately happened and ought to be discussed without passion. Everything may now come under controversy if it only assumes the form of scientific inquiry. Strangely enough, too, this does not increase our presumption, but tends to humiliate us. We take a lower place. Our earth, with its vicissitudes, is only a brief incident in the creation of the universe. We no longer flatter ourselves the world was made for man. And still further the human race, with its entire history, constitutes but a limited episode even in the experience in our own planet; the nations are but portions of mankind which we observe and study like individuals. We weigh carefully their tendencies, capacities, and achievements, coolly decide on their value or significance, and construct their history by representing these qualities as the moving principle. With all attainable means we endeavor to trace the earlier as well as later condition of the different nations. When in former days the theme was history, it was a narration of battles and the fate of dynasties; but now an infinite complication of causes and motives, acting one upon another, must be considered. It is a chase after new points of view. Once it was much to have found a practicable way through the woods, but now every leaf on the trees by the wayside must be counted; every stone must be turned over to see if anything lies concealed beneath it; every change in the weather is observed and registered. Countless years since an arrow-point, wrought by the hand of man, remained sticking in the body of an animal slain in the chase. Strata upon strata, sand and soil have heaped themselves above it. To-day we dig into this, find the arrowhead, measure the depth, and decide from the work and the strata of earth the nature of a departed race that lived thousands of years ago. Splinters of bone, according to their different forms, become hieroglyphics reporting an intelligible story. A dozen words, carved a thousand years since, perhaps, and not understood at that time, now show the nature of a language, or contain pregnant disclosures regarding the seat or spread of a people. We look about us on all sides with such unlimited freedom, that nothing any longer seems beyond our grasp.

It is exactly here, however, while carrying these investigations back to times whose remoteness we formerly dared not measure, that in connection with the positive results a negative side appears. The earlier historians, to be sure, worked with scant material enough,— seldom knew the facts exactly, and were forced to shape their pictures out of the nebulæ. Yet, on the other hand, our passions, which, after all, are the exciting elements in all human intercourse, were displayed in those early days in their unalloyed integrity, and history, which to us to-day seems the result of compelling laws acting one upon another from multifarious directions, was somewhat more free and comprehensible. No fact is willingly believed at the present time, if proof cannot be furnished that it occurred just as stated. We wish to feel that we understand an event so clearly that no point in it remains absolutely dark. The most brilliant elucidation of the growth and achievements of nations is found in Buckle's *History of Civilization,* which in its comprehensive introduction grasps the principles underlying the destinies of these various peoples and nations.

So long as Buckle limits himself to a comparison of the qualities of our planet with those of the people inhabiting the various parts of it, he finds startling and magnificent points of view. When, however, he enters the sphere in which for the interpretation of conflicts of spiritual origin not only a perception of the principal influences controlling the masses is demanded, but also a recognition of the individuality manifest in single leaders, he is powerless. He apprehends and explains only what relates to the passive in man, and his treatment fails altogether when extended to the active and creative. For here it does not suffice to consider man simply as an object of natural history.

It is very striking that, whilst in knowledge of the external conditions of life we have enlarged our horizon so vastly, we have rather fallen back as concerns the inner life both in keenness of insight and in the expression and delineation of it. At any rate, there has been no progress to speak of. The remotest accounts of spiritual things go back two or three thousand years; men would seem to have remained ever the same. Love, hatred, ambition, and the kindred passions, were felt by the old Greeks exactly as we feel them to-day, but were better observed than by us; they were greater orators, writers, poets, sculptors, architects, — yes, greater thinkers than we. The mysteries of human nature have not been solved through increase of knowledge. Many things in history are cleared up, owing to the immense enlargement of our resources; but the one problem remains, after all, unsolvable as of yore, — the secret of the vital growth of nations. To be sure, we are perfectly aware of this at the present day. We feel that the people have spiritual epochs, and that, even while realizing them to be of the utmost importance, they elude our grasp, notwithstanding a great amount of external and positive fact. Our own experience convinces us that a few men stimulate and direct the animus of their day, and are at once its type and most faithful reflection. We believe these men will give to coming generations their conception of it, and seek for such men in past centuries as have rendered this service to their times. It has been, and must remain, one of the chief tasks of a historian to find these men, and to study them in the true light. In order, therefore, to understand an era, we must first see the men who lived in it. This brings us back to Dürer.

Dürer's fame is of recent date, because it is only in our times that he has been recognized as the standard of the intellectual progress of his age. And so high has this ennobling distinction raised him, that he now ranks as a great painter without having actually furnished visible proofs of it.

In certain periods the men whom I designate as representative are at once evident. All are perfectly aware that Voltaire was the reflection of the intellectual movement in France in the middle of the last century; Rousseau, of the times preceding the French Revolution, whilst the beginning of the Revolution itself finds expression in Mirabeau. What Goethe, Plato, Pericles, and Phidias include and signify is familiar to every one. But take Italian history as mirrored in Dante, and, were we obliged to conceive the spiritual life of Italy through him alone, at the turning-point between the thirteenth and fourteenth centuries, the gloom and bitterness of his nature would prevent us from gaining a complete view of his times. We look about for a man who reflects the bright side of life in his day; the painter Giotto stands beside Dante, and affords the counterpart. But few indeed of his works are preserved to-day; as with Dürer, scarcely anything which in itself proclaims the great painter. But his place by the side of Dante confers upon him higher rank, and brings him forward as the indispensable man of historical significance.

Let us proceed with Italy. In the transition period from the fifteenth to the sixteenth century a man is wanting who includes, and at the same time represents, as much as Dante in former centuries. Michael Angelo was far too one-sided, and Machiavelli no less so; we ask for the man who reflects the brilliant side of life, — Raphael appears! These three men, however, embrace nearly the whole. I do not know of one who typifies the warlike element of the times. Certainly, neither Cæsar Borgia, nor Julius II, nor Bourbon, nor the Colonnas, nor any other of the renowned soldiers. Too much of the perishable makes a part of their natures, and what is really living in them seems a reflection of Machiavelli, without whom the times would be incomprehensible. Machiavelli, Michael Angelo, Raphael, include all the rest. Even Savonarola would grow indistinct without them as a background.

But now we will pass to Germany at the same period. A crowd of characters here seem to present themselves; yet, drawing nearer to scrutinize them, three only stand out as representative men, — living realities to their own and following ages, — Luther, Hutten, and Albert Dürer. They explain everything. Luther, the power, the will, and the self-consciousness; Hutten, the unrest, the pertinacity, and also the confusion; Dürer, the joy in productive labor, the integrity, and contentment, of the German people as they appeared to the world in that day.

Casting a glance back, there in Italy is Giotto beside Dante, then Raphael and Michael Angelo, and finally in Germany Dürer. To fathom the works of these men, and from them to gain acquaintance with the times which called them forth and constitute a part of them, is the science of art at the present day, long since well understood and applied to classic art whose merits have been proportionally realized. This study has not yet extended to the works of modern art, nor their wealth been fully recognized.

Albert Dürer stands before me in the perfect harmony of all the finest human attributes. When we think of Michael Angelo we are attracted to a lonely man, whose life, as a whole, forms a picture of almost painful isolation. If we should compare Dürer and Raphael to countries which limited, and limiting fill out their boundaries, and yet appear only as parts of a whole, sharing with others chains of mountains, rivers, and highways, we must compare Michael Angelo to an entire continent surrounded by water. Defective in many respects, but unique in all, — having its own inhabitants, its own vegetation, with vast solitudes and stretches of desert, and its own sky. All outward interests seemed of trifling importance to Michael Angelo, as it were superfluous. He bore no relation to his fellow-men which influenced his life. He was what he was from the beginning; no one guided him in the course he took, nor could he instruct any one how to follow in his footsteps.

On the whole, he appears poor and sunless. His favorite simile of himself in his poems is of one "born in the dark and wandering in the night." He could only envy others what had been denied to him. Where such a man comes forward with his colossal productions, and nevertheless is misunderstood and falsely judged, one finds every incentive to make the greatest effort to rend the dark veil behind which he seems waiting for the light. All that can be done for him, however, is much like entering a sombre hall in which a mighty statue stands, and, lighting a little candle at the foot of it, we see the outline grow somewhat clearer. Many things come out faintly illuminated, but on the whole only great masses separate the figure from the surrounding darkness. Who approaches sees just enough to surmise that here stands the image of a powerful man, but never perhaps will it be brought forward into the clear light of day.

Turn now, on the other hand, to Raphael and Albert Dürer! It is like stepping out of this stillness, darkness, and loneliness into the midst of a cheerful market-place, where the window-panes glisten on every side, fountains gush forth, and people mingle in the whirl of business. Nothing strange or replete with mystery comes here to meet us. We are only confused because unable at a glance to take in the whole;

one thing after another must be surveyed in turn. The crowd of genial, living faces, like the air of spring, seems infinite and exhaustless. How many dark, attractive eyes glance at us in all directions as we skim over in memory Raphael's works! How vividly the cheerful stir of German city life, both public and private, comes before us when we think of Dürer's! We see Michael Angelo once in youth and again in old age flying to Venice; the first time driven away by a frightful dream, the second with thoughts of the ruin of his country in his soul. Raphael, on the contrary, travels serenely through Umbria and Toskana, and radiant with hope enters Rome. Dürer rides gayly over the Alps to Venice, or, light of heart, with wife and maid, roves about in the Netherlands. To sit next to Michael Angelo at table would be like supping with heroes, where one weighs every word that he hears, and more conscientiously still that he utters. By the side of Dürer and Raphael one could have talked and enjoyed the wine. They are genial beings whom we joyfully rush forward to greet, just for a pressure of the hand, whilst with Michael Angelo we are contented to watch him at a distance, as we look at some grand statue drawn triumphantly through the streets of a city.

Dürer and Raphael are Italy and Germany side by side in the same epoch. No description makes the contrast between the two countries so clear as the sight of these men and their productions. Here and there a blossom shooting up suddenly, like the aloe, into supreme beauty to astonish and gladden the eyes of men. In Italy the son of a poor painter is transplanted from a narrow provincial town to Rome, where, in the space of fifteen years, he mounts all the steps leading to wealth and renown: he dies young, having had the prospect before him of becoming cardinal, and leaving palaces, money, and the pope in tears. All the influential men and nobles boasted of their acquaintance with him, or of the possession of his works, — if they had been so fortunate as to obtain them. Rome seemed empty after Raphael's death. And this side of the Alps, on the other hand, we find Dürer, son of a citizen of Nuremberg, a town in the heart of Germany, never touched by that concentrated flame of glory in the midst of which Raphael stood, but irradiated with a soft light, which penetrated to the north and to the south as far as Rome, so that Raphael caught its beams, sent gifts and exchanged with him words of friendship. He worked persistently, without ever receiving any large commissions, even from the community he helped to raise to distinction with himself.

Let us contemplate this artist and the various specimens of his work. What a bright, happy, self-sustained being he was from his earliest youth, even when, as an apprentice to Wohlgemuth, he had much to suffer from "the boys," up to his death, attributed by his friends to the excessive labor urged upon him by the parsimony of his wife. We do not, however, believe that Dürer ever allowed himself to be henpecked; for a merry, yes, roguish spirit, breaks forth in all his works. In reading his Venetian letters we cannot but think that a nature armed with such humor must have been more than a match for the bad temper of a woman. His diary in the Netherlands, in which he notes down all his expenses, seems to prove this. He often eats and drinks with boon companions, leaving wife and maid to take care of themselves; his losses at play are not infrequently quoted, while he buys collections of curiosities and whatever comes under his hand. Dürer must have had somewhat of the *gentilezza* which distinguished Raphael. Nothing put him out, and when he died (as with Raphael) his friends missed the man more than the artist. Pirkheimer, in elegiac verses on his death, lays great stress on Dürer's general superiority, on his many-sidedness, as if art had been only one of the many gifts and graces which adorned him. Luther, exclaiming at the horrors committed by the Anabaptists, writes, "God seems to have taken Dürer away to save him the pain of living to witness them." Dürer, dying, left a great void behind. Of how few this can be said those know best who have experienced with surprise how often after the death of the most distinguished man scarcely a token remains to indicate the loss.

What the word of a representative man, however, is worth to his times we discover from one of Luther's utterances. Much had been collected in those days in praise of Nuremberg, — a mass of very creditable material; but it was only relative, and did not give the city any special rank. But now we have Luther's words: "Nuremberg is the eyes and ears of Germany," *auris et oculus Germaniac,* and these conferred on Nuremberg that patent of nobility which all previous tributes had failed to insure it. And with his city's Dürer's position in Germany was also improved; and perhaps this explains in part his love for his native town, which did little enough for him externally.

Nuremberg must have had something of the keen, critical tone which made Florence in its palmy days so feared, and at the same time so productive. Here, as at Florence, too, the burghers' love for their city was proved by their constant desire to adorn and embellish it. They were nowhere so happy as at home. How carefully we find the streets and houses depicted in the works of their native artists! Dürer's, especially; and his own house was his favorite. We see in his precious, perhaps most precious, work that he has put St. Jerome and the Lion into his own little low-studded room, which, with a few additions, he has fitted up for the old gentleman's study. With what supreme satisfaction he proceeds to copy this room, so dear to him, even to the knots in the boards, and the rifts in its timbers! How warm and genially the sun streams in sidewise through the tiny panes of the broad, many-paned window upon the floor, touching lightly as it passes the strong, massive table. How the lion, blinking and drunk with sleep, stretches himself out, while a small terrier crouches at his side, both as if belonging naturally to the room. We seem to hear the buzzing of the flies and the gentle rustle of the leaves turned over by the bearded saint. How tidily is everything put in its place, — all freshly scoured, — wearing a Sunday air! Methinks, whoever had this etching in his room would find it a fast-nailed bit of sunshine, dispensing its beneficent rays even in the gloomiest hours.

And this composition is but one verse, as it were, in a long poem. Imagine all Dürer's engravings, drawings, etc., laid side by side; what a diary of his rich life! His portraits are a compendium of German characters of all sorts, from the emperor, whom he pictures in the little room of the castle at Augsburg, to the beggar and peasant in the street. Easy-going, block-headed monks, illustrious warriors, burghers, lansquenets, pedlers, and vagabonds; and with these, cities, villages, tracts of country. A humor for the fantastic finds expression in many of his compositions, and the belief in witches that held such sway over the minds of men in his day. The inability to conceive of the past otherwise than in the garb of the present, or history except as a romantic blending of truth and fiction, stand forth in his works clearly as leading characteristics of the times. We see how little there was to prevent the people from perceiving an immediate connection between the antique Roman empire and their own. We see what pleasure they took in the present; how firmly they believed that things had been so from all eternity, and so to all eternity must remain. Every house was built as indestructibly as possible, that it should last as long as church and empire, — powers of eternal origin, destined to be eternal! And how comfortable they seem to feel themselves in this world! What a respect they have for it! How absolutely they submit to the powers that be, on earth and in heaven! Dürer's soul apparently finds intense satisfaction in the production of these fresh works of art, arising from the feeling that they also will share to some degree in this immortality. With what care he prepares his colors! All the materials he uses must be as durable as possible. And this earnest striving to render earthly things imperishable extends, in a kind of practical sense, to their conceptions of a future life. Men of that day exerted their noblest talents in order to leave behind a worthy memory, and secure a reception in heaven; and the step over the boundary was never out of their minds, devoid, however, of all sentimentality. For the faith of that age pictured the life beyond as a festive state, to be attained with certainty, and bearing a likeness to our own in social forms and ordinances, — where each found his place prepared for him. The children had their toys, and their parents renewed the bonds of friendship with many who had left the world before them. Here, too, was no cause for anxiety, if only upright conduct had smoothed the way. Dürer moves about in life as in a garden, where one is secluded, but not imprisoned; he goes slowly, and his eyes rove far and wide; what he sees, he sees as pictures, and his hand is untiring in transferring them to paper.

And how naturally and modestly he fulfils this,— his mission! With every line he draws taking us deeper into the heart of his subject. Never has a plastic artist of equal genius looked at the world so ingenuously, and in a certain sense reproduced it with such truth.

This last assertion may possibly challenge contradiction. For, in point of fact, if the master is to be mentioned who, in those days, represented nature with absolute fidelity, only one name can be uttered, —Holbein's. Younger than Dürer, but his contemporary, the climax of his development was in Basle, where he painted a few magnificent compositions, on very large walls, but for the most part portraits and easel-pictures. He afterward went to England, where he died. Holbein is the man who in portraiture has exceeded every one in the reproduction of nature. But one defect is inherent in all his works: his portraits have a certain emptiness of expression, which with longer acquaintance inspires a mournful feeling. I have not seen all his works, but such as I have seen tend to confirm this observation. We seem to realize the fruitless struggle to lend a soul to these perfect reflections of nature. I have lately become acquainted with a portrait by his hand which was new to me. A work brought freshly before us in this way is studied in the most unbiased frame of mind. An unrivalled piece of work! Color and drawing unite to make it something perfect; the problem of how to bring out the face of a man from a flat surface in color, without letting the smallest particle of its life escape, is solved. Indeed, neither Raphael nor Leonardo were able to achieve what has here been done. But all these excellences fail to compensate for the want of a joyous soul in the work; and for this reason Holbein can never be to his generation what Dürer is. Holbein's works betray no palpable individuality. We feel no master behind them, to whom we would draw near to ask the solution of the secret involved in the picture. Holbein draws faultlessly; his conceptions are grand and full of taste, but beyond this he has no influence over our minds. Holbein's sketches are the studies of a painter; Dürer's roughest drafts, those of a poet. Dürer's figures become only more living the oftener we study them. Who does not know his portrait of Maid Fürlegerin, daughter of a Nuremberg patrician, whom he twice painted. Not beautiful, save the magnificent hair! He has intentionally arranged the light to fall in such a singular way upon the features that a multitude of faint shades come out, modelling the head with astonishing vividness. The hair is painted as if he had laid in each particular hair by itself, and the fingers of the hand are indescribably soft and delicately rounded. Critics may object that the portrait is too brown in its shades, and altogether more like a caprice than a work of art; but even so, what a lovely caprice! Suggested by the fondest, most ingenuous conception of nature.

This feeling for nature is, however, most strikingly conspicuous in Dürer's portraits of himself. I believe no master has so often and so carefully painted the portrait of his own person, and with such conscientiousness made the most trifling details as important as the essential features. Here, also, the hair is painted with the minutest fidelity, and his predilection for modelling hands, which chiefly distinguishes him, is apparent. Moreover, he especially delights to picture himself in rich and gorgeous attire, in fur-bordered mantle and cap of finest needlework, in French and Spanish cloaks, betraying a taste for fine clothes and a consciousness of his stately, aristocratic figure. In Venice he actually took lessons in dancing.

A portrait of himself opens the series of his works, so far as they are preserved. "I painted this likeness of my own face when I was nine years old," is written on the picture which is in Vienna. Drawn as a child draws, but already showing the attempt to bring the head out in relief by vigorous shading (which Leonardo made the test for the capacity of young people for art). The long hair is here as smooth as a thatched roof, so that possibly the curls of later years were not nature's unassisted work. Such vanity was quite consonant to the times when everything was overlaid with ornament, and the fancy for decoration extended to one's own person.

When Dürer drew this he was still at school. He had ten brothers and sisters at that time, and they finally numbered eighteen,— his mother having been married young. After the death of his father his mother came to live with him.

"Now you must know," we read in Dürer's journal, "that in the year of 1513, on the Tuesday before Passion week, my poor afflicted mother, whom after my father's death I had taken to live with me, because she was very poor, and who had been under my care nine years, was seized so deathly ill early in the morning, that we broke open the door of her chamber, since we could not get to her otherwise; we carried her down to a lower room, where both sacraments were administered,— for every one thought she would die; for she had preserved her health after my father's death, and her custom was to go much to the church, and she had always punished me faithfully when I did not do right, and had the greatest anxiety concerning me and my brother; and when I went out (or came in) her words were always, 'Go, in the name of Christ!' and she urged upon us constantly with all diligence holy admonitions, and felt always the greatest care for our souls and I cannot find words to tell all her good deeds, or her Christian charity, or worthily to praise her. This my pious mother had borne eighteen children, had frequently had the pestilence, and many other severe and noticeable diseases; had suffered from great poverty, scorn, derision, insulting words, frights, and great reverses. Yet was she never revengeful. From that day, namely, the one above mentioned as the one upon which she was taken ill, a year hence in the year of our Lord 1514, on a Tuesday, it being the seventeenth day of May, two hours before midnight, did my pious mother Barbara Dürer depart this life, absolved from pain and guilt by all the Christian sacraments in the power of the pope. She had before also given me her blessing, and wished me godlike peace, together with much good admonition, that I should keep myself from sin. She also desired to drink St. John's blessing, which she then did; for she much feared to die, but said that she did not fear to appear before God. And, indeed, her death was hard, and I observed that she saw something cruel, for she asked for the holy water, and yet had not spoken for some time. I also saw soon that death gave her two great blows on the heart, and how she closed her eyes and mouth, and departed with pain. I prayed aloud for her, but was in such grief as I can hardly describe. God be merciful to her! Her best joy was to speak of God, and she loved to see him in his glory. She was sixty-three years old when she died, and I have given her honest burial according to my property. God the Lord grant me also a blessed end, and may God, with his heavenly host, my father, mother, and friends, come to me at last. Almighty God, give us eternal life. Amen. And in death she looked much lovelier than she had done in life."

I have given Dürer's language in this quotation, with only insignificant changes, to make it a little more familiar to our ears to-day. Every one will see in it with what love he hung upon his mother. His striking portrait of her is to be found to-day in the Berlin collection just published of Dürer's *Sketches*.

Let us now turn to his father, whom he twice painted: a shrewd-looking old man with a little skull-cap in his hand; and the portrait of Wohlgemuth, in which with all imaginary care he has reproduced the aged, withered features. We need not repeat the words in which Dürer, before the death of his mother, describes that of his father, for if anything can testify to his love and fidelity it is these portraits.

It is no easy thing to paint men as they actually are. In surveying the entire realm of modern art, only about a hundred portraits of the first rank are found. Nothing is more instructive than a comparison of these works. Nowhere is the artist's own depth of nature shown more conclusively. It is the gauge of his genius, and this all the more veritably because portraits by the distinguished masters are, generally speaking, rather secondary things, over which they unbend to a certain degree. Professional portrait-painters are not here in question, as their works conform, more or less, to fashion, and do not aim at any special depth of meaning.

We were just speaking of Holbein. The want of love for his work, which is so striking when contrasted with its technical perfection, is not peculiar to him alone. Eminent productions in this department by Vandyck suffer from the same dissonance; so, too, many of Rembrandt's and Ruben's! It is likewise evident in Sebastian del Piombo and Andrea del Sarto, who in all other respects are to be counted among the first. On the other hand, Raphael, Rubens now and then, and Titian, make their portraits look at us with eyes that melt into our very hearts. And so also Dürer's! Like Shakespeare's creations, these portraits represent types, though in reality they give us only individuals. Dürer's *Maid Fürlegerin* is a type of modest burgher maidenhood in the sixteenth century; his *Holzschuher*, that of an honest and honorable German burgher. This portrait, which until lately has remained in possession of the family, gives us as clear an idea of the strong and solid basis on which German city organization rested as could be gleaned from the written archives. They are historical portraits, which exhibit common daily life in Germany, as Raphael's pictures Roman life in his day, and Titian's, which glow with the declining rays of Venetian splendor, whilst Rubens, Vandyck, Murillo, and Velasquez give us pictures of the men through whose aid, in the sixteenth and seventeenth centuries, the Hapsburg dynasty became all-powerful in Spain and the Netherlands. Rembrandt, on the other hand, is the historian of the free Netherlands. But if, turning to France, we study all the works of art produced in the Napoleonic era, we do not find one of those French painters able to furnish a real historical portrait.

And those earlier men were poets in the conception of their likenesses. Dürer's powerful *Kaiser Karl* whose face he invented as fitting the imperial robes above which it thrones, — does it not contain all that history, poetry, and tradition have combined to stamp on our imagination as united in the character of this great emperor? Is it not a type of the mighty legendary hero? — a kind of demigod, fountain-head of all German history, power, and glory? A St. Gothard from whose rocky clefts the Rhine breaks forth; then the main artery of Germany, as it promises again to become to-day.

When we examine Dürer's portraits, or in fact his pictures, as works of art purely, it would be infatuation not to grant defects in them. His faithfulness often runs into pettiness. He paints the window-frames as mirrored in the sitter's eye. If Rubens with a few bold strokes, or Titian in a riot of color, produced a magnificence, semblance to nature, which, when brought into comparison with it, really shows no points of correspondence, Dürer, at the opposite extreme, painted nature microscopically. It is not the pedantic minuteness of Denner, whose portraits, intended for effect, are feats of dexterity in reproducing the mere surface of the countenance; but, in Dürer, an excessive conscientiousness that overdoes it. Compared with other great masters, he lacks the command of technical aid, and his figures, therefore, have not perfect flexibility; they seem to be holding still, sometimes to the verge of nervousness. The reason for this may have been that he was conscious of not always at the first stroke creating what he wished. It is acknowledged that his portrait of Erasmus of Rotterdam is far inferior to that painted by Holbein. On the other hand, this fresh, free, vigorous handling produced many things which few other painters were capable of beside him. The pen-and-ink drawing of Felix Lautenschläger in the Netherlands, which Dürer "threw off," comes to mind; an admirable study of the nude, done with the pen on green paper and laid in in white. If inclined to find fault with Dürer for having put in the color at times with the point of a pen, we may now reverse the criticism, for the delicate strokes of the pen are here put in as if with a brush.

The observation frequently made that Dürer's works are more writings than paintings, may be a second reason why his pictures sometimes lack "technical finish," as the term is generally used at the present day. They hardly seem to have been conceived to the final point, and there is no indication of an aim at picturesqueness. What I mean to say is, that he does simply what he intended from the outset, and, this accomplished, lays his brush aside. Moreover, it may be remarked that perfection in technique can only be the fruit of long years of routine, and this kind of practice Dürer never had, because the commissions failed. That this failure was owing to circumstances, and not to any lack of capacity, is fully proved by some of his works, — for instance, parts of the picture of the *Strahower Madonna*, and above all the *Apostles* in Munich; in the former we find groups arranged with taste and historic in the best sense; in the latter, single figures, colossal conceptions wrought out with the power of Raphael or Michael Angelo. These Apostles show Dürer's genius to have been equal to the mightiest achievements. But no one demanded these great works of him. Here we may say, in a tone of regret, that we had at that time no emperor, no nobles, and no commoners, who had any appreciation of such things. As far as Dürer's fame is concerned, however, the proofs he has given suffice. Indeed, the feeling he inspires of what he might have done tempts us to see more almost than his actual works exhibit. The possible often stimulates the imagination more than the actual. Thus Goethe, who enjoyed giving his works every variety of poetical form, has really created in each form only one work; but that so perfect in itself that it seems to stand for a number of productions of the same kind.

Dürer felt himself freest when etching or drawing for wood-cuts. In the year 1509 he was to paint for Jacob Heller in Frankfort *The Ascension of Mary* (afterward destroyed by fire). "No one shall ever persuade me again to undertake a picture with so much work in it," he writes to the person who ordered it. "I should beggar myself. Of ordinary pictures I can finish such a pile in a year that nobody would believe one man could do so much; but here, with diligent painting, point for point, one does not make any progress; therefore, I will stick to engraving; and if I had done so hitherto I should be richer by a thousand guldens." But Dürer certainly did not work any less faithfully on his engravings. What he did in this line was popular, and established his reputation. Here he is free and full of life to the very marrow. His compositions stand quite by themselves, if I may so express it, and do not remind us of the small scale on which they are executed. They have an intrinsic magnitude quite their own. Had they been made life-size they would not have been greater than they are, as Raphael's *Tapestries* or Michael Angelo's *Sistina* really are no smaller in the smallest engraving than on the enormous surface the originals occupy.

In these works Dürer's imagination shows marvelous creative power. Whilst nowadays attempts are made to vivify New Testament events by introducing attractive foreign scenery with such artistic ingenuity and correctness that we are conjured into believing the lightly sketched figures in these landscapes to be equally real and unquestionable, Dürer, on the contrary, draws his figures sharply in the foreground, concentrates all the life in them, employing for effect German architecture, dress, and household furniture. His representations from the life of Mary are a series of charming idyls woven out of what he gleaned from the country people about him, or among whom he had grown up. Though he had never had a child, and his wife had little that was ideal in her nature, there is yet in these delineations a nursery poetry which is enchanting. No legend, no poem, of whatever kind, could depict so happily a young wife in the midst of the simple domestic surroundings of that age, as Dürer has done in these pictures of Mary. He introduces the angels like the ministering fairies in German legends, and they seem wholly in place; while in the accessories, where his fantasy achieves the most extraordinary combinations of German architecture and Italian Renaissance, we see how naïvely the most foreign of all foreign structures blend with the existing style; and there is something symbolic in this; it was the habit of that day in all things. Hans Sachs, who certainly is not to be placed beside Dürer, is yet to be likened to him in this one respect; if it had come to the point, he would with perfect coolness have introduced Homer, Pindar, Sophocles, and others into German doggerel for the benefit of the Nuremberg public.

In Dürer's works so much of the German life of his day is truthfully portrayed that they transport us into its very midst. He has no preferences, but exhibits just what offers, without a thought of displaying his special skill in one direction or another. His faces of Mary are every-day physiognomies, and we could pick out a number of them which are in no wise beautiful. It would have seemed an impossibility, in his eyes, to give an artificial elevation to his conception, or, for the sake of effect, to pitch the tone one degree higher or lower than was natural. He sketches whatever presents itself with a certain composure (a peculiarity also of Goethe), and paints it to the best of his ability without much ado. There are artists who cannot make a stroke without a dash of pretension in it; while Dürer's works seem as if he had done them incidentally, and found amusement in doing them. Indeed, this seems a distinctive feature of all the purely artistic German work. Goethe's best things, and the poems of Walther von der Vogelweide, of which I am always reminded when I see Dürer's works, inspire the same feeling. All three seem to have wandered through life without any fixed aim, slowly or in ecstatic motion as the spirit compelled. Almost unconsciously they pluck here and there a flower by the wayside, and in the evening lay the nosegay beside them on the table; not until the criticism of the world tells them so do they suspect that their eyes alone could have found these flowers.

Hence a reason why Dürer left no main work! He never seems to have entered into competition with others, nor to have envied any one. When in Antwerp the artists attended him to his house with torches, he was flattered, but neither Venetian ducats nor Netherlandish guldens, though temptingly offered, could prevent him from returning to his old friends in Nuremberg. Dürer's outward life had few incidents, — scarcely any that were at the same time epochs in his artistic development. I have earlier attempted to prove that his Venetian journey in the year 1506 produced a change in his views, and I still abide by these convictions. But in surveying his whole career from beginning to end, we feel that the man remains the same, and can only explain himself (as Goethe once said of him). Born in 1471, in 1506 he goes to Venice for a year, in 1520 to the Netherlands for the same space of time, and dies in 1528. He was fearfully emaciated, and Pirkheimer asserts had been hardly allowed by his wife to leave the house. At any rate, he was confined to his workroom by an ever-increasing sphere of labor; for towards the last he applied himself to writing on architectural and anatomical subjects, besides holding a position in the city, in some respects like that of Michael Angelo's in Florence; he had become a sort of indispensable authority in Nuremberg, and without referring to him few important matters were undertaken. But with regard to all this we have no precise information. At any rate, he was valued as a man of sagacity and tried disinterestedness; and when the world is once convinced that such men are not seeking their own advantage, they are sufficiently in demand. So much respectful consideration was manifested toward him by the council, that Dürer, to show his gratitude, felt it appropriate to make the city a present of a picture. Yet he never fought and suffered as Michael Angelo for Florence; no retinue of painters crowded him as around Raphael; and the few poems by his hand are so clumsy and uncouth, that Hans Sach's language in comparison has a Ciceronian flavor. But that Dürer knew how to express the most profound thoughts is proved by the introduction to his work on *Proportions*, and that his interest in everything going on in the world was most intense the pages of his diary show, — where, on Luther's being taken to the Wartburg, he bursts into lamentations over the loss of such a man. As we read his simple words, ending with the prayer that "God will have pity on the condition of Germany," we understand the character of the people among whom Luther arose.

We are accustomed to look upon the "Reformation" as a movement growing chiefly out of literary antagonisms. The political and moral incentives, whose combined working brought about the final great result, have often been analyzed; but what rôle art here played will be generally known only when the influence of religious art in Germany, and its peculiar nature up to the time of Dürer, has been thoroughly examined and its historical connection demonstrated.

Prior to the "Reformation" the ideas of religion and the contents of sacred history were familiarized to the people mainly through art. Painted walls took the place of books. There is an old Italian engraving, representing the painter Apelles, on which we find these words: "Apelle poeta tacenta," *Apelles who made poems without words.* This poetry without words was quite as intelligible at that time as any written poems. Temples in honor of God, or to the renown of the citizens, filled with little masterpieces of sculpture-painting, etc., were the manifestation of ideas in the silent poem, — symbols of the devotion, pride, and power which to-day finds expression in well-rounded sentences. The statue of a man, ornamental, honorary indeed, yet at the present time not adding a straw's breadth to the measure of his greatness, was at that time a monument which positively created and expressed the veneration of the people. No mere literary phrasing could then have given so clear an idea of the character of a man as Dürer's and Raphael's portraits gave. It would have been supposed impossible in Rome, as well as Germany, to make words suffice for what they were able to do with color, just as it would seem impossible to us to-day to exhaust Shakespeare's *Juliet,* or Goethe's *Iphigenia,* in works of plastic art.

Dürer in his pictures of scenes from the New Testament is not to be likened to our present illustrators. His compositions are at once picture and text. These engravings were scattered over Germany in thousands of copies, imitated everywhere, and etched in Italy even by Marc Anton, who had devoted himself almost exclusively to Raphael's works. These life-like, speaking pictures, with their wealth of meaning, prepared the people in a wonderful way for Luther's translation of the Bible. The German cities had long been overrun with representations of sacred history, many of them, of course, of rare merit. I need only remind you of Adam Krafft's *Stations*, replete with feeling that thrills the heart. Yet no artist was able to depict the events in the life of Christ as Dürer did, so connectedly and with a power which rivets them in our memories until, like Shakespeare's and Goethe's thoughts and creations, they become a part of our souls, and there lead an existence of their own. These Bible pictures by Dürer's hand were indelibly stamped on the minds of the people. Wholly free, at last, from any traces of Byzantine mannerism, they touched every chord in the soul, and gave to scripture history a new and more personal application. Into the midst of all this came Luther's Bible,— the first book in the German language read at one and the same time all over Germany; it contained the veritable text to their pictures. For no one at that time questioned that God had dictated the gospels, word for word, to the evangelists whose names they bear.

But what has made Dürer's influence of special importance is the service he rendered his time, like Giotto at the side of Dante in Italy. We have drolleries enough to be sure of that day, but no purer memorial exists of its higher graces than is to be found in Dürer's life and works, taken as a whole. We recognize in him the jubilant feeling, the spring-like freshness, with which the German people from all sides flocked about Luther, and they explain the child-like, playful vein in which Luther himself — the earnest man — used occasionally to characterize the situation of the moment.

When Luther describes the bird parliament under his window at the Wartburg, — the cackling of the crows, planning a crusade into Turkey, — it seems like one of Dürer's sketches. When hearing Luther tell how, upon the chase in the woods around the castle, a little hare sought refuge from the eager hounds in his wide sleeve, the scene comes before me as if etched by Dürer. It is a pet notion of Dürer to represent his angel-children playing with pretty little hares, when he paints the Madonna in the midst of her innocent court. When Luther speaks of old men and maid-servants, of his wife, the "dominus Ketha," as he calls her in jest, of the children and their little odd ways, of his professional brethren who lie abed terror-stricken lest they should take the English sweating-sickness, and how he persuades them to get up, I imagine his language to spring from the same source as Dürer's strokes upon paper. One man illustrates the other. Ordinary glimpses into the life of that period show a dull, heavy atmosphere hanging over the picture. The people about Luther appear quarrelsome and often vulgar, and in the universal, social, and political strifes, how bald, narrow-minded, and colorless seem the disputes. The general condition is, to a certain extent, dreary and forlorn. But whoever knows Dürer sees the sun still resting upon the picture, and all around the green, laughing fields of Germany. Even poor Emperor Max, in his old age, flitting from one leafless bough to another, like an eagle, holding out in the rain, knowing not where to get his daily food, receives a warm beam from this light and is more comfortable. Krafft, Vischer, Sachs, Pirkheimer, in fact, all the literary men and artists of Nuremberg, gain in freshness and become less professional. Even Holbein, who is so much in himself, cannot dispense with Dürer. Without him he pales, and his connection with the age loosens.

Holbein has also painted New Testament scenes. His compositions are executed with such skill that one might be tempted to try to discover in them some of the feeling which inspires Dürer's pencil. But such attempts would only lead to disappointment. Holbein worked with rare taste and marvellous knowledge of technique, but was personally indifferent to the spiritual significance of these thrilling events; and this dissonance is so striking as to have become his marked characteristic. Holbein has painted nothing that awakens deep enthusiasm. We note immense progress in him, but no development. His Dresden *Madonna* interprets nothing in his earlier or later productions. It stands by itself, a miracle of art. Dürer could not have done this; could not have approached it ever so remotely. Dürer never attempted to paint the beautiful simply for its own sake, or to produce a work whose sole aim was to charm the beholder. He was too childlike for this. He was not merely a painter, he was a Nuremberg painter, whilst Holbein had a universal genius, and was a cosmopolite, whose performances — like Leonardo da Vinci's — resembled rather those of a magician than of an artist human like ourselves. He disappears in England as Leonardo in France, and no record comes to us of their fate. After his stay in London the city rises before us veiled in fog, and just as unfamiliar as if he had never been a visitor within its walls. On the contrary, Dürer's journeys to Venice and the Netherlands are like rifts in clouds which else would wholly conceal the places from our sight. Warm human feeling is needed to render men and times intelligible. But placing Holbein by the side of Dürer, it seems as if they shared each other's genius, and we involuntarily attribute to the former a measure of the wealth of genuine feeling which overflows in the latter.

I return to my opening statement. Dürer's reputation, as understood to-day, is of recent date. What Dürer was to his time and his friends would have been transitory. Many a man, since passed into oblivion, was just as heartily, perhaps even more heartily, mourned and missed than Dürer. The knowledge was reserved for our generation, that Dürer, his works and his times, form as a whole a work of art, complete and indivisible; bearing the unique name of Dürer, but signifying an era.

The great men of Germany have never been renowned for their works alone. Raphael was a painter, Corneille a poet, Shakespeare a poet; but Goethe and Dürer were men. Who would dream of denying their right to this name to the former, but who would not feel that they must lay the greatest stress on the perfection of humanity shown in the two last. Goethe's and Dürer's greatness did not lie essentially in what they produced, but in how they produced it. They bequeathed to posterity but one single perfect work, — themselves.

The works of Raphael, Michael Angelo, Leonardo, and Titian separate from their authors and stand alone; those of Corneille, Racine, Cervantes, Shakespeare, and many others, do likewise. They are ripe, finished, self-sustained creations. The works are more conspicuous than the masters, as peaches beyond the boughs on which they have grown. But the works of the great Germans are below their authors, and make only subordinate elements, — integral parts of an indivisible, coherent life, which in itself occupies the highest place. This peculiarity belongs to German character, and we demand of an artist, if he is really to deserve the name in its highest sense, that he shall bring his whole life into harmony with his works.

What, then, is Dürer's mission in the world of art to-day?

All mature men, filling definite positions in life, feel that on their co-operative power the existence of the nation must rest, and long to be actively and efficiently laboring for the public good. No one can base his life on work which is performed only through the indulgence or the help of others. Such a condition is insupportable. The consciousness of the value of the work must stimulate the laborer. We desire with increasing years to grow into a position which commands universal respect, and constantly to enlarge our horizon.

But what rank do artists take among these progressive forces?

I reply, such as the success of their work gives them. The architect is not esteemed mainly for the beauty of his buildings, but for their technical importance and the money he earns by them; the painter and musician, by the prices they command; the poet and author, by the success of their productions. We have not only a right to consider this outward success, but it is our duty to impress upon those who would enter upon such a career the inevitable intrusion of these low motives. For such is life, and things cannot be changed. Just here, however, we must make an exception. No one would deny that there is a species of labor, elevated by its aim above the common pursuits of life, and whose fruits, although, perhaps, pecuniarily yielding less than nothing to their author, are really nobler than many others which receive the richest reward.

For if we ask what the world honors and esteems as the highest manliness, and the sign of the most aristocratic nature, it is this: to desire nothing from the world, and even to scorn what it offers. The novelist generally pictures the fate of his hero as perfectly tragic, or, to say the least, never represents him surrounded with all the luxuries and blandishments of life. It was Garibaldi's refusal to accept titles, promotion, or gifts, which made him appear so great. He lived a poor man on his rocky isle, and could conceive of no pecuniary reward for his rare achievements.

The number of those, however, who are able to rise to this height of unselfishness is extremely limited, and in any case it is attained only as the result of a life experience; men do not begin so. A man who in his earlier years does not strive to make himself of account in the world is either an invalid or wanting in capacity. To have something to do that yields honor or profit, or that will enable one, born to the gifts of fortune, to be of eminent service in public life, is a necessity to all healthily organized natures. Goethe, Raphael, Shakespeare, Michael Angelo, Beethoven, and many others, left behind money, houses, and estates, and made the acquisition of these a point of interest. Dürer also left a house and a considerable property he had fairly earned. All these men attained their position by indefatigable labor, and not one of them depended on outward support conferred on them for high esthetic reasons. They did occasionally receive gratuities. Dürer in his latter years obtained a sort of imperial pension, which was, however, irregularly enough dealt out to him. The way in which artists were assisted was by conferring upon them commissions worthy of their talent. Many were denied, however, even these, as for instance Dürer; yet this was more of a loss to the people than to the artist. Dürer, if he had nothing to paint in oils, etched or carved or wrote, and did whatever was desired of him. The beauty in his works he gave gratuitously, threw it into the bargain, we may say; for certainly he was no better paid for his works than the other masters. But the peculiar advantage which Dürer, and all artists in his time, had over those of our day (the best as well as the mediocre), was that plastic art, as I have already remarked, was very extensively used as the readiest vehicle for almost all forms of intellectual expression. The artist was as necessary to the people as the public amanuensis to the Roman peasant to-day, to whom is simply confided the subject of the letter, which he writes accordingly.

Dürer, although having the highest ideal conception of his profession, remained to the last an artisan. But whether the work intrusted to him was a large or a small one, whether he was to receive much or little for it, was of far less importance to him than that he should be able to make it a work of art. And herein lies the distinction between the artist and the artisan. Dürer puts his whole soul into his work, and the praise he strives to wring from himself of having rendered it in a manner worthy of his own nature and the subject, is after all his highest reward; which he takes beforehand, and in place of which no extra compensation could have made amends. The consciousness of being an artisan did not prevent him from associating with the learned men of his time, and attaching some value to his social position.

What, then, was Dürer's life? First apprenticed to his father to be a goldsmith, then with Wohlgmuth; after which he wandered about and worked with various masters in one city and another. But from the outset dependent on his own exertions. At last, established in Nuremberg, he became the master of a workshop, and by his glorious character acquired his reputation, constantly striving to come up to his own lofty standard, without which he might have been as unsuccessful, and his works as valueless, as the other innumerable productions of the masters around him.

Dürer was never the man to call himself an artist, or, because he carved and painted, to think he was doing anything remarkable. He was a Nuremberg burgher and master. He painted when pictures were ordered, etched, and sold his engravings singly or in numbers; but worked on steadily, without much regard either to criticism or renown. Not the encouragement

Dürer received made him a worker, but his innate talent, which must come out. Like a living spring, which flies upward all the same whether it is to fall again into a marble basin or be turned off into a horse-trough. It will up and aloft, what further as God will.

The views change which a nation holds of its men. At first Dürer was only the renowned engraver; to his friends, the truest and most delightful companion. Pirkheimer writes upon his tombstone, "What was mortal of Albrecht Dürer lies beneath this stone." A hundred years later this did not seem enough to Sandrart, and he added an epitaph extolling Dürer as the "prince of artists." Later still he was portrayed with dark, burning eyes, curls, and an imposing beard; but this, too, had been outlived. His pictures one by one have disappeared from Nuremberg, the greater part of them having been transported to foreign countries, till at last precious little remains there save his engravings.

Years glided by, when at last the interest taken by Goethe in Dürer awakened a fuller and more general appreciation of him. Goethe was the first to feel the artist in his works, and he proved from them the adorable nature of the man. At the close of the last century many of Dürer's manuscripts found their way again to the light. In the beginning of the present, when the opposition to the old school in Germany gained the ascendency, disciples of the new theories made Dürer their apostle. The excitement about him steadily increased, and at the three hundredth anniversary of his death the enthusiasm reached its climax in Nuremberg and Munich. A statue was erected to him; henceforth his name should herald the renaissance of German art.

This ardor has, to be sure, somewhat abated; but real appreciation of the man gains steadily. And yet, as I have said, Dürer is known to fame, while still unknown to the people at large; only the few having a comprehensive idea of his life, his works, his influence. Photography has made it possible to obtain the greater part of his productions. Photo-lithographic copies of the *Passion*, and especially of scenes from the *Life of Mary*, are now to be bought, and wherever they go kindle appreciation of the truth and intense feeling in Dürer's works. One must see the productions of a man before he can understand him; therefore, with all our veneration for the man, the full knowledge of his greatness is yet in the future. But those who love him will ever cherish the idea that in his personality, in his character, is to be found his highest worth. The unpretending nature of his works is a part of their excellence, as his almost uneventful career was one of the essentials in his development.

Who knows him not is deficient in a knowledge of German history; but those who do not know him will always hear in the name of Dürer the inspiring tones of Germany, — the Fatherland.

THE BROTHERS GRIMM.

On the 16th of December, 1859, at three o'clock in the afternoon, William Grimm died. He was buried on the morning of the 20th, in the Matthäikirchehofe in Berlin. The wind blew icy-chill as the coffin was borne up the hill, on whose gradual slope the new graveyard lies. Beside the open grave stood Jacob Grimm and William's two sons. Tears flowed from every eye when Jacob, uncovering his head, stooped down, and, taking up a handful of earth, threw it in after the lifeless form now to be left alone in the cold depth.

William Grimm was born at Hanau in 1786. The incidents of his external life are to be read in many places. They were few and simple. His father died early. With his mother and the other children he went to Cassel, where he attended school. Owing to a serious illness in his twelfth year, his health continued through life extremely delicate, and his labors and manner of living were regulated accordingly. His first visit to Berlin was in 1809, when he went thither to stay with his intimate friend, Achin von Arnim. The succeeding years he spent chiefly in Cassel. In 1825 he married there, and some years later removed with Jacob to Göttingen, which town he afterwards left with his brother to return to Cassel, from thence they were soon called to Berlin, here to spend the remainder of their days. The brothers had one house, one library, one purse.

In recalling William Grimm's career, however, it is not with the changes of the years or places of abode that our minds are occupied. Even his dearest friends, if they would know the exact sequence of these events, must hunt them up in encyclopædias. Our feeling at the loss of a man whom we have known and loved has little to do with the mere incidents in his career, which latter it is the work of a biographer to set forth. How few of those who most deeply lamented the loss of Humboldt knew more of him than that he was born in 1769, and, after extensive travels in Asia and America, spent the rest of his life chiefly in Berlin. The conception of a person retained by his contemporaries is no mere schedule, however long, of his achievements or vicissitudes, but a clear comprehension of their worth, position, and power while living, and of the void left behind at their departure.

This was the feeling when Bettina or when Humboldt died. The extent of what we had lost was measured by the magnitude of what we must henceforth live without. It is not a year since both passed away. As writer and poet, when Bettina died, her labors had long ceased; but as an intellectual power, as having the keenest eyes for whatever was great or fair, and the most eloquent lips to describe it, she might have lived on forever. Humboldt, the man of science, had embodied in the *Cosmos* the result of his long and gigantic labors, had apparently finished his work on earth; he was old and wearied, and had now a claim to immortality. We had no right to detain him longer; yet, as patron of all and every intellectual effort, we cannot but wish that he might have lived for centuries; there is no one to fill his place. He never repulsed any one, or overlooked genuine merit; and where he recognized talent, protected it. He often gratified men with flattering speeches, because, in his long experience, he had discovered the stimulating effect of this small coin; but he was far too sincere to give only this. He used his great influence at court to have superior ability rewarded and given the high position it deserved, lending personal aid and support freely whenever it was necessary. He expressed his opinion with courage, and openly. This was the irretrievable loss to us when his eyes closed in death.

And in William Grimm what we miss and passionately deplore is, not the man, who with untiring assiduity did all that in him lay for the glory of Germany. This he did, and his share was large indeed. He was almost seventy-four years old, and had a right to enter into his rest. From book to book he had pressed steadily forward; not a day of his life had passed unimproved. The *Kinder-Märchen* (the Danish songs which he translated), the German sagas, editions of old poems, academic treatises, and, finally, his share in the great German dictionary, unite to form a crown full and rich enough to cover his temples. It would be unreasonable to desire that he should further toil. And he, too, had reached a kind of terminus. Just as he dropped upon his bed, in his last brief illness, the letter *D* of the *Wörtenbuch* (his last undertaking) was finished, a new edition of the *Märchen* ready, which he examined, and selected the copies to be distributed among his friends; a new edition of Freidank's *Bescheidenheit* finished in manuscript, and finally, a lecture he intended to deliver in the Academy of Science on the 15th of December.

But who of those who knew him intimately regard even these as more than subsidiary to the nobler memories which cling to his life and person? We think of his gentleness, his repose, his broad, fair judgments, and the perpetual geniality which, like a fresh, beneficent atmosphere, surrounded him. His friends ascribe all this to him from his earliest years. An optimism of the most generous kind was born in him. Even when things were in the wildest confusion, he sought and found the way to a good issue. And in this tone he uttered his last words, while already rapt in dreams.

He denied what was evil as long as he could; but once fully recognized, threw no mantle over it, and if it threatened to approach moved out of its sphere. With marvelous patience he adapted himself to the inevitable. The conscientiousness with which he strove to perfect his work he extended to all the relations of life. Perhaps his most charming feature was his capacity of imparting to all who approached him his own tranquillity, and cheerful, grateful recognition of the blessings of life. He gladly went back to places he had once visited, and retraced the old familiar paths. He took a lively interest in recalling past events and interests. With what tenderness he spoke of the departed whom he had once known! How irrevocably strong in him was the tie of early friendship! It was cherished with sacred reverence. The nature of his social intercourse can never be described. William Grimm was *liebenswürdig* in the highest sense of the word. As in the *Märchen* he caught the poetry of the people, rendering their very words with an art which in itself was poetry, and which no one has since attained, although so much attention has been given to this branch of literature; so in his lightest narrations he caught the naïve aspect of things, and set them forth in the simplest and most natural manner. He loved to tell stories. He elevated the character of social intercourse by infusing his whole nature and soul into his words. In his strictly scientific works, in his more lightly conceived essays, prefaces and letters, always and everywhere we perceive the same delight in the contemplation of things, and the same felicity of expression in communicating this joy to others. And this capacity for happiness increases with his years. Ever more cheerful and more contented as his days roll on. Up to the last moment this serenity continues. How gladly he renders a friendly service! How willingly receives one in return when offered! He recognizes the smallest token of kindness, accepting it with heartfelt gratitude.

What has been here said is merely the image memory presents to those who, overcome by the blow which has fallen upon them so unexpectedly, can speak but of what is nearest to them. We do not eulogize such men, we only name them. Not a syllable of praise was spoken over his coffin; it stood close beside his writing-desk, the books still open upon it as if he had just been reading them, — the inkstand, the pen, the little scraps of paper bearing miscellaneous notes, the pictures on the walls, — each one a memento of beloved people or places; it was impossible to believe that he was nevermore to look at them. But this feeling must pass. The world is poorer by the loss of one man; others will step forward in his place. His friends will console themselves in the flight of years, speak of him less frequently; but his image will grow ever more and more distinct, until by degrees what he has done will concentrate itself in his very name. So long as the German language endures, so long will the name of William Grimm be in itself a word signifying a noble man, whose life and talents were consecrated to his people.

Berlin, Dec. 21, 1859.

APPENDIX TO

JACOB GRIMM'S ORATION ON HIS BROTHER.

DELIVERED IN THE ACADEMY OF SCIENCE, JULY 5, 1860.

ON beginning to speak Jacob Grimm had been, as usual, somewhat hoarse, and the words came with a certain hesitation. Only by degrees did the discourse flow on smoothly. He was the last to speak at the sitting, and it was already late. Many will ever remember him as he stood holding the written leaves turned toward the window to gain a better light, whilst the fading beams of day fell upon his white hair.

William's illness and death had come unexpectedly. On his return from a little journey in the autumn of 1859, he had seemed unusually fresh and vigorous. His malady at first appeared quite insignificant. Suddenly dangerous symptoms set in; a carbuncle developed on his back, which did not yield to treatment. At last, however, he believed the trouble overcome. "God be praised," said my father, sitting up in his bed; "I had really thought it would end fatally, and I have still so much to do." That he had had a presentiment he should not live through the winter is clear from certain directions found among his papers, which were later carried out for the printing of the new edition of *Freidank*.

In one night all was decided; violent fever set in, and on the morning of December 16th he died. He was not wholly conscious at the last. Jacob was sitting on a low stool beside his pillow, almost counting every breath he drew. He recognized him, but fancied it was his picture, and said, "It looks very like him." He spoke much, and, strange to say, just before his death, owing to the sudden working of some secret law, the confused thoughts arranged themselves clearly and succinctly. In well-formed, calmly-evolved sentences, he talked of himself, of what he had planned, what accomplished; glided from past to present, and gave his opinion of the political condition; taking the same serene, hopeful view of things he had always done, and ending so naturally that we had not seen he was struck with death. Such a revelation of thought must have implied full possession of healthily working powers.

The papers were filled with the most romantic accounts of Jacob's condition after the death of his brother. In despair, he was said to be wandering about in the lonely rooms, seeking for him who was no more. Nothing of the kind was true. He accepted the event very quietly, although he of all had least expected it. Toward the dawn of the last day, as I went to awaken him, I heard his quiet breathing; he was peacefully asleep. "Ah, my God!" he said, "I had thought all would now go on well." After my father was dead, he often went into the study where he lay to gaze at him long and earnestly. At the funeral, he walked between my brother and myself up the gentle slope of the burial-ground, in the piercing wind, stepping firmly over the crackling snow. It will also never be forgotten by those standing around the grave, how he stooped, and with his delicate fingers picked out a clod of earth which he threw after the coffin. There was no change perceptible in his general demeanor. He immediately resumed his customary work, and went on with it in the old way.

This calmness under his heavy trial, and which rendered it possible for him to speak of it publicly, surely arose from the feeling that, at most, the separation was only for a very few years. How passionately, in earlier days, the thought of William's dying before him had excited him. I read in a letter to Lachmann, with whom he maintained unbroken correspondence from 1820 to 1840, and to whom he opened his heart as to no one else.

My father was also in correspondence with Lachmann, and all the letters and answers are before me.

"How long, dear Lachmann," he writes 21st February, Göttingen, "I have striven to find a leisure day or quiet hour in which to reply to your consoling letter of December 28th, and to inform you of all that has befallen us. On the day when the in every respect disgusting riot in this place came to an end, William, who had probably taken cold during the previous night watching over the threatened library, went to bed ill. The first few days inspired no alarm. We supposed it a return of the catarrhal fever which from time to time had troubled him; but after one fit of coughing came a hemorrhage,—a dangerous sign of inflammation of the lungs, and his life was manifestly in danger. Heaven graciously listened to our supplications, and improvement soon appeared; since then he has by degrees, but slowly, recovered, although he has not yet his full vigor. With what anguish of heart I sat during these heavy days at his table, covered with his work; how everything I looked at pained me,—his books, his writings, the order and neatness everywhere, absorbed as I was with the idea that perhaps all this might end at one fell stroke, and that my own life must be spent in mourning and longing for him. I cannot describe my feelings; I can only say, that I prayed to God ardently, and thanked him fervently for the mercy he has shown us. After such days one breathes freely, as after a terrible thunder-storm, and is prepared to endure bravely other trials, which do not take the very heart out of us."

What he has here said is repeated in the preface to a new part of the grammar then in progress, which was dedicated to William. In this he says, that he almost believes he wrote all his books specially for him, since nobody else accepted them in such a true spirit. The dedications of their books form a record of their friendships. Scarcely one of the intimate friends has been omitted.

The lives of both up to the time when they left Cassel for Göttingen they have themselves related in autobiographies composed for Justi.

What I shall here attempt to give is merely a glimpse of their last years, by way of introduction to Jacob Grimm's discourse upon *Old Age*, of which he could not have written so eloquently had it not been his own experience.

Jacob speaks of those first years in Cassel as being the happiest in his life. The position offered in Göttingen was in every respect an honorable reparation for the injury which made a longer stay in their chosen home impossible; on the other hand, they missed the leisure for their special work, which they had there enjoyed in the richest measure. Instead of three working hours, and even these devoted for the most part to their own matters, twice that number was demanded in Göttingen. It was hard to accustom themselves to it, and in the letters to Lachmann this is often expressed; hence when upon their banishment to Göttingen they returned to the old place, where, wholly undisturbed, they might once more dedicate their lives to their own work, amid all the sad circumstances by which it was attended, they really at heart felt it to be a blessing. The most painful part of it all was, that from now on between the old Cassel friends who took their side, and those who openly, or covertly, drew back from them, there must be a separation. They lost many friends at this time, but fresh ones came in their place, and from this period date most of the close friendships which were the joy of their latter years; the intimate union with Dahlmann and Gervinus, with whom they had long been acquainted, was now formed, which remained unbroken to the last. I here introduce part of a letter to Lachmann after the first impression had somewhat subsided, and the brothers (who did not leave Göttingen together) were reunited, and firmly established in Cassel.

CASSEL, May 12, 1840.

The sun which for three weeks has shone unintermittingly, and brought forward the most beautiful spring I think I ever knew in my life, since yesterday is again behind the clouds, and all too quickly cold weather has set in upon us. Yet your letter has been like the warmth of the sun to me, and I rejoice that you still love us; for in my heart is the old friendships and affection. There have been some things which grieved and annoyed me, but they were not great ones; most painful to me has been the occasional suspicion that you were more and more drawing back from us, and no longer taking the same interest in our life and work. It would be natural, I suppose, that just now we should be very sensitive. Had you come alone and stayed longer with us last autumn, everything would then have been satisfactorily explained. I have indeed never had the slightest cause to reproach you as to your conduct in this matter; your opinion was always given openly and honestly, and in so many essential points coincided with ours, that it has afforded me much satisfaction; it was neither to be expected, nor was it necessary, that you should agree to everything at once. But reticence and the refusal to give a distinct opinion, though coupled with a sympathy which I am sure was intended to be sincere as was my experience with ——, wounded me. In all he said he seemed to imply that he had been kept in ignorance of the facts necessary, for complete insight into the matter; whilst they lie so openly and fully before the world that I cannot conceive how anybody can withhold his decision in this case, if he has the courage to pronounce judgment on any historical event whatsoever. I have never yet repented our step for an instant, and when I think of Göttingen praise God that he has taken me away from the place which I should now feel to be insufferable. I still stand the trial when I ask myself what a Greek or Roman would or would not have done in our situation. The act to me, at the time of its occurrence, seemed much more insignificant; simply natural and right, and I believe nothing avails men and nations but to be just and brave; this is the basis of all sound policy. Whether any or what kind of fruit shall come of it lies in God's directing hand; there are trees which spread out their broad arms according to their strength, which bear no fruit, and are only to afford shade and verdure in the land. I cannot, however, restrain the thought (and it makes me so much the more humble) that this may prove a spark without which the fire of resistance would not have been kindled that is now becoming a blessing to our whole country. For the future of the German nation depends on the public regard for the sentiments of honor and freedom.

I am not hostile to the world, and cling with ardent love to my country. But, after my Göttingen experience, once more in the peaceful retirement of Cassel I feel that I am so much happier here, that if we Protestants had the institution of monastic life, without other monkish worship, I would gladly pass the rest of my short span of life thus apart from the maddening crowd. It is my nature to learn less from intercourse and teaching than from my own efforts. It has also disinclined me to social intercourse, that almost all talks or discussions are brought to bear upon these public affairs of ours, which is most disagreeable and painful. And what should I be in the turmoil of Berlin? I could accomplish nothing there, either for myself or others, which could not be done more agreeably almost anywhere else. Heaven grant and help that Prussia may not hinder, but guide and stimulate, the rest of Germany!

Some months after these words were written, however, came the call to Berlin, which was accepted.

Among Jacob's papers I found one directed to Savigny, in which he gives his reasons for refusing the summons to Bonn in the year 1816. The salary in

Cassel was extremely small, but he writes: "I confess the money consideration influences my decision very little, as my limited wants make this of trifling importance, and I am confident that I shall always have enough to live honorably." Nor would they have gone to Berlin in 1840 had their circumstances left them any choice. William had been there in 1809 to visit Achin von Arnim; the city had pleased him so little, that when not long after Savigny was called from Landshut thither, he sincerely pitied him. Since that time, however, great changes had taken place in Berlin; but the brothers shrank from the turmoil of the large, distant city, where they feared they should always feel themselves to be strangers. Jena or Leipzig, or best of all Marburg, would have seemed very much nearer; they would gladly have remained in Hesse, which is, perhaps, the country in all Germany most passionately loved by its inhabitants. Notwithstanding this attachment, which never diminished, after they had made their choice and entered Berlin, the first unfavorable impression was wholly reversed; they found retirement, comfort, and resources in a far greater degree than they had enjoyed in Cassel. Both the brothers were very happy in Berlin, and my father especially often represented to strangers in the clearest light the advantages this city afforded. Independent, absolute masters of their time, relieved from every social obligation, they soon created for themselves a true home, and, as compared with former years, the health of both had so much improved, there remained little to wish for.

Over twenty years their labors in Berlin went on continuously. Journeys infringed but little, the longest interruption for Jacob being a visit to Italy and a stay in Frankfort, when he was elected member of Parliament in 1848. He lectured in the university only a few years, but rarely failed to be present at the sittings of the Academy of Science, and often delivered the treatise. Of these dissertations he enjoyed giving his friends printed copies, and it was his intention to have published a collection of them; but as he wished to remodel them, this was postponed from time to time, and he was never able to accomplish it. His published works, ranged in serried files, stood all around his work-table so that from his chair he could comfortably reach any one of them. He, and William also, had the *Wörtenbuch* printed with very broad margins, and the separate sheets lay in piles beside his writing-desk, these margins quite covered with supplementary remarks. After William's death Jacob laid his brother's copy beside his own. All these books, objects of reverence to us for so many years, now stand orphaned, with a dubious fate before them. For to whom will all this labor be of value? Among Jacob's papers was found one of an early date containing the express command that after his death all his notes should be burned. To be sure, they would be of little use to others, as he alone had the key to them. His books he thought might again be used.

He loved his books — the word is not too strong — dearly, and the joint library was under his special protection. He had the different works bound in a variety of ways after his special directions, and indulged his taste in this matter to the point of luxury. The good or better opinion he entertained of a book was indicated by the less or more costly bindings.

Occasional things intended for presents were bound in purple velvet. The *Freidank*, printed after the death of my father, received the most costly binding which could be made. It was quite natural that he who for many years had been a librarian should regard his own library as a kind of personality. He often surveyed with satisfaction the rows of books, took down this or that volume, looked into it, closed it, and put it back again in its place. It pleased him to jump up and find the book which others had searched for in vain.

When upon my father's death his room was added to the library, he arranged the books with his own hands after a new plan. He could lay his hand in the dark upon every book in his library. He did not like to lend them, because he was in the habit of writing in them, and inserting scraps of paper covered with annotations. Many volumes bear on the fly-leaf a double index, one in William's and one by Jacob's hand. In a letter to Lachmann, he speaks jocosely of the future auction of his books, and how the people will wonder that such costly volumes as the magnificent edition of the *Nibelungen* should be found among them; he also once said to me that the books would be scattered after his death and my father's, and that no one else understood the system according to which the collection had been made; when on such occasions he was contradicted, he let it pass. Many times we had assured him that the books should not be divided or sold at auction, and still, even in his last hours, while his eyes showed that he understood all that was said, and we were trying to say what would please and quiet him, we repeated the promise that the library should be reverently preserved. Perhaps a place will be found for it in some university, where it will be serviceable and help to perpetuate the remembrance of its founder.

With my father, the apprehension was natural that old age might deprive him of his freshness and working power. He had not so well resisted the effects of time. Whilst formerly he had enjoyed spending his evenings in society, he now gradually withdrew from it; he first gave up going out, and afterwards limited the reception of guests at home to a small circle. It was no deprivation, but a change. With Jacob this was not so, however; from youth up somewhat more reserved, his habits remained unchanged to the end. He worked all day, but was not unwilling to be interrupted, and was always ready and happy to receive visitors. The course of political events he followed with interest. When the newspaper came, he usually laid his pen aside to peruse it without delay. His temperament was one of uniform cheerfulness. It was easy to give him pleasure. Both brothers loved to have flowers at the window, and tended them with care. My father was specially fond of the primrose, which blooms continuously and unfolds its leaves in graceful symmetry; while Jacob had a preference for the yellow wallflower and heliotrope. Upon their writing-tables, which were covered with a variety of keepsakes, they were glad to have a few fresh flowers in a glass. These friendly mementos at last took much room, but they enjoyed seeing them increase, and always found place for the new-comers. Jacob, in his last years, took great delight in small photographic portraits. A considerable number was soon collected, and he lost no opportunity to add to the store. He brought everything that was sent him over to show us, even books in unknown languages, from which he would read a sentence here and there, laughing heartily because none of us understood a word. He was fond of reading aloud; not long chapters for their special eloquence or beauty, but terse, pithy sentences which startled us. He spoke French fluently, and when the Japanese embassy, during their visit to Berlin, called on him, addressed them in Dutch. Most moving and beautiful were his words when on birthdays and like occasions he gave the toast; it was always something unexpected and weighted with the accent of sincere affection.

My father needed repose for his work; interruption disturbed him; he thought everything had its time, and did not like sudden resolutions. Jacob, who, if he had a journey before him, often resolved upon it only the preceding night, and who wrote all his books at once just as they were to be printed, without a fresh draught or changes, was always willing to be interrupted at any time. To pause in his work for the sake of giving a bit of information here, or to gather news there, or glean from strangers accounts of their work, which he would follow up with genuine interest, — all this was to him agreeable relaxation. In later years these chance interruptions were not enough; my mother and sister systematically enticed him away from his writing-table, since if left to himself he worked all day long, and then the infirmities of age showed even in him. Perhaps he might have been preserved to us for many years yet, if he had consented to work less.

Toward the last, his rest at night was not always unbroken; he would wake up, and could not go to sleep again.

"How beautiful the long summer days, hailed with joy by birds and men! They recall the spring-time of life, when the hours drink in light and flow slowly away; it is only what remains over that is swallowed up in the gloom of winter and old age. Now I shall soon be seventy-eight; and when I lie sleepless in bed the dear, soft light comforts me, and inspires thoughts and recollections. JACOB GRIMM."

June 3, 1862.

These words were found written on a little card in his pocket-book. From his youth he had a fondness for gazing at the stars. In a letter to Lachmann he complains that he had lost the view from his chamber window of the glorious Pleiades. As an old man, when he could not sleep, he would sometimes get up and go to the window to look at the heavens.

We had thought that he might live on thus for many a year. In the spring of 1863, when his brother Ludwig Grimm, painter and professor in the academy at Cassel, died, he said, "Now I am the only one left," but without a thought that his turn was to come so soon. When collecting what had been written on old age, prior to rewriting his own essay on the subject, he received as a present Flouren's book *Sur la Longévité*, in which the average age of man is computed at one hundred years, he jokingly remarked that he intended to live so long. That he would sometimes lie down for a while, or sitting at his table rest his head on his folded arms, indicated to us rather the natural need of repose than any decline of strength; for when it seemed to him essential, he could work all day without interruption. Little did he anticipate himself that he should so soon be interrupted forever! He had still much work in view. He would go on with the *Wörterbuch*, a new preface to the *Märchen* was to be written, another volume of the *Weisthümer* published, for which a comprehensive and far-reaching introduction was to be prepared. He had also intended writing a book on German habits and customs, a work on Ossian lay in the future, and probably plenty of other things known only to himself. His last printed essay was a criticism of the work of Jonckbloet, about Reinhard, in the Göttingen *Anzeigen;* he would next have written on Goethe's correspondence with Carl August. I found upon his table a freshly folded sheet with the title of the book at the top. For this end, he was anxious to read Goethe's correspondence with Frau von Stein, and begged me, if I meant to buy the book (as had been my intention), to do so at once. The last things he read were some leaves sent to him, of a collection of Greek myths, which he had looked through with great interest, and covered with pencil-marks. It was his habit to read books as soon as received, and he always did so, with pencil in hand. In this way he has left behind innumerable scraps of notes and citations.

As in my father's case, a little autumn journey just before his final illness had seemed to be of special benefit to him. He caught cold soon after his return, and inflammation of the liver set in, which, however, seemed to subside. His days were good, he was able to read for hours together in bed, but his nights were restless and feverish. The physician advised his getting up a little, in the hope of making the nights more comfortable. On Saturday afternoon, when he attempted this for the second time, my sister, sitting near the window, felt him falling against her. It was apoplexy which had struck the right side. He passed into a state of drowsiness; he could move his leg at moments when awake, but his arm less easily, and he spoke with difficulty. He often touched his right arm with his left, as if to discover how it was with him. This was through the night. Towards Sunday morning his consciousness apparently grew clearer; he turned his eyes upon us all, and the friends standing around him; seemed to understand what we said to him. Once we thought we had lost him, when he suddenly took up a photograph of William, brought it close before his eyes, as he was wont to do, looked at it for some moments, and laid it down upon the coverlet. Sunday, September 20th, at twenty minutes past ten in the evening he drew his last breath. His final resting-place has been prepared beside his brother's, according to his express desire.

BETTINA VON ARNIM.

BETTINA VON ARNIM, according to Lewes, fills a larger space in the literary history of the nineteenth century than any other German woman; but her works are not greatly read to-day, and even in her lifetime the distinction she won was to be attributed, in part certainly, to her altogether rare and elevated nature. Gifts she had indeed, and was both intellectual and accomplished; but, better still to those who knew her, she was a very sunbeam in the flesh, and gave not only light, but a spark of Promethean fire, to all who approached her. Through a wretched translation of her principal work, she appears to the English reading public only as the most exaggerated sentimentalist of a sentimental age, — the Dorcasina Sheldon of modern times. That this was neither her character nor style is proved by the abundant testimony of many talented men still living, who speak of a debt of gratitude to her such as they are conscious of to no other. — *Translator's Note.*

BETTINA was born at Frankfort-on-the-Main April 4th, 1785. She married Achin von Arnim 1811 in Berlin. The correspondence of *Goethe with a Child* appeared in 1835. She died on the 20th of January, 1859.

Her correspondence with Goethe had been preceded by one with her brother Clemens Brentano and with the Stiftsdame Caroline von Gunderöde. In these three books is contained the narrative of Bettina's childhood and youth; of these times she gives the most graphic and pleasing description. Her mother was the Maximiliane von La Roche, whom Goethe pictures so charmingly between childhood and maidenhood, as she first came to greet him in her mother's house, and whom he afterward held so dear when a young wife in Frankfort. Maximiliane's character afforded material which completed his picture of Lotte in the *Sorrows of Werther*, while her husband, Brentano, (Bettina's father) gave the final emphasis to the uncomfortable Albert of the romance. She was Brentano's second wife, and after her early death his quickly followed. Many brothers and sisters, all distinguished for beauty and wit, — and in the idiosyncrasies of their natures best understood by one another, — formed a large and closely linked family which attracted into its circle a host of dearly beloved relations and friends. The old family mansion of the "Golden Head" in the Sandgasse in Frankfort was the central home of this republican community, within which Bettina's nature unfolded itself freely.

In a kind of idyllic narration of personal events the genius of Bettina and her brother, Clemens Brentano, shines forth most brilliantly. An inexhaustible vitality and freshness favored her desire ever to behold the world under new aspects. Bettina was never ill, never ailing, until during the very last years of her life, and not even variable, like most of us, in temperament. A victorious soul dwelt in her. She was brimming over with a happy confidence that things were taking the right direction. She demanded large intercourse with people, and an active participation in important affairs. She was a cosmopolite, and from childhood accustomed to change of place. We find her on the Main, the Rhine, in Bavaria, Austria, Thuringia,—always and everywhere surrounded by friends and relatives.

The scope which had been allowed her as a maiden Bettina looked upon as proper and essential to her through life. The future must stand before her rich in anticipations if she was to be content. The state of society in her day favored these views. Old forms in Germany were disintegrating. Fresh talent springing up everywhere, and not to be diverted from its proper channel, or monopolized or quenched by party spirit. Each pursued quietly his own path, while a great aim was common to all. Poetry, philology, natural sciences, philosophy, and politics formed one great sea, over which each took his own course, with the sails of all the others constantly in sight. The young and gifted, heedless of the past, lived in the expectation of tremendous events which the next day was to bring forth. Now, as I read the early letters of my father and uncle, I realize how all interest in the past had disappeared, while prosperity and happiness seemed to lie only in the future. Bettina was permitted to enjoy an intimate friendship with the noblest of those who thought and worked in this spirit, and she penetrated even into the processes of their intellectual labors. Both Goethe's and Beethoven's letters to her, known to us to-day as genuine, prove how much earnestness they found in her. Earnestness was the sign-manual of that day. Bettina possessed the power to absorb the ideas of her epoch, and to develop them in many directions. Her acquaintance with Goethe was the goal toward which all her youthful efforts and strivings had tended.

Bettina came to Berlin at the same time with Savigny, who had been called to the new university. Savigny's wife was Bettina's sister. Thither also repaired Clemens Brentano. He was seven years older than Bettina, and like herself had been for years an intimate friend of Achin von Arnim. Among Arnim's letters to my father and uncle the most beautiful certainly is that in which his marriage with Bettina is described. When my father spoke of Von Arnim, it was always in a peculiarly reverent tone, as if the stately form of his friend rose upon his inward sight. Goethe and Arnim were his most precious memories. Hallowed seem the great talents of men who have been too early snatched from earth. There was in Arnim's nature the all-conquering, joyous tone, which distinguished Bettina, although it found a different expression. Bettina was a child of the South, with dark hair and dark eyes; she was fearless and direct, and sought to mould circumstances to her will. Arnim was of the North, and more reserved. He was born for a country life. He was the genuine Prussian nobleman. Wherever he appeared, I have heard it said, men felt that a good spirit had come among them. A certain atmosphere of distinction surrounded him, and a happy, soul-stirring energy, which he communicated to others. He was courteous, elegant, handsome, free, brave, and single-hearted. His style of writing had all these qualities. No greater contrast could be found than between his writings and Clemens Brentano's, as exhibited in their correspondence. Arnim's name is surrounded with a peculiar lustre in our literary history, but his works are not widely known, and the best things in them have not been winnowed out.

When Bettina came to North Germany the struggle with Napoleon was just beginning, and Berlin was full of excitement. Then came the war, with its triumphant issue; but after this elation passed away Germany relapsed into a state of monotony and dreariness, which increased day by day. Naught remained of the gigantic hopes which for long years previous had stimulated the people, and whose sure fulfilment the war for freedom seemed to prophesy. As early as 1820 Goethe spoke of the "utter worthlessness of the present."

Bettina now threw herself into her family life. With her children around her she lived for many years in the retirement of their country home. Of these quiet years she tells us little. The most important event which marked them was her acquaintance with Schleiermacher, who confirmed her sons, and with whom she exchanged letters full of interesting matter, which are as yet unprinted.

Immediately after her marriage Bettina had become estranged from Goethe. She went to Weimar at that time with Arnim, and displeased Goethe by her manner toward his wife. I have letters in Arnim's own hand to Riemar, in which he strove to gain, at least, a meeting with Goethe; but Goethe refused, the old friendship was broken, and Bettina and Arnim mourned the loss bitterly. It was most natural that they should look forward to a reunion. In the beginning of 1820 the idea was seized upon in Frankfort of erecting a monument to Goethe in his native city. In Boisserel's letters, as well as in Rauch's *Life of Eggers*, we read many of the details concerning it. In the last pages of the diary which forms the third part of *Correspondence with a Child* Bettina tells how the sketch for a monument to Goethe arose in her mind, which she afterward took to Weimar; she would show the world how Goethe had appeared to her from the beginning. For years she pursued this matter, into which Arnim entered with a like enthusiasm. In 1831 Arnim died, and in the following year Goethe. Chancellor von Müller returned to Bettina her letters found among Goethe's posthumous papers. The thought now came over her to erect, in her own way, this monument to Goethe, which they had not been able to execute in marble. Her sketch should find a place on the first leaf of the *Correspondence with a Child*, and face the title-page bearing the dedication, "Scniem Denkmale," *For his Monument*. Doubly bereft, Bettina found in this work the occupation she needed. Thoughts of the far-off days of youth awoke in her soul as she pored over the old letters. What she would have said and written to Goethe, but never did, and at the same time what, according to her own conception, Goethe might have said in reply, should now find expression. The fruits should hang riper and sweeter on the boughs than in her early days, and weigh down the branches to meet the hand which was to pluck them. This was the key-note to this unique book of which Mensebach, in closing his review of it, said justly, that "it would with difficulty escape immortality."

In recalling the days of our youth Fancy sits like Penelope at the loom, drawing out of the web the old threads in order to weave them over anew. Even the most exact memory, when gathering up and laying together the things which have constituted its earthly experience, will join the threads so as to produce something like a work of art. Goethe in *Dichtung and Wahrheit* has acknowledged the necessity and naturalness of this process.

Let us now consider what Bettina's personal share in this work really was. She had related to Goethe the stories of her childhood, just as her mother told them, at the same time giving him her rendering, and saying how she had reconstructed the legends to suit her fancy. Goethe received these letters with delight, and as we see the use he made of them, it is quite possible that it was Bettina who first struck the tone in which he later wrote his biography. Certain it is that the desire to make experience conform to what "it *might have been*" moved Bettina to write this *Correspondence*. She never dreamed of any one's regarding this book, in which Goethe is made the inspiration of her young life, as anything but a work of art. She freely confessed what she had added to it, saying that in truth she had never loved Goethe passionately.

We will now pass on to examine what Goethe's real letters to Bettina contain, which Dr. Von Loeper has published, so far as they could be obtained, together with those to her grandmother, Sophie von La Roche. "Thy letters," Goethe writes to Bettina, May, 1810, just as he was leaving for Carlsbad, "travel with me and shall keep thy refreshing, lovely image ever before me. I do not say more to thee, for truly one can give thee nothing, because thou either takest or createst all within thyself. Farewell, and think of me." The letter was sealed with a little amor, but neither by Bettina nor Goethe was this symbol interpreted seriously; and, precisely as the letter stands, how much of what may be called fatherly love is expressed in Goethe's words, and how much he acknowledges equality also. We have at hand a vast amount of material, and can compare what Goethe said to others in letters; to whom, after the times of Frau von Stein, has he declared that he could give nothing? He appreciates Bettina's mental wealth, and allows her to feel the closest affinity with him, — nothing more. The passion which fills Bettina's letters did not come into play between the actual Goethe and herself as they met in life, but between the imaginary Goethe and a feigned Bettina, later born.

We know how Goethe himself, in the writing of *Werther*, was transported with a passion for Lotte, which he had long ceased to feel, — perhaps never had felt so powerfully as he represents. He writes of what might have been. It was almost a year, before, free from the reality, his poetic imagination acquired intensity enough for the romance. Bettina had borne these things in her mind over twenty years ere the fitting opportunity came to give them expression, and she was capable in a far greater measure than Goethe of transforming real experiences into myths. In fact, to such an extent did she possess this gift that often in the very midst of events they assume to her a legendary form. Her grandmother, Sophie La Roche, had given evidence of this talent long before; but she was of a passive nature, while Bettina was active and accepted life bravely, with the power of a sovereign will to rule its accidents. Granting that the Clemens of Frühlings kranzes, that her *Gunderöde*, her *Frau Rath*, and her Goethe, are fictitious creations, what vigorous handling, and what light and shade these figures receive in her modelling of them! Her treatment of her subjects is only a little more daring than Goethe's, for Marianne von Willemer complained to me that an element of passion was subsequently introduced into the poems addressed to her in the *Divan* which, in reality had been wholly foreign to their intercourse on both sides.

Bettina was in her fiftieth year when her book appeared. With a large family, of which she was the light and centre, she had been settled for many years in Berlin, where she was surrounded by a brilliant circle. Her renown came like the reviving spring rain which falls at night, and the enthusiasm awakened spread far and wide in Germany. It was assumed, as a matter of course, that this was only her first work, and expectation was eager as to what would follow. The *Gunderöde* found a public ready for it. This book had just appeared when my father and uncle were called to Berlin in 1841.

They were both among Bettina's oldest friends. I myself from a child had looked upon Bettina as a near relative of a superior order, — as a kind of double of my mother, as my uncle Jacob seemed of my father. Without Bettina's energetic assistance we should probably never have reached Berlin. I considered her house as an annex to our own, and saw her daily from 1841 until her death, except when journeys intervened. I can never express how much I owe her, or find it possible to recount the wealth of new and interesting matter I learned and enjoyed in her house.

The revolution of 1848 put an end to the glorious period when a free exchange of ideas, through personal intercourse, gave the tone to public opinion in Berlin. In truth, a censorship so strict and vigorous was maintained as to make it difficult to discuss things as exhaustively in the public journals. Bettina never had much to do with newspapers; what she wrote appeared in book-form. She claimed the privilege of saying many things forbidden to others. Bettina and Alexander von Humboldt were the two distinguished individuals whose private views determined the current of public opinion. It was believed that they knew more than others of the brilliant future in preparation, and that paths lay open to them which were closed to common sight. All who wished to attain anything, or who desired free scope, or felt themselves misunderstood, applied to them. Year after year have I seen missives of this kind flood in upon her. Both Bettina and Von Humboldt had the gift to suddenly kindle a spark in beings by no means extraordinary, which raised them far above their ordinary level. From her youth Bettina looked upon herself as the natural counsellor and friend of the unfortunate. Her letters give proof of this. Sad, forlorn people exercised magnetic power over her, and she gave with liberal hand.

It was not from this proclivity to succor and sustain that the political ideas arose and took form which in later years dominated her. In this respect also she went back to the thoughts of her youth. As a child she was almost contemporary with the French Revolution, which now in Germany (between 1840–50) was glorified as having been the creative epoch of modern freedom. With holy awe these conflicts were once more regarded, and men sighed for a German Mirabeau. What is meant by "politics" to-day interested Bettina very little. The emphasis of her work, in which the title was also the dedication, — "This Book belongs to the King," — and whose publication created the greatest sensation, did not lie in anything which admitted of being brought into paragraphs.

In the year 1830, when the cholera first appeared in Berlin, Bettina fearlessly undertook the relief of the sick and the needy. From this hour dates her sympathy with the people. Arguing from her personal knowledge of the condition of the laboring classes in Berlin, who had no work and nothing to eat, she came to regard the whole nation as without political will of its own; as diseased and helpless. These were the days when it was all the fashion to speak of Germany as personified in Hamlet. Bettina's suggestions were made from this point of view. To-day this book is simply a testimony to her noble intentions, and shows what radical confusion the want of a healthy public life caused among us. This was the last of her works which created any sensation, and with the year 1848 Bettina's career in this direction closed. Her *Discourse with Demons* scarcely found a public. Happily for Bettina's last years, this change in public favor came on neither suddenly nor in a way to wound her, nor even to make her conscious that she was no longer indispensable.

Many energetic natures find themselves in old age confronted with a new generation and new conditions, which they cannot understand. They isolate themselves, and turn aside with bitterness to live in recollections of the past. Bettina was spared this. Her mind was so rich, her interests so universal, that the domain was still large enough upon which she could draw. To the very last she looked forward to new events and experiences, eagerly and full of hope. She was always writing. Next to editing her own works, those of Arnim claimed her care and attention.

Whenever her picture rises before me, I see her seated at her desk. Every letter of her hand-writing was legible, fully formed, and energetic. She copied and recopied what did not please her until she attained that grace and ease which lent to all she wrote its peculiar sprightliness and fascination. Her style in hastily written letters is much more ponderous than in her books. She read uninterruptedly the new literature as well as the classics. Goethe, Shakespeare, and the Greek tragedians were her favorite reading. The book whose style she most admired was Hölderlin's *Hyperion*. She had cherished a predilection for Hölderlin from her youth, and when the new edition of his work by Schwab appeared it became a yet stronger feeling. From this moment it was her inseparable companion. One book lay on her table, from which she often read, that I never met elsewhere,— *Klinger's Observations and Thoughts*.

In her early days Bettina drew, and cultivated such a keen eye for plastic art that her criticisms were wholly to be relied on. In later years musical interests became supreme, together with her literary occupation. Among her compositions, which are no longer known, that which moved me most deeply was on the words of Faust, *O schaudre nicht*, — a motive in a violin sonata of Beethoven's, played by Joachim. In her estimation Beethoven held the highest place in the musical world.

It seems strange to me that, out of Bettina's manifold experiences, scarcely one presents itself which affords a complete illustration of what it was to live with her. I have found it impossible to give to those who did not know her an idea of her personality. How is one to describe the power in a being which renders every moment spent with them of the richest significance; the attractive charm which no one can resist; the gift, above all, of entering into the feelings of the young, of influencing and elevating them? She brought light to men, and made them trustful and happy. Others who knew her confess themselves as little able as myself to describe wherein lay this power to inspire, and yet, like myself, even to-day are aware of its magic potency. One might speak of the affluence of imagery that streamed from her lips, of her skill in detecting new phases in common things and the like; but these were only secondary, after all.

I have found that with natures of the highest order

the actual source of their attractive power lies in their clearer perception of the value of existence, and that, having ever present to their souls the importance of the great thoughts which have been revealed to mankind, they find refreshment in consecrating themselves to their further interpretation. It is the supreme joy to know ourselves participating, if only in the smallest measure, in these thoughts. Hence in intercourse with such natures we seem to attain to it.

One recollection occurs to me oftener than any other. In the beginning of the year 1850 Bettina with her family had reached Weimar on her return from a long journey. Thither I went to meet them. It was in October. I found her in "The Elephant," on the market-place, — the old classic inn, — where she had taken possession of the first *étage*. I remember entering the parlor in the twilight, before the lamps had been brought. A variety of guests were there, to whom I was introduced without seeing them. There was music, and I heard for the first time a violin sonata of Beethoven's, by Joachim. I sat quietly in my corner. The delight of meeting once more those with whom I felt so closely united, the softly-stealing, entrancing music, transported me into a new world. Weimer was still the residence of Goethe, and his spirit hovered about us there.

The next morning at six o'clock Bettina knocked at my door. We went through the park that borders the Ilm. The rustling yellow leaves of the poplars were glistening in the sun's first rays, while all beneath still lay in damp shade. We took the narrow path which leads to Goethe's garden-house. All was solitary. The small, dark shutters were closed, the garden-gate fast bolted, but near it there was an aperture in the hedge, through which we pressed into the garden. The earth was thickly strown with leaves, yellow, red, brown, and all the colors intermingled. It seemed as if no one had been here for ages; the branches of the trees had grown until they hung low over the path. Behind the house stood a half-broken bench; here we seated ourselves. Under our feet the ground was paved with the little erect river pebbles, between which moss had sprung up. Bettina said that Goethe once told her he had passed many a night here in the open air, and when he awoke how beautiful the stars appeared twinkling through the branches of the trees. We then strolled through the wet, faded grass about the house until the sun began to shine. Roses and vines on trellises ran over the chalk-white walls, and where the wooden frames no longer held them fast the vines drooped in clusters and hung down as if to detach themselves wholly. We discovered close to some withered roses bunches of grapes, with rotten berries among them, as if nobody cared to pick them. Bettina took some of them in her handkerchief. I see the vines still trembling in the morning light, as Bettina grasped them and plucked the fruit.

She was at this time not far from seventy years of

age, but in the possession of her full vigor and activity. She spoke of Goethe without the slightest tinge of sadness, as is so often the case with old people when reviewing the days that are gone. The present, which was hers, still enchanted her.

Bettina saw in Weimar Steinhäuser's colossal execution of her monument to Goethe, now so unfavorably placed, awaiting the time when it will have a better position. With Wichmann's help she had herself made the plaster model of it, and among the many statues intended to glorify Goethe Bettina's alone seems to me to embody what he was to his age in the second half of his life. The final execution of the work (for which the group of Goethe, with the Genius at his knee grasping the chords of his lyre, was intended to form only the crowning point) engrossed Bettina's thoughts completely in her last years. Steinhäuser came to Berlin and stayed at her house; where by their united efforts the whole was erected. A plaster model of the statue stood in the great hall of her house, and she constantly found something to improve in it. Ever new plans were formed to obtain the means for it. Bettina listened to nothing with so much pleasure as when I pictured to her our all going to Rome, to watch the execution of the monument in Italian marble. Feeble, and no longer able to walk alone, she was many times led up to the work, and, supporting herself by resting her hands on the staging upon which the model stood, she would move slowly round it, scrutinizing it from all sides.

Beside this statue they placed her coffin before it was borne to Wiedersdorf, the country-seat of the Arnims. The family had gone on in advance. A heap of laurel-wreaths and long leafy vines lay there, which I nailed about the casket.

I cannot say that I have been conscious, in thus giving my recollections of Bettina, of intending to write her eulogy. The feeling would have been natural indeed; but, after the flight of twenty years since her death, my glorification would come somewhat late. All the more, because after a period of misapprehension, something like a true appreciation of her has again been awakened, chiefly through Loeper's short life of her in the German biographies.

Like all mortals, Bettina had her weaknesses, and there would be no reason why we should be silent in regard to these, if anything decisive in her life had grown out of them. But as they never affected her innermost nature, we can pass them over. All the thoughts of her which arise in me are of a loving, joyous being. I see her ever before me, occupied with serious interests. Never, even for an instant, did I find her exercised about trifles, or for her own selfish advantage. In this she resembled Goethe, in my eyes, whose every act was determined by that same bright, inward illumination, which, streaming from his own soul, irradiated everything around him.

Only of the few spirits "elect precious" in all ages can this be said.

DANTE,
AND THE RECENT ITALIAN STRUGGLES.
I.

POLITICAL conditions in past epochs are often so closely analogous to our own, as to tempt a comparison. History shows a repetition of the stages of development; things stride forward, and do not fall back into the old ruts, but wind along in new tracks with a similar movement.

Thus mankind has experienced more than once the transfer of the government from the hands of narrow-minded aristocracy into the broad grasp of the masses, or the rise of tyrannical authority upon the disunion of parties no longer able to maintain the balance of power among them. And individuals at the coming on of such revolutions sometimes strike into devious paths; a parallel may not unfrequently be drawn in this respect between isolated characters, as between nations separated by hundreds of years. Positions on this chess-board of life surprise us as being almost mathematically analogous, in view of which we forget how differently here and there the game began, and how very different was its issue. It is by comparing such crystallizations of events that results are arrived at, which, assuming the appearance of higher historical laws, not only explain their own time, but throw such unexpected light on the dim and distant past as to persuade us that we understand it.

To be sure, history, in dealing with such comparisons, has usually political ends in view; yet it is conceivable that one may labor to obtain such formulas of universal development merely for the sake of gaining a just and clear apprehension of things. Historiography is, after all, nothing but a reflection of past events in the mirror of the present, and unconsciously even the most impartial historian makes his own day the background for the figures he wishes to introduce. Why not occasionally bring out all in clearer relief, by making the past, or a definite epoch of the past, the background to which our present political excitement furnishes the front and moving scene. We usually begin as far back as we can go, and come gradually up to our own times. Why not, for once, reverse the process? Everything, that in itself has real value of any kind admits of practical and natural treatment. Comparisons of different epochs, of our day with former days, or former days with our own, of persons, of nations, or of countries with one another,—all this can be made instructive and serviceable; it is the most natural way to discover the progress of humanity, and to convince ourselves of the advantages we enjoy in the present. No better illustration of the marvelous facilities for warfare nowadays than the contemplation of Cæsar's campaigns, or those of a hero of the Middle Ages, or even of Frederick the Great, with the supposition that they had at their command our present highways, railroads, steamboats, and all the improvements in guns and cannon.

But what would be said to an attempt to-day to solve the question whether Frederick the Great would have preferred rifled or smooth-bore cannon? whether Charlemagne would have acknowledged the kingdom of Belgium, or whether Frederick the Great would have sworn allegiance to the present German constitution? Wherein lies the absurdity of such questions? It seems natural, when the Prussian Liberals are pointing to Frederick's bold policy and tolerance, to retort, "If you had expressed these views to him while living, he would have stopped your mouths." "Quite right," they answer; "but he would not do so if he were living now." And so the Liberals continue to quote Frederick as if he were one of them, while the opposite party will have nothing to do with the king, who truly was, in every sense, an absolute monarch, and granted more privileges to his nobles and soldiers than it would be possible for any king nowadays to grant.

Whence these contradictions? Under what conditions may the political parties of the present appeal to the great men of the past?

I have been moved to put this question by a brochure just published by professor Carl Witte upon *Dante, and the Italian Question* (Halle, 1861), wherein Dante's name is connected with the late revolution in Italy, and the writer has undertaken to prove that the great poet and statesman, so far from being in sympathy with it, would have turned aside in disapproval, and regarded it as a ruinous change in the destiny of his country. Instead of hating the Germans he is said to have been filled with love and gratitude toward them, and to have ardently longed for their rulership; that he opposed the overthrow of existing things, and that united Italy, as proclaimed to-day, was a conception which never could have entered his mind, since he believed the only salvation for Italy was in subordinating its different rulers under the German or Roman German Empire. That it is to be looked upon, not merely as an error, but as a conscious deception, if the Italian Liberals, the founders of the great revolution just accomplished, honor Dante as having been its source and inspiration.

Our author enumerates the distinguished Liberals who had been devoted students of Dante: Mazzini, who published a posthumous work of Urgo Foscolo's on Dante; Tommaseo, the ex-dictator of Venice, and one of his most gifted modern interpreters, and others. Here we have, in brief, the contents of this little volume.

It would naturally seem that whoever tries to draw such conclusions must be inimical to the new form of Italian unity. The very subject involves it. But our author does not at once reveal himself in this light, and on the contrary expressly denies any imputation of the kind by his answer to the question, in how far

Dante may be referred to for decision as to some of the perplexing questions of the day, by those who have given to Italy its present form. He avoids passing sentence of condemnation on the late proceedings or existing government; objectively, and as a scholar merely would he discuss the position that in all probability Dante would have taken toward the recent movement. Yet the way in which he carries out his purpose can hardly be called "objective," hence a contradiction appears at the very outset which deprives his treatise of all clearness as to the main question.

Italian unity, he asserts, as Dante heralded it, was a wholly different thing from that which has been brought about by the revolution; or, as he affirms in other places, "is now to be achieved by right and might." These words clearly enough reveal his opinion, however much it may have been his intention to withhold it, and this standpoint is maintained throughout the book. In such a task as he proposed to himself the promise to remain impartial could not be fulfilled. Impartial we can only be when the things we contemplate are entirely divorced from the passions seething about us. Impartially might Dante's times be considered, if we were convinced that Catholicism, aristocracy, imperialism, and citizenship signified entirely different things in the thirteenth century from what we understand by them in the present; that the fiery feuds between the Guelphs and Ghibellines, the cities and the nobles, the emperor and the pope, were burnt-out volcanoes. But the moment they are looked upon otherwise, and the question is asked whether Dante, author of the work on *Monarchy*, could have been the friend, or possibly was the spiritual father, of the late triumphant movement, all impartiality is at an end, and it seems to me it would have been far better to confess this plainly than to disclaim what he was unable to conceal.

For Dante's book on *Monarchy* not only contains no word which could lead us to regard him as an adherent of the present so-called legitimate princes, but really nothing in any way applicable to the present state of things, or from which Dante's attitude to recent Italian policy could be argued.

II.

The times in which Dante lived were those, when, after the fall of the Hohenstaufens, who had been the last to maintain the idea of a world-embracing empire, not an arm could be found wielding the imperial sword and ready for the fight.

But the idea did not die out; it was too deeply rooted. As in our own day, a genuine Catholic, even if he has never had anything to do with Rome, recognizes only one indivisible church, with its imperishable head, — the Pope of Rome, — so at that time all mankind, as a state organism, considered the Roman emperor to be its head, — whether one existed or not; and even those acknowledged his divine right who would not obey his mandates.

Men still clung too firmly to the spots which gave them birth, and to ideas inherited from their fathers, to part quickly with one so firmly established as that of "the Empire." It continued to exist for centuries, long, long after the actual substance of the Roman Empire had become either a myth or a faint dying echo of the past. In those days the ordinary man had as little definite notion of the import and tenor of the public life of which he was a part, as infants of the property of their parents. Ancient laws, habits, and customs, dating from immemorial time, which nobody thought of attacking, were encountered everywhere. The nations stood in a kind of nebulous light to each other, and this atmosphere of unreality tinted all their views. Like some grand, mysterious power, the emperor moved through the different countries, always in motion, the highest tribunal wherever he appeared, and like a distant sun irradiating the whole, the papacy sat enthroned in Rome, eternal and immutable.

The rise of cities, — that is to say the gradual development and concentration of culture within fortified walls, — formed the first blessed islands in this sea of political confusion. The dwellers in these cities soon came to feel how strong they were in themselves, and how easily the emperor could be dispensed with. The cities united in friendship or made war upon each other without asking the permission or arbitration of the emperor. And soon the different nationalities grew more and more conscious of being self-sustained corporations; conducted their wars independently,— scorning resort to any higher authority. Everywhere self-consciousness, and a falling away from the old dogmas. The Crusades,—those grand repeated strivings for a common external goal,—were to harmonize once more the inward discords. For a time they had this effect, but finally only served to add to the general disunion. It was from the Crusades that Venice and Genoa,—to quote the two most brilliant examples,—absorbed into themselves the power of independence. The last of the Hohenstaufens carried on their wars, not to maintain their supremacy over other nations, but as representatives of their dynasty, which, through the possession of Naples, was able to lord it over Italian politics. The cities, the pope, and France disputed this possession. After the fall of the Hohenstaufens, France entered Naples as victor in their place. Germany resigned the grand rôle she had played in Europe. With her power her culture also waned, whilst that of the Romanic nations rose in splendor. All the while, however, for the state form men had before them the old image of an indivisible, overruling empire, and for this the parties in Italy fought.

What men in reality contended for, however, was simple possession. The French party, the National, the Guelphs who adhered to the Pope as being a power superior to the Emperor, believed themselves absolved from any recognition of rights or privileges which, without the confirmation of the Church, were only imperial feoffs. The German party (the Ghibellines) held fast, or tried to recover, what had slipped from its grasp. It was this which made these conflicts so tedious, and in theory so interminable. It was a struggle for existence. Submission meant banishment, and banishment waiting for a chance to return as victor. And as this state of war and tumult lasted through decades, it became the habitual, yes the normal, condition of Italy. Everywhere we see two camps, with changing fortunes, as if one half of a ship's crew swam by the side of the vessel, until they found an opportunity to jump in and throw the others overboard, who now, in their turn, must swim alongside until fortune favors them. So it was with the cities. It was not simply the nobility as Ghibellines opposing the citizens as Guelphs, but both parties split asunder. And as lack of public funds, of high-roads, the want of one leading authority, all made a well-planned war impossible; isolated local skirmishings took its place, and camp-fires flared up everywhere. This unfortunate condition of things went on in hopeless activity for centuries, — mere petty feuds. Great armies, if they did form, as often happened, were only a conglomerate of the smaller detachments, and without inward organization, they often vanished as suddenly as they had come together. The earth sucked them up, as it were. The emperor to-day at the head of a long troop, to-morrow had not a single man. Each soldier made war on his own account, led on to battle with his own arm, and at his own cost. Between the firm rank and file of the nations to-day and those of the old Roman Empire, these centuries are a curious middle point betwixt disintegration and formation. Under just such circumstances, however, do characters assume the most distinct form.

Florence, Dante's home, was an imperial fief. Together with the rest of Tuscany, the city belonged to the notorious inheritance of the Countess Matilda, who bequeathed her land to the Church. The emperors would never acknowledge the gift; the popes, on the contrary, accepted it, and the contests went on within the city between the nobles which adhered to the Pope and those faithful to the Emperor, both, according to their own notions, entitled to rule, — that is to say, having the right to drive each other away. To either party the destruction of the opposite meant freedom. It was a war in which souls fought as well as bodies. The Guelphs tried to insist that the Emperor must obey the Pope, that the Pope was the greater light, without whose blessed help the Emperor had no real authority. The Ghibellines theoretically separated the two powers, and stood up for the independence of the Imperial policy. The Emperor was to come and sustain them; this was why they so ardently longed for his presence. Dante, in his youth a Guelph, was — it would seem more through change of parties toward one another than any sudden political conversion — gradually carried over from a central position among the Guelphs to the other party, until at last he found himself in the very midst of the Ghibellines. Passionate by nature, conscious of his own power, and of what service he had already rendered in fighting and by negotiations, he would continue to labor for his party as he had always done; his book on *Monarchy* is one of these efforts. With logical scientific acumen he vindicates the justice of his cause; as the substance of his whole great poem is the condemnation of his political enemies and the glorification of his friends. The latter was written in exile, the former, it may be, in days when he was more tenderhearted, and before he had reached the decisive turning-point in his fate.

III.

Dante's work, entitled *De Monarchia*, is written in Latin, and is in three books.

The first book opens with proof of the special necessity of the Imperial government. Dante founds it on Aristotle, Homer, and general philosophic grounds. He conceives mankind as an unseparable whole needing a head. This unity of the human race, which he assumes as prevailing over all distinctions of nationality, is used in his argument as an understood and well-established fact.

After these philosophic reasons he passes on to the religious. God, he says, being the primal source of all

Good, the Good must as far as possible seek to be like him. God is one, "Hear, O Israel, God the Lord is one God." God has created man after his own image, therefore creation must strive to be like him also in this; under the sovereignty of a single ruler, the human race is most God-like. Every son must follow in the footsteps of his father, so also mankind, which is the son of heaven.

Lastly, the utility of Imperialism is made an argument. Whenever a dispute arises, a decision must be possible. Between two princes of equal rank, if a quarrel breaks out, who is to settle it? There must be a third, standing higher than either, — a Monarch, or Emperor, whose word shall be final.

Bur nothing is so apt to cloud our sense of justice as selfish desire. The Emperor, argues Dante, alone is free from such temptation; he only has nothing left to desire; for are not his possessions boundless? The Emperor only can be perfectly candid and impartial. His sway is one of love and peace. All men stand equally near to his heart: under him only is absolute freedom conceivable.

For the source of all freedom is in the power to determine one's own purposes. We first covet something, seize it, then judge whether it is good or hurtful; and after that either drop it, or live and die for it. Only when our satisfaction with a thing springs from the judgment we have formed of it can we be said to be free; but if, on the contrary, our desire for it has led to the judgment, all freedom is lost. Hence only the Emperor's judgment is free; he desires nothing because nothing is denied him.

On these and many other grounds Dante explains why monarchy is the most salutary form of government. It makes the substance of the first book, whose conclusions and final argument show how very directly the world was based at that time on antique principles. Once, says Dante, monarchy existed in its most perfect form; it was the time under Augustus, which the Son of God had chosen, or perhaps (because this, too, was in his power) had shaped for his appearance. Under this emperor peace reigned throughout the entire globe, and the human race was happy, as Paul himself testifies, calling the time "Blessed." "In truth," exclaims Dante, time and earthly rulership then arrived at its fulfilment, and man possessed all the essential aids to happiness. But what vicissitudes this world has undergone since those days, when the seamless robe of the Saviour was first rent in twain by the hands of carnal passion. O that we might read of this only, and not be forced to witness it with our own eyes! O hapless mortals! through what storms, what tribulations, what shipwreck of hopes, have you passed to become this beast with many heads, striving and contending against each other, sick in mind and in soul! What care you for the spiritual understandings of things with their irrefragable proofs? what for the knowledge, for the sweetness, of the

Heavenly voice which through the breath of the Holy Spirit the words ring out, "Behold how good and how pleasant it is for brethren to dwell together in unity."

In these words from the translation of the second book, which treats of the legitimate right of the Roman people to the sovereignty, Dante explains the meaning of the Law or the Right. It is the will of God in its earthly manifestation! What runs counter to this cannot be Right, since only what happens among men by his will is Right. Now God's will is in itself invisible, but it may be recognized in temporal affairs; hidden and concealed from us is the seal, the impression only is perceptible; therefore we must seek for the tokens which reveal the imprint of this mystic ring.

The first proof that the Roman people gained the rulership over the earth by right, that is by the will of God, Dante sees in an inward quality of the nation. *Nobilissimo populo convenit omnibus aliis præferri,*— "The foremost place belongs to the noblest people." The Romans were the noblest, therefore entitled to the first rank. For, since honor is the reward of virtue and bravery (*virtus*), and since every preference is an honor, preference is the reward of virtue; and now begins the praise of the Roman people, its nobility, its antiquity. Æneas, the glorious king, was its progenitor, as the godlike poet Virgil has immortally engraven on our memories. Livius also testifies to this. But the nobility that dwelt within this *invictissimo et prissimo patri,* Æneas, is proved not only by his own superiority, but also by the advantages transmitted to him from his ancestors and bestowed upon him by his wives. The passages in Virgil are now quoted in which Æneas's nobility shines forth. It is curious how Dante, according to the views of his time, substantiates, through the different marriages of his hero, his claims to universal sovereignty. Through Creusa, Priam's daughter, his first wife, he won a claim to Asia; through Dido, his second, to Africa; through Lavinia, his third (who was born in Italy, the noblest country in Europe), the right to Europe. *Summa summarum* Æneas won by his three wives for the Roman people, to whom he bequeathed all that was his, — a claim to the sovereignty of the world. Fortuntely Australia and America were unknown at that time!

On Virgil's testimony Dante points to the direct leading of God in history. The mission of the Roman people could only be sustained by miracles. But these miracles took place and manifested the will of God; thus establishing the lawful claims of the Romans to supremacy.

And first the wondrous shield which under King Numa fell down from the clouds; then Rome, saved by the geese of the capitol; after that the hail, which prevented Hannibal from pursuing the Romans, ripe for destruction; finally, Clœlia's flight.

Dante closes with finding still another proof in the political conduct of the Romans. "He who has the public welfare in view" (*bonum rei publicæ*), thus begins the fifth chapter of the second book, "will also have in view the carrying out of the Law. Law defines the personal and outward relations of man to man: where these relations are cared for and prescribed, the human race is benefited; where they are neglected or violated, the opposite. If, now, the end and aim of society is the general good of all its members, then the aim of the Law must be the common weal. He who cares for the good of the state desires the fulfilment of the Law; and that the Roman people in subjugating the whole earth had this in view is plain from all their deeds, by which we see that this holy, pious, and glorious people, disregarding all selfish aims, actuated solely by a desire for universal peace and happiness, really created it for the human family, and therefore it may with truth be said that Roman supremacy sprang from the fountain of piety." It reads like a French manifesto.

Dante, however, does not make this assertion without authority. Cicero's *De Officiis* is quoted. "So long," he writes, "as the rule of the republic was distinguished by benefits, and not by injuries, the wars, whether for ourselves or our allies, ended in a conciliatory spirit. The Roman senate was the refuge alike for kings and people. Our generals and magistrates made it their pride, faithfully and conscientiously, to defend the lands and provinces of our allies. Our imperial government should have been called the 'protector of the world' rather than the 'sovereign ruler of the world.' Cincinnatus, Fabricius, and Cornelius are named as brilliant examples; Brutus sacrificing his son, Mucius Scævola, and Cato. Taking it for granted, then, that the Romans on subjugating the earth had the Law at heart, it follows that whoever has the Law at heart also carries out the Law; therefore, that Rome by Law has gained her dominion, and that this conclusion must be looked upon and maintained as arising from the very nature of the case.

The proof that the Roman people were predestined by nature to rule continues. "It is clear," says Dante, "that in organizing a state, not only the rank of the members is to be taken into consideration, but their fitness for office as well. With similar foresight nature proceeds; she arranges things according to the measure of their special fitness. Hence it follows that this natural arrangement is according to Law, and that what has been determined by nature is lawful, consequently after God's will."

Further proofs of this! As he would be imperfect in his art who considered only the final form, leaving out of sight the means by which to represent this form, so nature would fall short of full accomplishment if in producing the general form of the godlike she neglected to give us the means by which to attain it. Nature, however, is imperfect in nothing. Accordingly she has in view the means to her end, and not the end alone: in short, Italy is the fittest land, the

Romans the fittest people; their rule, ordained by nature, consequently justified, and in as far as this rule is maintained, the will of God is fulfilled.

All these, says Dante, are the revealed proofs of God's will. He will now tell us what are God's hidden decrees, some of which are to be understood at once, whilst others we can only arrive at by faith and a study of the Holy Scriptures. For as no one, even the most excellent, can be redeemed without faith in Christ, so no one is able to discern "the law" without it. *Impossibile sine fide placere Deo*, is written in Hebrews. We read in Leviticus: "What man soever there be of the house of Israel that killeth one ox, or lamb, or goat in the camp, or that killeth it out of the camp, and bringeth it not unto the door of the tabernacle of the Lord as an offering unto the Lord, is guilty of blood." By this door of the tabernacle is here meant Christ, as the entrance to the heavenly kingdom; and by the killing of the animals, the deeds of men. This is clear; but the secret decrees of God are only revealed by special grace, either freely vouchsafed or in answer to prayer. By a variety of tests, however, this knowledge may sometimes be arrived at, as by casting lots or by competitive strifes, which are of two kinds, — the duel, and that in which several contend for the same aim.

The first duel of which we hear was that of Hercules with Antæus; and the first race or match between Atalanta and Hippolytus. By the judgment of

God the victor conquered. The Romans conquered all other nations, therefore God had so ordained it, who allowed the destruction of single small parts that his one great purpose might be fulfilled. Many other nations had set out with the idea as the Romans, but they alone reached the goal.

Ninus, king of Assyria, was the first to strive for universal rulership. He subdued Asia. Dante states this on the authority of Ovid and Orosius. The second was Vesoges, king of Egypt; the third, Cyrus; the fourth, Xerxes; and the fifth, Alexander. We here read a new account of Alexander's death; he demands the submission of the Romans, but before receiving their answer suddenly dies. The mere collision with this chosen people destroys him. Sixthly and lastly come the Romans; the whole earth obeys them; their claims are of divine origin.

In like manner the duel is cited as a vehicle by which the Divine will is made manifest. The duel of Æneus and Furnus is the oldest on record, and its issue affected all Europe. Scipio's fight with Hannibal is explained to have been a duel *en masse;* by means of which the sway over Africa was gained. But why all these proofs? It was Christ's will, as St. Luke testifies, to be born under a decree of the Roman emperor. Christ himself recognizes through this the lawfulness of the decree. But since only a lawful ruler can issue a valid decree, Augustus was this lawful emperor.

And further, Christ died to redeem mankind from the eternal punishment entailed upon us in consequence of the first sin. Dying he said to John, "It is finished." This *consummation est* signifies there is nothing left to do. In that He suffered punishment without guilt was the redemption complete. Had this punishment been decreed by one not authorized to pronounce such sentence, it would have been simply a wrong inflicted upon him, and not the just punishment of sin; and our sins, from which we are redeemed through the punishment of His innocent body, would have had no just atonement, and our salvation could not have been secured. But if our salvation is a truth, and Christ's words, "It is finished," a truth, then must also the judge who condemned him to the cross have been lawfully invested with his office. This judge was Pilate, chosen by Tiberius, and Tiberius governed as legitimate emperor, and according to God's will.

Nevertheless, both he and the Roman people were innocent of the death of Christ, for Herod was by no means vice-regent of the Roman emperor or senate, but installed by Tiberius as an independent king, who alone had to bear the responsibility of his deeds. Therefore, continues Dante, those of us who call ourselves "Sons of the Church," should abstain in future from casting unjust reproaches on the authority of the empire, seeing that Christ, the bridegroom of the Church, recognizes it in life and death. He closes the second book with these words: "I believe to have clearly enough proved that the Romans gained rightfully their sovereignty over the earth." "O happy people!" he exclaims; "O glorious Italy! O would that he had never been born who weakened thy power, or would that, at least, the pious intention which he thought he was fulfilling had not led him into such delusions!" The third book teaches us what these words mean.

If Dante, a man holding some of the highest offices in the state, far more learned than most of his contemporaries, — truthful by nature, frank almost to harshness, a declared enemy to all the lying tricks by which the papal party sought to establish its claims, with a clear logical brain, could still forge together such a mass of fantastic proofs, what must have been the confusion in the fanatical minds of the great mass of the people? Criticism of original sources was an idea which at that time had scarcely entered into anybody's thoughts. What the old authors had written was not questioned. They might be church-fathers, heathen philosophers, or poets, and their works legends, history, poetry, or philosophy; men accepted them as a great whole, to which they gave an artificial organization and inner connection, thus gaining serviceable material which they made use of with implicit faith. Here we find Old Testament characters in closest family connection with those of Greek mythology; Roman and Greek history interwoven with the romances of the people and their legends; the gaps of centuries overleaped; chronology unknown; yet all this accepted with a wholesale confidence, such as is hardly accorded to the most authentic narrations nowadays. Dante appears utterly to forget that Augustus and Tiberius were not Christians. This fact vanishes before the dazzling truth that they were the rightful emperors over the rightful people. Not a word of the Jews, who surely reckoned themselves of some distinction too. There is only the one chosen people, the Romans; only the one country, Italy; only the one city, Rome; all the others subordinate. But we must not forget that men in Dante's times did not see beyond the geographical horizon of the ancient Romans, and that as Italy was the centre of the earth, so the earth was still the stationary centre of the universe around which the rest of the solar system revolved.

The third and last book of the *Monarchy* treats of the pope. "One question," it begins, is yet to be handled, which to accuse truthfully may cause some to blush, and possibly awaken indignation against me. It conceives the two great lights, the Roman High Priest, "Pontifex Romanus," and the highest temporal ruler, "Princess Romanus," the question whether the power of the Roman emperor be derived immediately from God, or from his vicegerent or messenger,— that is, from Peter's successor, who holds in his hand the keys of the heavenly kingdom.

To decide this, Dante again starts with a principle

from which he evolves his arguments. God cannot wish what is contrary to nature. He then discusses the difficulties which beset the treatment of this question. In general he says, disputes arise from ignorance, but in this case ignorance grows out of the dispute. Men do not see, or will not confess, that they are blind. Three sorts of people are here opposed to the finding out of the truth, and present it. First, the pope himself, Christ's vicegerent and Peter's successor (to whom we owe merely what we owe to Peter, not what we owe to Christ), and with him other shepherds of the Christian fold, who are opposed to the truth out of blind zeal, and not, as Dante willingly admits, out of pride and arrogance. Secondly, those in whom the light of reason has been extinguished by persistent cupidity, who call themselves "children of the church," though the Devil himself is their father; to them the very name of the most Holy Empire is an abomination, and they deny in the most barefaced manner the principles on which this and the foregoing questions are based. Thirdly, those who are called "Decretalists," who, without any theory or knowledge of philosophy, rely wholly on their certainly venerable Decretals, and because of them insist on ascendency of the Church over the Empire.

This was the party of the Guelphs, the pope at their head. They refused to hear of Imperialism, or to enter into any discussion regarding it. When they required the sanction of Law they brought forward the Decretals. These they say are the fundament on which the Church rests.

Dante disposes of them very briefly. The Decretals, or Traditions, came into life long after the Church was founded; how, then, can she be said to rest on them? How can Decretals which derive their authority from the Church invest the Church itself with authority? He then goes on to deny the symbolic interpretation of the creation of the moon and sun; both were respectively for the benefit of mankind; yet moon and sun were created on the fourth day, man himself not until the sixth; would God have sent into the world a mere accessory of man, before creating man himself? Besides the two supremacies, the imperial and the papal were only corrective means for human sinfulness, and since on the fourth day man was not yet a sinner because he did not yet exist, how could God apply the remedy before there had been any hurt? Therefore it is impossible that Moses could have meant to give this meaning to the creation of the moon and sun.

But, granted that it were so, is the moon because she receives her light from the sun therefore a part of the sun? It is only a single property of the moon which is derived from the sun; beside her borrowed light she possesses her own light, as is clearly proved by an eclipse of the sun; it is an increase of light which she owes to the sun; as to be sure the Emperor owes to the benediction of the Pope.

Dante hereupon refutes other passages from which

the supremacy of the Church over the empire had been deduced. I omit these, to us mere theological subtleties, and come to what he has to say about the donation of Constantine, who, after being cured of leprosy by Pope Sylvester, gave to the Church the city of Rome, and more too. The bequest by the Countess Matilda is not mentioned by Dante, and in regard to Constantine's donation, he says that this must be looked upon as an act violating the idea of an all-embracing empire, and for this reason bearing on its very surface the stamp of incredibility. The Emperor had no right to give, nor the Church to accept, worldly possessions.

Following out this principle, he declares that Charles the Great could never have made a gift of the kind described to him to Pope Hadrian. On the other hand, would anybody deny that Otto deposed Pope Benedict and reinstated Pope Leo? The empire had existed before the Church, therefore could not have derived its power from the only God himself, or the unanimous will of mankind could have invested the Church with a supremacy of this kind, and we nowhere find the traces of such a transfer. Christ, whose earthly career is symbolized in the life of the Church, said to Peter, "My kingdom is not of this world; if my kingdom were of this world, then would my servants fight that I should not be delivered to the Jews." Man is formed of body and soul, each having its prescribed end and aim, each exposed to corruption; for both God has provided leaders; the Pope is to lead the soul to eternal blessedness, the Emperor, to earthly prosperity; the former according to the teachings of Scripture, the latter according to the measure of worldly wisdom; and because to the attainment of both repose and peace are essential, to insure these must be the highest striving of the Pope and the Emperor. Nevertheless, so closes Dante, the separation of the two powers must not be conceived too strictly, since earthly happiness has in a measure been granted only for the sake of the heavenly; therefore the Emperor must approach the Pope with a reverence such as the eldest son should cherish toward his father, that, cheered by the light of paternal favor, his reign may be so much the more glorious; for he alone has been ordained to govern the earth, and we must revere him as being in all temporal and spiritual affairs the supreme disposer. This exhausts, it seems to me, the contents of his work on *Monarchy*. We do not know when Dante wrote it, whether in the days when he was lingering in Florence awaiting the advent of a German emperor, still far in the distance; or later, when Henry of Luxembourg had appeared, and the Ghibellines demanded of him the fulfilment of their hopes.

IV.

In Karl Witte's essay the general complaint against the Italian liberals is summed up under three heads. In the first place, they must not pretend to derive from

Dante their burning love for Italy as a united country; secondly, their antipathy to foreigners, especially Germans; thirdly, their opposition to the temporal power of the Pope. These three are represented as the creed of the Italian revolutionary party, who in their enthusiasm for Dante turn back to him as the earliest authority for these principles.

Let us begin with the Papal States.

Dante in the *Monarchy* declares himself opposed to the Church's having worldly possessions. By the following train of arguments our essayist now tries to undermine his authority. "Even assuming that our veneration for the poet of the *Divina Commedia* was great enough to prevent us from disagreeing in the slightest degree with his manner of thinking, we still could not carry our idolatry so far as to make his words our standard of judgment for the present condition of things, however true and reasonable they were five hundred years ago."

"We should," he continues, "be guilty of an injustice towards Italy, were we to identify the position of arbiter and imperial protector of the whole peninsula, and indeed of Catholic Christendom, which the old emperors enjoyed, with the possession merely of a small Italian territory, which has reduced the power of the Austrian emperor to a level with that of the other Italian princes, and involves him in their quarrels simply as a partisan.[1] All this is correct; and were

---

[1] This sketch of Dante in political life was first published by Professor Grimm, in Berlin, in 1861.

the writer to conclude, therefore, that, because the circumstances differed so wholly, it would not answer to quote Dante to-day. No objection could be made when he adds in conclusion: "Still greater, perhaps, would be the wrong done to the temporal power of the Pope, if we were to make the views of the fourteenth century our standard to-day."

But the remainder of the essay does not coincide with these apparently fair and impartial utterances. If Dante actually stands so entirely out of relation to the politics of to-day, why does the writer try to define what his attitude would have been toward them? What right has he to affirm that Dante would surely have been opposed to the present monarchy? According to his own showing, he has no more right to make this assertion than the Italian Liberals to make theirs; — nay, had he begun with these words, there would have been nothing further to say, for they entirely exhaust the subject as given on the title-page.

But as it is, he is only disposed to use this kind of logic with regard to the single question of the Papal States, and it is exactly here that I maintain this logic is out of place. In taking the pains to prove Constantine's donation illegal, Dante does seem antiquated indeed! The Church has long since dropped this argument altogether. It is a matter of fact that in the sixteenth century the Papal States were brought together by all sorts of manœuvres, which even the most enthusiastic Catholics acknowledge were, in part, contemptible enough. But when Dante argues against the political sovereignty of the Church, with reasons deduced from the nature of Roman Catholicism and the simple words of the Gospel, he may yet be quoted, and continue to be, so long as the States of the Church exist. For there are certain general views of human relations which never change. Men will never differ in opinion that children should love their parents; that men should be true and loyal to one another; that Christian priests should be pious, chaste, peace-loving people, quite above seeking worldly and vulgar advantage. Hence, when Karl Witte speaks of misapprehension and intentional deception on Dante's part, upon this point he has no right to make such an accusation.

But even less, when he seeks to prove that Dante wished the "subordinate membership" of Italy under the German Empire.

He grants that Dante seldom mentions the Germans as a race. Instead of "seldom" he should have said "as good as never." Dante only refers to us in the *Inferno* (17 – 21) as a people, where he honors us with the soubriquet of *lurchi*, drunkards and revellers. Here, however, we are alluded to simply in a geographical sense, to indicate a certain locality. Yet, in spite of this, Dante is said to have desired above all things the subordination of Italy to German sovereignty. And why? Because he thought it right a German emperor should rule the world, — consequently, Italy.

"German" or "German-Roman" the writer calls this emperor. This designation is so current in Germany, that we may allow him to translate the Latin *Imperator* or *Imperator Romanus* in this way. But to attempt to build up historic proofs on this superficial use of language, without even an allusion to the different meaning of the words, cannot be permitted in science; and least of all when attempting to prove intentional deception. Dante nowhere speaks of a German or German-Roman Empire, of an Imperial Tedesco, Germanico-Allamannico, or Tedesco-Romano, etc.; but wherever in Karl Witte's essay this is imputed to Dante he uses either the word *Imperium* or *Imperium-Romanum*, without the faintest hint of the fact that the person of the emperor must be German; or, more than all, that the rule of an emperor was synonymous with the political preponderence of the Germans in Italy. If Dante could not conceive the imperial crown on any but a German head, some such distinct declaration was necessary at a time when the French kings and other princes, not German, were on the point of attaining to this dignity. Once he addresses Albrecht, Rudolph of Hapsburg's son, "O Alberto Tedesco,"[1] and reproaches him for not coming to Italy to be crowned as emperor and to establish peace. I should be inclined (although I by no means insist on it) to translate even these words in an unfav-

---

[1] *Purg.* vi. 98: "O Alberto Tedesco, ch' abbandoni. Costei ch' è fatta indomita e selvaggia."

orable sense: "O Alberto, you are a true German, an irresolute procrastinator, leaving Italy in her dilemma, and never coming to help us Ghibellines;" still, the Tedesco may here mean that Albert, because he did come to Italy, had remained a German; he ought to have come to Rome, and been converted into a Roman.

These, however, are conjectures, for nowhere else does Dante allude to the peculiarities of the German character. Nowhere, for instance, does he acknowledge, what he must often enough have had occasion to observe, that German soldiers fought better than Italian, nor do the Ghibellines, as a party, manifest any personal favor toward the Germans. In what respect do they ever give us the foremost rank? Dante's favorite expression for his emperor, — this instrument of providence, towering over all nationalities, — is *Imperidore*, whose office par excellence is called *Imperio*, without further additions, — " *Cui ufficio è per eccellenza Imperio chiamato senza nulla addizione.*" I quote these words from his work entitled *Il Convito*, or "The Banquet," which, unlike the *Monarchy*, is no purely literary work, divorced from the politics of the day, but bears directly upon contemporary events, and is couched in maturer language, — more concise, more passionate. The *Convito*, rather than the *Monarchy*, should be quoted, if Dante's views of the Empire are to be discussed. Here we are made to feel clearly what special emphasis belongs to the word Roman, as an attribute of the Emperor's, and that it would have been impossible for Dante to have used the terms "German" or "German Roman" indiscriminately as our essayist does.

Dante troubled himself as little about the nationality of his Emperor as our strictest ultramontane Catholics do about the nationality of the Pope, who would never dream of wishing to establish the sovereignty of Italy in Germany, because the popes had usually been Italian. The Church is the sole consideration; Rome, as the residence of its supreme head, is outside of any political chart. Rome is the dwelling-place of the highest spiritual power, before which all nations are equal. So the Ghibellines regarded the Emperor. Dante says it expressly. All who belong to the Roman Empire are Romans; but the Italians have the advantage of direct descent from the ancient people who founded the Empire, and made its centre. Italy is the garden of the Empire — *il gardino dell imperio*, — Rome its capital. Italy to Dante was the old predestined nest in which the fate of the world was incubated; Germany, the soil which was to furnish the representatives of the highest temporal power. The political institutions of Germany, a knowledge of which would surely have been of the first importance, if Italy was to become a "subordinate member" of the German Empire, were entirely beyond Dante's horizon.

And now, in conclusion, the Italians, in their zeal for a single free, united kingdom, Italy should not appeal to Dante as one to whom this single, free, and great Italy was in his day an object of enthusiasm.

By means of a brief sketch of Italian history, our author seeks to prove that Dante never advocated this distinction-levelling isolation of Italy, but the already so often mentioned "subordinate membership" of Italy under the German empire. But here it should first have been proved that Dante knew anything about this so-called "subordinate membership;" and, secondly, that the rule of the whole earth by an emperor, which he desired, was totally unlike the form of government recently consolidated in Italy Dante's empire, and the centralization of the government under Victor Emanuel, are two such utterly different things that we cannot even speak of contradiction or contrast between them, any more than between an infant borne upon the arm of its parent and the same individual fifty years later on horseback.

Different times simply produce different conditions. Dante indeed complains that Italy is full of tyrants.[1] But it does not follow from this that he would have helped to expel the several dukes and the Bourbons to-day; nor that his enthusiasm for the ancient empire would have disinclined him personally to Victor Emanuel. The union which has been achieved in our day would have been something inconceivable to Dante. To bring together under a central government states so unlike as Genoa, Venice, Pisa, Florence, Rome, and Naples would have seemed as impossible to

---

[1] *Purg.* vi. 124: Ché le terre d' Italia tutte piene son di tiranni.

him as to us the suggestion of a universal empire, with London, Paris, or New York for its capital.

V.

Dante's political wishes were dreams even to his generation; to us they are historic curiosities! How very greatly the imperial policy, as he conceived it, differed from that which the Emperor himself thought politic and practical, is shown by the conduct of Henry of Luxembourg, — the long looked-for helper of Italy.

Perceiving clearly enough that the Ghibellines did not care so much to obey him, as through him, and for their own advantage, to subdue the Guelphs, he awarded to both parties the strictest justice. Regardless of their hostility toward one another, he sought with the help of both to establish firmly the imperial authority, and soon the accusation arose among the Ghibellines that the Emperor was a Guelph. Dante himself urges him to pursue a different course, but Henry remains true to his own policy, to the success of which an early death put an end.

He did not restore the Ghibellines to Florence. Dante died in exile. Two popes — a Guelph in Avignon, a Ghibelline in Rome — stood at a distance, inimical to one another, — personifications of the contest between France and Germany. The French kings attempted to usurp the imperial crown in vain; when these contests came to an end, however, the Roman popes could no longer pretend to the supremacy in Europe, but small princes, with a purely local political power. They yield to the new idea of higher spiritual freedom, gained through a reawakened interest in classical studies, whilst the German emperors in their turn allowed their claims to jurisdiction over the whole earth to lie dormant. The structure which Charles the Fifth two centuries later erected was of a different nature; with him disappeared the last traces of those gigantic proportions Dante had in view when he composed his *Monarchy*. Yet how firmly the original conception of one grand empire still clung to the mind is shown by the various notions, evolved from old imperialism, which sprang up in the very times of the Reformation; these not only prove how immensely strong that first foundation was, but also how in harmony with the nature of things had been this ruler of rulers, who issued irrevocable decrees for high and low, and was a match for the Pope.

Dante's way of treating politics, philosophy, and theology must appear to us childish and old-fashioned. In such a maze of proofs we should not expect to-day to entrap the smallest fly. Neither is it to be assumed that Dante, were he alive to-day, would entertain ideas in the remotest degree like those we find in his writings. If the specific weight of a great spirit is to be ascertained, we must once and for all reject the idea of burdening the scales with the transitory conditions under which he lived.

What was the actual attitude of the man toward the eternal questions which agitate mankind? Did he love his country? Did he love freedom? Did his intuitions guide him to the right, or did he arrive at it only through calculation? And finally, could anything have induced him to act contrary to his convictions? We may not even take into account the peculiarities of character, which, although apparently independent of outward circumstances, in truth were to be ascribed wholly to the nature and conditions of the period. For example, Frederick the Great's predilection for French literature, the cruel manner in which Barbarossa conducted his wars, or, if we take Dante, the severity with which he attacked his enemies, through exile, loneliness, and poverty increased almost to the point of savagery. One might say that Dante advocated in his lifetime an impractical, ideal, reactionary policy; and why should he not do the same to-day? Wholly carried away by one-sided party passion, he was blind to the good in his opponents, and overlooked or palliated the wrong in his friends. Why should he not to-day have argued from the same prejudiced standpoint? But such hypotheses are false; they do not go deep enough. If Dante is to be named in connection with the present state of his country, we must ask, How would a man such as he, — not the old Dante, embittered by experience, but the man in his prime, untrammelled by any past or future, — how would he have decided? For the freedom and unity of Italy, or for submission to those who, as opposed to this unity and freedom, have either fled the country, or are still there, openly or secretly working against it? We must free him from all earthly alloy, and regard him neither as the man who experienced what he experienced; nor even in a certain sense as the man who wrote what he wrote. We must try to discern only the spirit in which he wrote and acted if we wish to invoke his assistance in determining the vexed questions of the present day.

VI.

Dante was Ghibelline, representative and defender of the holy ancient empire. But what vestige remains of this old idea to-day? Compare the cause of the old Ghibellines with that of the present Legitimists in Italy; is there a glimmer of this shining ideal left? Where, now, the frantic spirit of the Ghibellines? where the brilliant past they recalled with pride? Dante was an impassioned believer in a divinely appointed emperor, the most purely ideal of monarchs, whose rule, whether he looked into the past or the future, seemed eternal; but what of all this would he find to-day? What trace of anything ideal has there been in the governments of the kings of Naples or the grand-dukes of Tuscany? Tuscany has been built upon the ruins of the freedom of the old independent city of Florence, destroyed by lies, treason, and violence. The glory of Tuscany ends with the beginning of hereditary sovereignty in the country.

How the Papal States came together has been already alluded to, and how they were governed is well known. Naples belonged by sheer accident to the Bourbons; from Spain, as foreigners, they had forced their way to the Neapolitan throne. Lastly, Venice and Milan were deprived of their freedom. Venice was given to Austria, which for centuries had been her natural enemy. Milan, first through Charles V made a Spanish possession, thus passed over to Austria.

If in either of these countries prosperity of any kind had attended the government forced by these various rulers upon the people, I would willingly hear it called providential, and look upon such rulership as hallowed by time and success. But where do we find the slightest claim to such high sanction? And could a man like Dante have been so blind to the last centuries of Italian history, as now, that his people are recovering from their long oppression, to wish a return to weakness, dismemberment, and spiritual bondage; and to see in it any likeness to the obedience paid in his time to the Roman emperor? Dante was a patriot. This makes him a hero for all time, without further historic inquiry. An instinct finer than the subtlest scholarly acumen leads the people to discover their representative men and put them in their right places. Arminius, Charles the Great, Barbarossa, Frederick, have become to us symbols of German liberty, wholly apart from the political relations of their day, with which only the few are familiar. To others the memory of Charles V or Louis XIV may be strengthening. Having verified themselves as men who had absorbed the nature of their people until their deeds appeared as an emanation of the national mind, we must assume that they would stand forth in every age alike in defence of freedom and country, and think and act in harmony with all true patriots.

The present Italian question is not one in which we Germans actively participate. God be praised, the times are outlived when we were ready to help others that we might forget ourselves! These recent Italian struggles have interested us greatly because of their similarity with our own. When a country is undergoing a radical transformation, the dregs often come to the surface, and blind zeal on both sides leads to wrongs and injustice. The Queen of Naples showed herself in Gaeta, a woman of courage and energy. Every one must have sympathized with her, when as a queen without a throne she was forced to leave her country; just as we pity the last king of Grenada, obliged to surrender his kingdom to Ferdinand and Isabella, or even the last king of the Vandals when we see him a prisoner in Byzantium, led along in the triumphal procession. It is always pitiful to behold the downfall of an empire, and an ancient dynasty wandering in exile. But, notwithstanding, the King of Sardinia, Garibaldi, and Cavour were the saviors of their country. What would Italy have been had the Bourbons continued to rule in Naples, or the popes in the States of the Church? Whoever has known the condition of things in Italy, if only as a traveller, must feel that without a total change the people would have been lost. It is not necessary to hate the benevolent Grand-duke of Tuscany, nor to feel any the less sympathy with the courageous Queen of Naples; the transformation was one of the inevitable necessities. Even our affinity with Austria cannot blind us to the well-authenticated fact, that it was the Austrian policy which for many years actually suppressed by force all mental development in Italy.

To realize half the misery contained in this one word "force" we need only glance at some of the recent Italian literature. Take the works of a man like Leopardi, who was neither conspirator nor revolutionist. In reading these poems, essays, and letters we feel the anguish to which those are condemned who, in the midst of a people bound down in spiritual slavery, with the love of freedom gnawing at their hearts, strain weary eyes for a glimpse of liberty beyond their prison-walls. For all this Austria was to blame in regard to Italy, as well as Germany; not the Austrian people, but their rulers. It was they who strove for centuries to weaken and humiliate Prussia and North Germany. Karl Witte says rightly, that the hatred of the Italians for the Germans is a product of modern times. They hate the Germans because the common people confound the words *Tedesco* and *Austriaco*. Nobody hates the Prussians, nobody would hate Austria if Austria had not provoked the feeling.

VII.

What men long for to-day is *Liberty*. When a great nation has once become conscious that it is a unit, — an intrinsic whole, — it must be insufferable to find itself sundered by boundaries, different laws, and a splitting up of its military force. These boundaries, this want of uniformity in the laws, this scattering of power, seem arbitrary, — contrary to its nature and hindrances to its natural growth and highest welfare. The people chafe under them. There have ever been epochs when by a suddenly aroused and marvelous spirit of coöperation among the people every member has exerted himself to the utmost to restore natural relations, and when everything sank which did not possess the power, to maintain outright its proper existence. Neither repugnance to regal authority, nor hatred of nobility, nor clergy, nor indeed impatience with any kind of authority, agitates mankind to-day; but a wholly new feeling has grown up and spread to an extent unparalleled in the history of the world. A stress is now laid on the importance of self-direction, independence of traditionary rules and customs, on release from all that is arbitrary, on freedom in thought and deed, and justice to every human claim. Men will sacrifice themselves, but it must be voluntarily; men will subordinate themselves, but only to the worthiest; they will dwell where they choose, and go and come without being driven. That every human being is to share in the rulership of the world, according to his possessions, that each is in truth a part of the whole, without whose assistance the public welfare is not to be maintained and the necessary progress insured. All this is granted to-day without grudging, even by those whose personal interests would at first seem to stand in opposition. The astonishing feature in the present movement is that practical ways for achieving this resolution open on all sides as if by magic, and while resistance shrinks into nothingness, unity of action promises to bring the unattainable within reach. This convergence toward the truth, from all directions, is the glorious fact in our present experience. The light which has penetrated everywhere has reduced our wishes and expectations to normal dimensions converting secret discontent into openly avowed love of country; indifference into active effort for its highest good; despondency into confidence in a future by whose light the present appears a historic epoch fruitful and elevating beyond all conception.

Would Dante have held aloof from all this? In dark, perplexing conditions he stood forth boldly, an ardent partisan. His poem is a trumpet-call to vengeance on his opponents; with implacable rage he pursues them beyond this life, and pictures them as eternally damned. And yet wherever he rises to the height of the purely human, undisturbed by party passion, he is unconstrained and gentle. Could his imagination have gone so far as to have conceived the possibility of all nations being united in one grand treaty of peace, all the inhuman means of compulsion, which his narrow-minded century dragged along with it, gone, — a favorable development of one's own nature made the aim toward which each individual in the uncounted millions on our planet was striving, — must he not have hailed the picture with enthusiasm, and, overwhelmed by its splendor, have joyfully allowed it to replace that of the papacy and "The Empire"? I have wittingly given the most ideal view of our future, because Dante's conception of the empire was so extravagantly ideal. To him Italy was still ever the central point of the flat disk, with countries to right and left only dimly visible, the past a chaos without road or track, the present a general struggle for personal supremacy. Thoughts of a higher freedom almost unconsciously crowd into his verses, and lie so deeply imbedded therein, that their interpretation has been the chosen task of those who bore the proud consciousness of being the truest sons of Italy, and by the genius which set him free and raised him above the strifes of the hour he has drawn to himself the passionate love and enthusiasm of all parties.

In Guelphic Florence itself men very soon felt that Dante's Ghibellinism was something quite different and superior to the selfish, wavering policy of those into whose midst he had been thrown. As Dante conceived Imperialism, it would indeed have been the salvation of his country. The form of government which he imagined was the culmination of Romanic ideas, and would even to-day be the highest conception of the Romans, if it had not been for the final breaking through of Germanic ideas. According to the latter we no longer need any pope or emperor as personal forces. Public opinion, that is, a general judgment formed on broad and wide-cast knowledge, is the monarch to-day governing the nations. As, despite the differences of creed, one universal, invisible Christian Church unites the majority of men (a substitute for Pope and Catholicism), so, in political affairs there rules a code of morals, which finds expression in the public opinion of the Germanic nations. No power can successfully oppose it. Inexorably it judges princes and people neither resistance nor deception can restrain or lead it astray. To Dante's generation the undisputed sway of a mere sentiment was incomprehensible. Pope and emperor, armed with the spiritual and temporal sword, seemed indispensable powers.

Dante conceived them as purely and spiritually as the idea admits; to have soared wholly beyond it he must have been more than human.

If, returning to the life that now is, he saw the peaceful intercourse of nations with one another, the flight of thought over whole communities, and the unanimity of thousands in spiritual concerns, where formerly here and there only an individual troubled himself about them; if he saw the cities without walls connected by air-line roads, the entire disappearance of that envious hostility with which they once pried into each other's affairs, the light of science penetrating fields which were unknown wastes to him, the immense influence of individuals whose genius is universally appreciated; if, above all, he saw his country, hitherto crushed and fettered by selfish tyranny, suddenly dropping her chains to share in these noblest blessings, would he devote the life-giving power of his spirit to replacing those walls of separation which hemmed the way to her developments?

As during his lifetime he tried to embrace all the sciences, and by their aid to corroborate and fortify his opinions, he would also seek the means now afforded for raising himself to the same height. His dim, childlike notions of the past would resolve themselves into luminous thoughts of what had been, and truer anticipations of what was to be, while his narrow-minded Florentine patriotism would broaden into a love for united Italy such as fills the breasts of the noblest men of his country to-day.

BIOGRAPHICAL BOOKS.

GRACE A. OLIVER. A Study of Maria Edgeworth. With notices of her father and friends. Illustrated with portraits and several wood engravings. 3d edition. 1 vol. pp. 567. Half calf, $5.00; tree calf, $7.50; cloth $2.25

——————————— A Memoir of Mrs. Anna Lætitia Barbauld. With many of her letters, together with a selection from her poems and prose writings. With portrait. 2 vols. 12mo. Half calf, $7.50; cloth, bevelled, gilt top 3.00

——————————— The Story of Theodore Parker. 1 vol. 12mo. Cloth 1.00

——————————— Arthur Penrhyn Stanley, Dean of Westminster: His Life, Work, and Teachings. With fine etched portrait. 4th edition. 1 vol. 12mo. Half calf, $4.00; tree calf, $5.00; cloth 1.50

E. B. CALLENDER. Thaddeus Stevens (American Statesman, and Founder of the Republican Party). A Memoir. With portrait. 1 vol. 12mo. Cloth 1.00

ANNA C. WATERSTON. Adelaide Phillipps, the American Songstress. A Memoir. With portrait. 1 vol. 12mo. Cloth 1.00

MARTHA PERRY LOWE. A Memoir of Charles Lowe. With portrait. 1 vol. 12mo. Cloth. pp. 592 . . . . 1.75

JOHN LE BOSQUET. A Memorial: with Reminiscences, Historical, Political, and Characteristic, of John Farmer, an American Antiquarian. 1 vol. 16mo. Cloth . 1.00

JUDITH GAUTIER. Richard Wagner and his Poetical Work, from "Rienzi" to "Parsifal." Translated by L. S. J. With portrait. 1 vol. 12mo. Cloth 1.00

A. BRONSON ALCOTT. Ralph Waldo Emerson: His Character and Genius, in Prose and Verse. With portrait and photographic illustrations. 1 vol. Small 4to. Cloth 3.00

CHARLES H. BRAINARD. John Howard Payne. A Biographical Sketch of the author of "Home, Sweet Home." With a narrative of the removal of his remains from Tunis to Washington. With portraits and other illustrations. 1 vol. 8vo. Cloth . . . 3.00

☞ *Any of the above works sent postpaid to any part of the United States or Canada on receipt of the price.*

CUPPLES, UPHAM, & CO., Publishers, Boston.

WORKS OF FICTION.

ANONYMOUS. MR. AND MRS. MORTON. A Novel. 9th thousand. 1 vol. 12mo. Cloth $1.25

GEORGE G. SPURR. THE LAND OF GOLD: A TALE OF '49. Seven illustrations. 1 vol. 12mo. Cloth 1.50

IVAN TURGENEF. ANNOUCHKA. A Tale. 1 vol. 16mo. Cloth 1.00

FREDERICK ALLISON TUPPER. MOONSHINE. A Story of the American Reconstruction Period. 1 vol. 16mo. Cloth . . . 1.00

MRS. H. B. GOODWIN. CHRISTINE'S FORTUNE. A Story. 1 vol. 16mo. Cloth 1.00

——————— DR. HOWELL'S FAMILY. A Story of Hope and Trust. 3d edition. 1 vol. 16mo. Cloth 1.00

——————— ONE AMONG MANY. A Story. 1 vol. 16mo. Cloth 1.00

PHILIP ORNE. SIMPLY A LOVE-STORY. 1 vol. 16mo. Cloth 1.25

WILLIAM WILBERFORCE NEWTON. PRIEST AND MAN; OR, ABELARD AND HELOISA. An Historical Romance. 3d edition. 1 vol. 12mo. pp. 548. Cloth 1.50

CARROLL WINCHESTER. FROM MADGE TO MARGARET. 3d edition. 1 vol. 12mo. Cloth 1.25

——————— THE LOVE OF A LIFETIME. A Story of New England. 1 vol. 12mo. Cloth 1.25

ANONYMOUS. WHEELS AND WHIMS: AN ETCHING. An out-of-doors story, dedicated to American girls. With illustrations. 1 vol. 12mo. Cloth 1.25

ANONYMOUS. SILKEN THREADS. 1 vol. 16mo. Cloth . 1.25

SALLY P. McLEAN. CAPE COD FOLKS. A Novel. Illustrated. 1 vol. 12mo. Cloth 1.50

——————— TOWHEAD: THE STORY OF A GIRL. 5th thousand. 1 vol. 12mo. Cloth 1.50

——————— SOME OTHER FOLKS. A book in four stories. 1 vol. 12mo. Cloth 1.50

☞ *Any of the above works sent postpaid to any part of the United States or Canada on receipt of the price.*

CUPPLES, UPHAM, & CO., PUBLISHERS, BOSTON.

WORKS OF FICTION.

E. A. ROBINSON AND GEORGE A. WALL. The Disk: A Tale of Two Passions. 1 vol. 12mo. Cloth . . . $1.00

MRS. GREENOUGH. The Story of an Old New England Town. (A new edition of "The Annals of Brookdale.") 1 vol. 16mo. Cloth 1.00

ANONYMOUS. The Widow Wyse. A Novel. 12mo. Cloth   1.00

WILLIAM H. RIDEING. A Little Upstart. A Novel. 1 vol. 16mo. Cloth 1.25

HEIDI: Her Years of Wandering and Learning. How she used what she learned. A story for children and those who love children. From the German of Johanna Spyri, by Mrs. Francis Brooks. 2 vols. in 1. 12mo. Cloth. pp. 668. Elegant   1.50

> This work was the most successful book for the young issued during the season. The whole edition was exhausted before Christmas. To meet the steadily increasing demand, the publishers now offer a popular edition at a popular price, namely, $1.50, instead of $2.00.
>
> The *Atlantic Monthly* pronounces "Heidi" "a delightful book . . . charmingly told. The book is, as it should be, printed in clear type, well leaded, and is bound in excellent taste. Altogether it is one which we suspect will be looked back upon a generation hence by people who now read it in their childhood, and they will hunt for the old copy to read in it to their children."
>
> A leading Sunday-school paper further says: "No better book for a Sunday-school library has been published for a long time. Scholars of all ages will read it with delight. Teachers and parents will share the children's enjoyment."

BY THE AUTHOR OF "AMY HERBERT." A Glimpse of the World. By Miss E. M. Sewell. 1 vol. 16mo. Cloth. pp. 537 . . . . 1.50

——————————————————————— After Life. 1 vol. Large 12mo. Cloth. pp. 484 . . . . 1.50

CUPPLES HOWE, MARINER: A Tale of the Sea. By George Cupples, author of "The Green Hand." 12mo. Cloth . 1.00

☞ *Any of the above works sent postpaid to any part of the United States or Canada on receipt of the price.*

CUPPLES, UPHAM, & CO., Publishers, Boston.

BOOKS OF TRAVEL.

DANIEL E. BANDMANN. AN ACTOR'S TOUR; OR, SEVENTY THOUSAND MILES WITH SHAKESPEARE. With portrait after W. M. Hunt. 1 vol. 12mo. Cloth $1.50

HATTON AND HARVEY. NEWFOUNDLAND. By JOSEPH HATTON and M. HARVEY. 1 vol. 8vo. Illus. pp. 450. Cloth . 2.50

ALFRED D. CHANDLER. A BICYCLE TOUR IN ENGLAND AND WALES. With four maps and seventeen illustrations. 1 vol. Square 16mo. Limp cloth 2.00

J. E. L. TEN DAYS IN THE JUNGLE. A journey in the Far East by an American lady. With vignette. 1 vol. 16mo. Cloth . 1.00

WILLIAM HOWE DOWNES. SPANISH WAYS AND BY-WAYS, WITH A GLIMPSE AT THE PYRENEES. Finely illustrated. 1 vol. Large 8vo. Cloth 1.50

S. H. M. BYERS. SWITZERLAND AND THE SWISS. Historical and descriptive. By our American Consul. With numerous illustrations. 1 vol. 8vo. Leatherette 1.50

HENRY PARKER FELLOWS. BOATING TRIPS ON NEW ENGLAND RIVERS. Illustrated by Willis H. Beals. 1 vol. Square 12mo. Cloth 1.25

THOMAS W. SILLOWAY. THE CATHEDRAL TOWNS OF ENGLAND, IRELAND, AND SCOTLAND. A description of Cities, Cathedrals, Lakes, Mountains, Ruins, and Watering Places. 1 vol. 8vo. Cloth 2.00

CHARLES W. STEVENS. FLY FISHING IN MAINE LAKES; OR, CAMP LIFE IN THE WILDERNESS. With many illustrations. New and enlarged edition. Square 12mo 2.00

WILLIAM H. PICKERING. WALKING GUIDE TO THE MOUNT WASHINGTON RANGE. With large map. Sq. 16mo. Cloth 0.75

JOHN ALBEE. THE ISLAND OF NEWCASTLE, N. H. Historic and picturesque. With many illustrations by Abbott J. Graves. 1 vol. 12mo. Cloth 1.00

WILLIAM H. RIDEING. THACKERAY'S LONDON. With portrait. 1 vol. 16mo. Cloth 1.00

Descriptive of the novelist's haunts and the scenes of his books, prefaced by a new portrait of Thackeray, etched by Edward H. Garrett.

☞ *Any of the above works sent postpaid to any part of the United States or Canada on receipt of the price.*

CUPPLES, UPHAM, & CO., PUBLISHERS, BOSTON.

RELIGIOUS BOOKS.

JAMES R. NICHOLS. WHENCE, WHAT, WHERE? A VIEW OF THE ORIGIN, NATURE, AND DESTINY OF MAN. With portrait. 9th edition, revised. 1 vol. 12mo. Cloth $1.00

NATHANIEL S. FOLSOM. THE FOUR GOSPELS. Translated from the Greek text of TISCHENDORF, with the various readings of GRIESBACH, LACHMANN, TISCHENDORF, TREGELLES, MEYER, ALFORD, and others, and with Critical and Expository Notes. 3d edition. 1 vol. 12mo. Cloth. pp. 496 . . . . 2.00

E. J. H. FIRST LESSONS IN THE ARTICLES OF OUR FAITH, AND QUESTIONS FOR YOUNG LEARNERS. By E. J. H. With Introduction by Rev. PHILLIPS BROOKS, D.D. 16mo. Boards . . 0.30

"A child who studies these pages, under wise directions, can hardly help being drawn into the presence of Jesus, hearing him speak, seeing him act, and so feeling, as the first disciples felt, the strong impulse to love him, to trust him, to obey him, and to give the heart and life into his care." — *Extract from Introduction.*

LOVING WORDS FOR LONELY HOURS. Oblong. Leaflet, tied. 22 pp. Printed in two colors. 6th thousand . . . 0.50

Second Series. 22 pp. 2d thousand 0.50

KNAPP. MY WORK AND MINISTRY. With Six Essays. By Rev. W. H. KNAPP. 3d edition. 16mo. 327 pp. 1.50

NEWTON. ESSAYS OF TO-DAY. Religious and Theological. By Rev. WM. W. NEWTON, Rector of St. Paul's Church, Boston. 12mo. Cloth. 253 pp 2 00

"LET NOT YOUR HEART BE TROUBLED." Square 12mo. Leaflet, tied. 48 pp. Printed in two colors. Illuminated covers. 4th thousand 0.75

REV. D. G. HASKINS. SELECTIONS FROM THE SCRIPTURES. For Families and Schools. 1 vol. 12mo. 402 pp. 1.50

G. P. HUNTINGTON. THE TREASURY OF THE PSALTER. 12mo. Cloth 1.25

BY THE AUTHOR OF "AMY HERBERT." THOUGHTS FOR THE AGE. New edition. 12mo. 348 pp. 1.50

☞ *Any of the above works sent postpaid to any part of the United States or Canada on receipt of the price.*

CUPPLES, UPHAM, & CO., PUBLISHERS, BOSTON.

BOOKS FOR THE YOUNG.

SEVEN AUTUMN LEAVES FROM FAIRY LAND.
Illustrated with etchings. 1 vol. Small 4to. Cloth. pp. 136 . . $1.50

MRS. H. B. GOODWIN. CHRISTINE'S FORTUNE. 1 vol. 16mo. Cloth 1.00

———————— DR. HOWELL'S FORTUNE. A Story of Hope and Trust. 3d edition. 1 vol. 16mo. Cloth . . . 1.00

———————— ONE AMONG MANY. A Story. 1 vol. 16mo. Cloth 1.00

CARROLL WINCHESTER. FROM MADGE TO MARGARET. 3d edition. 1 vol. 12mo. Cloth 1.25

———————— THE LOVE OF A LIFETIME. An old New England Story. 1 vol. 12mo. Cloth 1.25

MARY S. FULLER. FIVE LITTLE FLOWER SONGS. For the Dear Wee Folk. Large 4to. Pamphlet. Beautifully embossed pages 0.50

> CONTENTS. — I. The Merry Sunflower. II. The Mayflower's Hiding-place. III. The Golden-rod and Purple Aster. IV. Out in the Old-fashioned Garden. V. Ragged Robin.

BY THE AUTHOR OF "AMY HERBERT." A GLIMPSE OF THE WORLD. By Miss E. M. SEWELL. 1 vol. 16mo. Cloth. pp. 537 . . . . 1.50

———————————————— AFTER LIFE 1 vol. Large 12mo. Cloth. pp. 484 . . . . 1.50

☞ CUPPLES, UPHAM, & COMPANY keep always in stock a large line of Juvenile Books. Sunday-school and other libraries supplied at special rates. Send for catalogues and price-lists.

☞ *Any of the above works sent postpaid to any part of the United States or Canada on receipt of the price.*

CUPPLES, UPHAM, & CO., PUBLISHERS, BOSTON.

BOOKS FOR THE YOUNG.

CUPPLES. DRIVEN TO SEA; OR, THE ADVENTURES OF NORRIE SETON. By Mrs. GEORGE CUPPLES. Illustrated. Cloth, full gilt sides. Large 12mo. 11th thousand. $1.00

——————— THE DESERTED SHIP: A Story of the Atlantic. By GEORGE CUPPLES, author of "The Green Hand." Handsomely bound in cloth, gilt, extra. 12mo. Illustrated 1.00

"In these two absorbing sea stories — 'The Deserted Ship' and 'Driven to Sea' — the peril and adventures of a sailor's life are graphically described, its amenities and allurements being skilfully offset by pictures of its hardships and exposures, and the virtues of endurance, fortitude, fidelity, and courage are portrayed with rough-and-ready and highly attractive effusiveness." — *Harper's Magazine.*

NEWTON. TROUBLESOME CHILDREN: THEIR UPS AND DOWNS. By WILLIAM WILBERFORCE NEWTON. With ten full-page colored illustrations, and fifteen plain engravings by Francis G. Attwood. 1 vol. Thick oblong 4to. Exquisitely colored covers . . 2.00

Being wholly without cant, affectation, or any attempt to enter into the subtleties of religious creeds, the purity, sweetness, and combined tenderness and humor, together with its high moral tone, will give it an entrance to our homes and our American firesides in a way suggestive of the welcome accorded to the "Franconia" stories and "Alice's Adventures in Wonderland"

HEIDI: HER YEARS OF WANDERING AND LEARNING. HOW SHE USED WHAT SHE LEARNED. A story for children and those who love children. From the German of Johanna Spyri, by Mrs. FRANCIS BROOKS. 2 vols. in 1. 12mo. Cloth. pp. 668. Elegant 1.50

This work was the most successful book for the young issued during the season. The whole edition was exhausted before Christmas. To meet the steadily increasing demand, the publishers now offer a popular edition at a popular price, namely, $1.50, instead of $2.00.

The *Atlantic Monthly* pronounces "Heidi" "a delightful book . . . charmingly told The book is, as it should be, printed in clear type, well leaded, and is bound in excellent taste. Altogether it is one which we suspect will be looked back upon a generation hence by people who now read it in their childhood, and they will hunt for the old copy to read in it to their children."

A leading Sunday-school paper further says: "No better book for a Sunday-school library has been published for a long time. Scholars of all ages will read it with delight. Teachers and parents will share the children's enjoyment."

☞ *Any of the above works sent postpaid to any part of the United States or Canada on receipt of the price.*

CUPPLES, UPHAM, & CO., PUBLISHERS, BOSTON.

MISCELLANEOUS.

ARTHUR LITTLE. NEW ENGLAND INTERIORS. A volume of sketches detailing the interiors of some old Colonial mansions. Thick oblong 4to. Illustrated $5.00

"To those far distant, unfamiliar with the nooks and corners of New England, this work will be a revelation." — *Boston Daily Advertiser.*

ROLLO'S JOURNEY TO CAMBRIDGE. A TALE OF THE ADVENTURES OF THE HISTORIC HOLIDAY FAMILY AT HARVARD UNDER THE NEW RÉGIME. With twenty-six illustrations, full-page frontispiece, and an illuminated cover of striking gorgeousness. By FRANCIS G. ATTWOOD. 1 vol. Imperial 8vo. Limp. London toy-book style. Third and enlarged edition . . . 0.75

"All will certainly relish the delicious satire in both text and illustrations." — *Boston Traveller.*

"A brilliant and witty piece of fun." — *Chicago Tribune.*

W. H. WHITMORE. ANCESTRAL TABLETS. A book of diagrams for pedigrees, so arranged that eight generations of the ancestors of any person may be recorded in a connected and simple form. 5th edition. 1 vol. 4to. Boards 2.00

"Cupples, Upham, & Co., Boston, we are glad to learn, are about to issue a new and improved edition of Mr. W. H. Whitmore's 'Ancestral Tablets.' No one with the least bent for genealogical research ever examined this ingeniously compact substitute for the 'family tree' without longing to own it. It provides for the recording of eight lineal generations, and is a perpetual incentive to the pursuit of one's ancestry." — *New York Nation, March 26, 1885.*

JOHN WARE, M.D. HINTS TO YOUNG MEN ON THE TRUE RELATIONS OF THE SEXES. 11th edition. 1 vol. 16mo. Limp cloth 0.50

STARDRIFTS: A BIRTHDAY BOOK. 1 vol. Small quarto. Imitation alligator, full gilt sides, $2.00; full calf 5.00

An exquisitely made book, compiled by a committee of young ladies, in aid of "The Kindergarten for the Blind." Only a few copies remain for sale.

FRANCES ALEXANDER. THE STORY OF IDA. By FRANCESCA. Edited, with Preface, by JOHN RUSKIN. With frontispiece by the author. 16mo. Limp cloth, red edges 0.75

——————————— THE STORY OF LUCIA. Translated and illustrated by FRANCESCA ALEXANDER, and edited by JOHN RUSKIN. 16mo. Cloth, red edges 0.75

☞ *Any of the above works sent postpaid to any part of the United States or Canada on receipt of the price.*

CUPPLES, UPHAM, & CO., PUBLISHERS, BOSTON.

www.ingramcontent.com/pod-product-compliance
Lightning Source LLC
Chambersburg PA
CBHW030803230426
43667CB00008B/1042